between banat

Queer Arab Critique and

between

Transnational Arab Archives

banat

MEJDULENE BERNARD SHOMALI

DUKE UNIVERSITY PRESS DURHAM AND LONDON 2023

Printed in the United States of America on acid-free paper ∞
Designed by Aimee C. Harrison
Typeset in Portrait Text by Westchester Publishing Services

Library of Congress Cataloging-in-Publication Data
Names: Shomali, Mejdulene Bernard, [date] author.
Title: Between Banat : queer Arab critique and transnational
Arab archives / Mejdulene Bernard Shomali.
Description: Durham : Duke University Press, 2023. | Includes
bibliographical references and index.
Identifiers: LCCN 2022028076 (print)
LCCN 2022028077 (ebook)
ISBN 9781478019275 (paperback)
ISBN 9781478016649 (hardcover)
ISBN 9781478023906 (ebook)
Subjects: LCSH: Women, Arab—Social conditions. | Women—
Arab countries—Social conditions. | Lesbianism—Arab
countries. | Feminism—Arab countries. | Lesbianism in
literature. | Lesbianism in motion pictures. | Queer theory.
| Sex—Arab countries. | BISAC: SOCIAL SCIENCE / Ethnic
Studies / General | HISTORY / Middle East / General
Classification: LCC HQ1784 .S493 2023 (print) | LCC HQ1784
(ebook) | DDC 306.76/6309174927—dc23/eng/20220804
LC record available at https://lccn.loc.gov/2022028076
LC ebook record available at https://lccn.loc.gov/2022028077

Cover illustration by Aude Nasr

for banat arab
and for the arab women who have loved me into possibility

1
2
3
4
5

contents

acknowledgments

Writing a book requires immense support, and this book has benefited from the assistance of many organizations and individuals. I am grateful to the Institute for Citizens and Scholars for the fellowship and financial support that allowed me to complete this project. I am grateful for the financial support from the University of Maryland Baltimore County (UMBC) via the Dresher Center for the Humanities, the College of Arts, Humanities, and the Social Sciences, and the Provost's Office. Thank you to *Multi-Ethnic Literatures of the United States* and the *Journal of Middle East Women's Studies* for publishing early versions of chapters 1 and 2, respectively. Thank you to Will O'Neal and Ideas on Fire for editorial work. Thank you to Elizabeth Ault, Benjamin Kossak, Annie Lubinsky, and the many others at Duke who brought this book to fruition. My gratitude to Aude Nasr for creating the beautiful cover illustration, and to Aimee Harrison for the thoughtful design that coheres the book's visual register.

    Between Banat would not have been possible without the writerly companionship and feedback of many interlocutors. Thank you to Rebecca Adelman, Evelyn Alsultany, Tiffany Ball, Umayyah Cable, Carol Fadda, Roderick Ferguson, Amira Jarmakani, and Nadine Naber for offering feedback on various parts of this project. Thank you to Amber Jamilla Musser, Therí Pickens, and Mimi Thi Nguyen for reading the whole thing and offering crucial commentary that cohered the book to its current iteration. Thank you to Sony Coráñez Bolton for support during my workshop and outside it. Thank you to Katie Lennard for pomodoros in the final hour. Maryam Griffin and Josen Diaz, thank you for funny and heartfelt support during the finishing stages. Thank you to my anonymous readers for their comments and engagement with my work. Extreme gratitude to Evelyn Alsultany, Sony Coráñez Bolton, Jenny Kelly, Nadine Naber, and Sarita Eschavez See for helping me navigate the publishing process. Thank you to those folks with whom I have presented at conferences, those who have organized panels, and those who have attended them. Your engagement with my work at the conferences of the Arab American Studies Association, American Studies Association, and National Women's Studies Association revitalized the project in key moments of its journey. I am grateful to Nadine and Jacquie Mattis at Easton's Nook for providing space and nourishment to work on this project.

Thank you to the artists and writers whose work I discuss in this book: in chapter 1, Susan Muaddi Darraj, Mohja Kahf, and Alia Yunis; in chapter 2, directors Niazi Mustafa and Hasan El-Seifi with beloved performers Tahia Carioca, Dalida, Kouka, and Samia Gamal; in chapter 3, Seba al-Herz, Elham Mansour, and Samar Yazbeck; in chapter 4, the writers and organizers of Aswat and Meem; and in chapter 5, Maamoul Press, including Leila Abdel-razaq, Christina Atik, Lina Habazi, and Aya Krisht; Nöl Collective; and the writer and director of *Bar Bahar*, Maysaloun Hamoud, as well as its exquisite cast: Mouna Howa, Sana Jammelieh, and Shaden Kanboura. I am especially grateful to Leila Abdelrazaq and Christina Atik for allowing me to reproduce some of their art in these pages. There are many Arab and Arab American artists and writers who I do not write about but whose work moves me and inspired this book in intangible ways: thank you for making space for us with your work. I am especially grateful to the queer, trans, and nonbinary artists and writers of the Arab and Arab American community who continue to forge new ways of living and loving. It is a gift to be a fan, to see the self in public, and to recognize like, when for so long one felt invisible and alone. Likewise, I am indebted to the Arab American National Museum, the Arab American Studies Association, Habibi House, Maamoul Press, and Mizna for doing incredible cultural, political, and community work.

As a scholar, I have been lucky to have generous, brilliant mentors. Nadine Naber and Evelyn Alsultany, thank you for lifting me up since graduate school. I could not have done this job, or this book, without your guidance and love. You model ethical feminist scholarship, and I am lucky to follow in your path. Likewise, Carol Fadda, Amira Jarmakani, and Sarita Eschavez See have been stalwart supporters. Roderick Ferguson and Mimi Thi Nguyen, thank you for taking me on as a mentee and continuing to support my work. I could not have gotten to this point without the early mentorship of Jami Anderson, Bob Barnett, Victor Roman Mendoza, Scott Russell, and Stevens Wandmacher.

I am grateful to the many intellectual interlocuters I have been fortunate to think with and learn from in various settings, including graduate school, conferences, fellowship and writing spaces, art and poetry circles, and sometimes hotel lobbies and karaoke bars. Rather than experiencing friendship and scholarship as separate spheres, I have found my scholarship and self constituted by multiple forms of sociality. I am grateful to my friend-thinkers, including Deena Al-Adeeb, Lanice Avery, Dima Ayoub, Meghanne Barker, Ahimsa Timoteo Bodhrán, Karisa Butler-Wall, Louise Cainkar, Brian Chung, Scott De Orio, Josen Diaz, Keith Feldman, R. Benedito Ferrão, David Green, Emily Hue, Doug Ishii, Joe Kadi, Maryam Kashani, Tala Khanmalek, Kareem Khubchandani, Jina Kim, Ashvin Kini, Neveser Köker, Jenny Kwak, Isabel Milan, Orquidea Morales, Deena Naime, Rachel Norman, Allison Page, Michael Pascual, Jennifer Garcia Peacock, Elliott Powell, Rachel Afi Quinn, Angela Robinson, Tyler Rogers, Kiri Sailiata, Steven Salaita, Rebecca Scherm, Kyera Singleton, Matt Stiffler, Stephen Sheehi, Wendy Sung, Thea Quiray Tagle, Malcolm Tariq, Leila Tayeb, Urmila Venkatesh, Pauline Vinson, Lee Ann Wang, Cookie Woolner, and Kathy Zarur. Regarding broader forms of intellectual community, I am indebted to the many scholars working in Arab and Arab American studies and adjacent fields, and the beautiful, bountiful queer of color and transnational feminist scholarship that provides the theoretical and methodological backbone of this work.

During my time at UMBC, I have been fortunate to work with generous colleagues. Thank you to the Gender, Women's, and Sexuality Studies Department, including María Célleri, Kate Drabinski, Elle Everhart, Katie Kein, and Carole McCann. Outside my department, I am grateful to colleagues Rebecca Adelman, Kristen Anchor, Shawn Bediako, Jessica Berman, Tamara Bhalla, Bev Bickel, Dawn Biehler, Rachel Brubaker, Bambi Chapin, Gloria Chuku, Lindsay DiCiurcci, Keegan Finberg, Sarah Fouts, Amy Froide, Jo Gadsby, B. Ever Hanna, Chris Hawn, Courtney Hobson, Nicole King, Tania Lizarazo, Christine Mallinson, Keisha McAllen, Susan McCully, Susan McDonough, Kimberly Moffit, Thania Muñoz, Jess Myers, Lisa Pace Vetter, Elizabeth Patton, Tim Phin, Jules Rosskam, Michelle Scott, Sarah Sharp, Orianne Smith, Brigid Starkey, Sharon Tran, and elle trusz. My students at UMBC have also inspired me to keep at it. It is an honor to work with students, especially ones as intelligent as those at UMBC.

I wrote the majority of this book during a global pandemic, though it had ideated in me since graduate school, if not earlier than scholarly interest can trace. The process of doing so exhausted me. It brought me moments of great joy and great sadness, moments of intense self-doubt and, very occasionally, a sense of thinking, "Maybe this is fine and not total trash." When I felt like it was impossible, I thought about my ancestors. I was bringing to bear a future we couldn't have imagined. So, I thank my ancestors and my family. ألف شكراً لدار الشاعر, to the Shomalis and Rishmawis at home and in the diaspora, and for all my Palestinian ancestors who are dabke dancing and za-hgretting for me and my book. I believe in our joy, and I believe our freedom is coming. تحيا فلسطين حرّة.

Thank you to my father, Bernard, whose lyricality and joy of life inspires my writing. Baba, who was a teacher before me and taught me more than this or any other book can express. I thank my mother, Mariam, the core of strength in our family. When I am at odds with myself and the world, I call my mother and she brings me to the center of myself, which is us. I thank my sisters, my ghanamat, my nancies: Lubnah, Maysoun, Lemma. Without you, I simply could not be. I thank my brother, Farid, for his spirit of fun and his determination. All my niblings: Rachel, Marie, Jacob, Carlos, Tammer, Leila, and Zaina: thank you for being wild and lovely and weird. Kathleen, my tender heart and #tsr, I am grateful for your infectious enthusiasm and the ways you care for our little family. Thanks for road-tripping through this world with me.

I am lucky to be queer, and this book would not be possible without my queer ancestors, without queer Arab women, banat, and femmes. Those I know and those I do not. It would not be possible without the vibrant and warm queer Arabs I have been fortunate to meet and befriend. But beyond that, just knowing you exist changed my life. For this, I am grateful to the list for teaching me that I am not alone. I am also thankful for all the people I met through it, who shared their stories and their time and their hearts online and in person when possible. Thank you for helping me see I could be queer and Arab and OK. Thank you for creating queer Arab joy. Special shoutout to Charlotte Karem Albrecht, Umayyah Cable, and Lamise Shawahin for being my first queer Arab friends/hummusexual habibis. This book is for my queer Arab community, and I hope I did us justice. Where I have not, please attribute it to my head and not my heart.

I am so fortunate that my family exceeds the normative structures of het-erosexuality. My family has held me in ways I did not imagine the world could. Tahereh Aghdasifar, when I met you I knew I wanted to be your friend, and I'm so glad you let me fulfill that dream. Thank you to Kristen Anchor for being my first and best friend in Baltimore. Thank you to Tiffany Ball for being my dream wife and companion in grief. Brooke Baker, thank you for keeping me across time and space. Sony Coráñez Bolton, thank you for sharing this book journey and for all the care you have provided as a friend and colleague since our earliest days of grad school. Umayyah Cable, thank you for being a touchstone in our very strange profession and even stranger world. Lynn Eckert, your compassion and friendship feel like the most luxurious of gifts. Kristopher Geda's support, warmth, and thoughtfulness has sustained me for years. Maryam Griffin, habibi bro. Thank you to Amanda Healy for being my heart anchor and home away from home. Andy Jih's dry wit is exceeded only by his generous spirit, which tolerates Kristopher's and my tendency to talk A Lot and Loudly. Thank you to Ashley Smith for being my most steadfast, loyal friend and for hiding the bodies. Amber Williams, thank you for always holding space for me, in joy and sorrow.

During the course of this journey I have found kin and made community with many beautiful people. These intimacies have many shapes and forms, and they morph over time, yet each is vital to the project of me as a human, and therefore to the project of this book. My gratitude to Cass Adair, Rebecca Adelman, Charlotte Karem Albrecht, Rahne Alexander, Erin Ashmore, Stevi Atkins, Nadia Awad, Kay Ulanday Barrett, Leila Ben Nasr, Pam Butler, Bonnie Applebeet Cameron, Matthew Chin, Simone Chrisitian, Meiver De La Cruz, Kelly Fayard, Margot Finn, Joshua Fortney, Chris Finley, Jess Giusti, Staci Grandstaff, Lloyd Grieger, Candice Haddad, Lennox Hardin, Marwa Helal, Martha Jerrim, Dashini Jeyathuri, Anand Jay Kalra, Jenny Kelly, Ken Laatz, Marisol LeBrón, Katie Lennard, Beatrix McBride, Darren Meade, Anne Mitchell, Mindy Mizobe, Helene Murtha, Nkiru Nnawulezi, Dana Olwan, Jessica Pickett, April Reitano, Heidi Andrea Restrepo Rhodes, Elisabeth Saab, Jna Shelomith, Caroline Su, Dédé Tetsubayashi, Lani Teves, Sang Truong, Jenny Wagner, Dale Weighhill, Brian Whitener, Byron White, Stephen Wisnewski, and Bradley Woodruff. Many of the names here could have appeared in the earlier paragraph on friend-thinkers, but I hope you'll imagine yourself at the center of the Venn diagram of my head and heart.

To commit fully to the queerness of this project, I am going to thank my pets. Finn and Boone: we miss you so much. My perfect femme cat, Lolita, died during the copyediting phase of this project. She was my constant companion during the writing of this book, and I wish she could have been here for the last leg. I love you grrr. Dexter and Max: you are why we cannot have nice things and also why I have asthma, but you bring us joy. In a similar queer relationality, my capacity to write this book was replenished by objects, activities, and spaces with affective registers and alternate geographies to those of writing and scholarship. My gratitude to baking, my bike, Baltimore Clayworks, and the Harvest Community Garden for giving me different forums for flight.

Reader, are you still here? As it became more obvious *Between Banat* would indeed exist as an object in the world, I found myself embarrassed to imagine people would read it, and equally embarrassed they would not. Reader, thank you.

introduction

I began this work in search of ancestors. I wanted to find other queer Arab women. I wanted to hear their stories as evidence of my own history, as hope for my future. But I looked for ancestors without knowing their names. Many queer women eschewed the names available to them in Arabic or English: lesbian, gay, سحاقيّة (sahaqiya), شاذة (shaatha). Others did not publicly or politically articulate their sexualities for fear of violent reprisals. Some chose to live queerly, but their queerness was "unremarkable." By this I mean they were remarkably strange: spinster aunts and حسن صبي (hasan subi) cousins whose sexuality was left pointedly without remark. I could not figure out how to call to other queer Arab women, and so I was at a loss to find them. Instead, over time I discovered my kin calling to me. A knowing glance in a conference hotel lobby. A playful wink on-screen. A double entendre intended just for my ears. Someone familiar, someone kin called to me from many spaces and texts. Even when I could not speak them, I felt their resonance. This book is the story of queer Arab women's becoming as I found it, but it also the story of unbecoming: the unbecoming ways we are erased in Orientalist and Arab heteropatriarchal thought and the unbecoming of identities and practices that do not serve us. *Between Banat: Queer Arab Critique and Transnational Arab Archives* is my love letter to my unnamed ancestors. It is the knowing glance, playful wink, and double entendre between us. It is the ways we call one another, not only for recognition and community, but to action and movement toward a joyful and pleasurable queer Arab future.

Queer Arabs, and especially queer Arab women, face a discursive double bind that often invisibilizes or undermines their presence: Orientalism fashions Arab cultures as abject via queerness, and Arab cultures often reject queerness as symptomatic of Western assimilation. This double bind produces "queer Arab" as a site of anxiety. How do we call someone queer when the act of recognition can produce misrecognition, stigmatizing the subject as inauthentic or assimilated? How does one search for "queer Arab women" when the language and categories available for search are ahistorical and at risk for positing epistemic violence on their subjects? Queer sexuality, particularly women's queer sexualities, are understudied within Arab and Arab American scholarship and do not function in parallel to Western iterations of LGBTQ history and identity. They require an alternative methodology and archive, a different kind of story/telling. That is, a different kind of story and a different kind of telling.

In order to study queer Arab women, *Between Banat* develops queer Arab critique grounded not in individual subjects, but in attentiveness to the between: desires between bodies, bodies between nations, words between languages, nations between one another. Through queer Arab critique the book fashions queer Arab archives, which are ever moving, ever circulating. Indeed, it is only through movement and relation that queer Arab archives can be constituted at all. The archive is a living record that constantly changes because it's constituted between bodies, in movement, in the transnational.

Queer Arab critique is affirmative insofar as it insists on the historical, contemporary, and future presence and relevance of queer women in and of Arab cultures. It is tentative insofar as I do not offer conclusive and exclusive definitions of what constitutes Arab or queer cultures. I maintain elasticity as a foundational premise to understanding queer Arab women's subjectivity, desires, and lives. The certainty in this work then is derived not from a prescription toward how we must discuss or think queerness in Arab cultures, but rather a certainty that dialogue is already ongoing, has been, and will continue. I offer points of conversation and invitation within the dialogue of queer Arab studies: What has precluded queer Arab subjects from being visible in mainstream Arab cultures? What possibilities for queer life happen outside of conventional earshot? How do queer women and femmes narrate their lives? How do we move beyond survival, visibility, and inclusion to imagine a joyful and free queer future?

In this work queerness and Arabness are interstitial subjects, formed in and out of tension. The book demonstrates how heteropatriarchies, Arab nationalisms, and Orientalisms work in relation to mire queer Arab women's horizons. It catalogues the challenges toward seeing and imagining queer Arab life in the past and present. At the same time, queer Arab women and femmes teach us how to surpass our foreclosure by rejecting authenticity, respectability, and inclusion as adequate tools or strategies for queer futures. *Between Banat* uses literature, art, and films about queer Arab women, created by Arab women, femmes, and nonbinary people, to articulate queer Arab critique and fashion queer Arab archives. Through critique I substantiate the archive, which includes the limiting discourses that arrest and occlude queer Arab women's lives, techniques for locating queer Arab women's stories amid heteronormative imperatives, vignettes and analyses of queer life as imagined by Arab subjects, and axioms for inspiring a queer Arab future with women, femmes, and nonbinary people at its center. Queer Arab critique is both an analytic frame that allows us to see queer Arab histories and presence, and the underlying premise of this work: attention to women's desires, bodies, and experiences gives us critical tools to live and forge queer futures.

Between Banat is as much an archive of queer texts as it is an archive driven by longing and desire for queer representations. In addition to its concentration on women and femininity, the archive assembled in this book is bound and cohered by affective attachments: the longing and desire for queer Arab women's historical and future company; the anxiety and ambivalence associated with trying to isolate or categorize a queer Arab woman as such; and the evasive tactics and maneuvers used by writers, characters, and myself to maintain some levels of opacity and privacy about the intimacies of queer Arab women's lives. In *Between Banat*, feelings abound and shape both the objects that are archived and the arguments that I offer.

Namely, I consider feeling aesthetically and analytically useful in the deployment of queer Arab critique and the assemblage of queer Arab archives. Sianne Ngai asserts that "feeling can be used to expand the project of criticism and theory."[1] The feelings the texts produce and the feelings the texts circulate are diagnostics for what animates and ails queer subjects. Because of its association with femininity, feeling is disparaged in both public cultural spaces (e.g., political spheres) as well as in cultural texts (e.g., "women's literatures"). For example, the Arabic novels discussed in chapter 3 are devalued in Arab criticism because they explore the emotional lives of women, usually in stream-of-consciousness narration. Drawing from Lauren Berlant's work on sentimentality, Sara Ahmed's work on complaint, and Ngai's work on "ugly feelings," I reject the disparagement of "feminine" and negative feelings. Instead, I use feeling as a means by which to understand femininity and the demands placed on feminine subjects in heteropatriarchal contexts.

I build on feminist and transnational feminist theorizing to explore how Arab queerness is associated with certain affects and how affective positions inform how we imagine and articulate our queerness. Transnational feminist thinkers have explored how feeling becomes racialized, how Brown and Black peoples are erased and harmed through the affects and emotions written on their bodies. In *The Promise of Happiness*, Ahmed considers the plight of the melancholy migrant, a subject whose diasporic longing, rather than imperial and racist violence, allegedly undermines their capacity for happiness in the new nation.[2] In *Arab and Muslims in the Media*, Evelyn Alsultany articulates how pity is mobilized in Orientalist and anti-Arab representations to undermine the agency of Muslim women.[3] Dina Georgis writes of shame as an affective marker of queer Arab identity that might be usefully recuperated by queer subjects.[4] In *The Better Story: Queer Affects from the Middle East*, Georgis considers primarily queer pain and racial suffering. Queer Arab subjects sit at the affective crossroads of such texts: discourses about them—Orientalist, imperial, and Arab nationalist—conscript their capacities for existence, let alone joy. Homonormative notions about queer life formulated in Western LGBT spaces regard some of the primary emotional registers of queer Arab life—shame and ambivalence—as markers of failed or bad queer subjects. Instead, following the model set forward in Jennifer Nash's *Black Feminism Reimagined*, I consider how queer women's lives, cultural production, and activisms are informed by their affective postures.[5] Queer Arab critique is an affective posture marked by ambivalence. Though ambivalence might open queer Arab archives to criticism regarding their "authenticity" as queer or Arab subjects, I demonstrate how ambivalence is productive rather than constrictive. *Between Banat* uses emotion as a way into queerness, where "good and bad feminine" feelings alert us to moments of queer emergence, queer presence, and queer joy. Feeling, like gesture and ephemera, is fleeting and mobile and thus imminently suitable to the ambivalence of queer Arab critique and the queer archives mobilized here.

Beyond an attention to how texts and subjects "feel," feeling operates as imperative—that which motivates and shapes action in both literary and material instances; feeling is that which curates the archive itself. In *An Archive of Feelings*, Ann Cvetkovich notes that an archive can be constituted through the affective investment of the archivist who creates it.[6] My "feel" for queerness in Arab cultures draws objects into this archive. Yet, this book is a reluctant archive, and I am a reluctant archivist. Here, the work of making queer Arab archives is coupled with a simultaneous commitment to their unmaking. Thinking alongside Anjali Arondekar, I understand *Between Banat* both as a recuperative gesture, a reading against history to make history, and at the same time, a worried contribution to the archive it imagines.[7] I borrow gestural from Juana María Rodríguez's *Sexual Futures, Queer Gestures, and Other Latina Longings.* Rodríguez identifies the gestural as a socially legible and kinetic form of communication, one that sometimes captures what cannot be said and what we do not want others to hear.[8] In this way, gesture captures queerness as a relation between rather than a sedimented end. In "Ephemera as Evidence," José Esteban Muñoz refers to the queerness of ephemera—that the fleeting nature of an object with shaky ontology is queer. He too proposes "queerness as a possibility, a sense of self-knowing, a mode of sociality and relationality."[9] This form of queerness is essential for queer Arab critique and its archives, particularly because of the discursive limitations queer Arabs face and because of the ambivalence around identity queer Arabs often express. *Between Banat* studies and operates as an ephemeral and gestural archive, producing legibility in its specific moment of enactment, but with the clear realization that legibility is neither the end goal nor a stable, infinite state.

Between Banat is necessarily an affective archive, one most often marked by ambivalence. While my investments in queer ancestry hail and manifest texts, I maintain some fuzziness about the subjects of those texts. As a vulnerable population, queer Arab women sometimes proceed with caution around legibility or transparency. As Rodríguez notes, communities of color often worry about what we make available for consumption, and to whom.[10] The selection of texts, the analyses provided, and the obfuscations maintained are themselves part of the archive, but they also construct it. That structure is "necessarily inchoate."[11] On the one hand, the archive can be an amulet against queer women's erasure in Arab histories, a testament to the ways we have always existed. It is a celebration of presence, in both the record and the present. In "Venus in Two Acts" Saidiya Hartman discusses how critical readings of the archive mine history to "both tell an impossible story and to amplify the impossibility of its telling."[12] Hartman suggests we can never recover a lost or impossible subject, but we might paint as full a picture as possible. *Between Banat* harbors no doubt that queer Arab women survive and live and love. On the other hand, the book acknowledges that we have not always existed in the same ways, or in ways legible to those who survey our histories and lives. The archive does not repair historical injury or invisibility, nor produce clear identities from its pages. The evidence of our experience is situational, historical, mediated by me and many other interlocutors.[13] We are here and not. We are queer and not. We name ourselves and we don't. The project of constructing an archive assumes a rigidity that I do not ascribe to the subjects within it. I have tentatively gathered texts that circle around the signifier of queer Arab women, but I am ambivalent about how we understand and use those modifiers.

If *Between Banat's* archive is ambivalent, queer Arab critique is a skeptical method, a side-eye toward itself. There is absurd capacity in Arab, but Arab also occludes many subjects under its broadness, its troubling ethnic primacy in the Arab nations. I focus on women and femininity, though like some writers featured here, I note that woman is not always the sign under which the subjects travel.[14] I discuss nonnormative iterations of gender and sexuality in Arab women and call this queer even while remaining slightly skeptical that such a word can encompass or adequately render the beauty, intimacy, and desires represented. I use queer knowing that it can never really render a clear subject in part because I am committed on some level to our privacy, our secrecy. If the book has a closet, if the closet is an archive: it is disorganized, overfull, cluttered. Things are forever accidentally falling over or out, and the reader only has access to a microscopic slice of what is inside. Sometimes I shove everything back in and close the door.

Between Banat constructs queer Arab critique as a tool to make and unmake queer Arab archives. Making the archive takes the shape of affectively gathering and consolidating texts under the umbrella of "queer Arab women"; unmaking it takes the shape of poking holes in the fabric of Arab, women, and queer. Underneath the umbrella, the book is wet. Its subjects, its canons, its definitions are slippery and elusive. I want the book to feel like a good soak, but I do not imagine it is always useful, necessary, or possible to quantify the rain. *Between Banat* operates in tension with the difficult binaries that animate discussions of Arabness, queerness, and femininity. Each of these terms comes from robust genealogies and are ongoing sites of critical interrogation. I offer the following comments on my use of each.

Arab Is a Transnational Relation

Between Banat suggests that Arabness is a relational quality or subject position rather than a fixed, essential definition open to authentication. Despite some legitimate differences shaped by geography and national origin, Arab is a meaningful ethnic attachment for many subjects, one that shapes and is shaped by Arabs' relationships to geography, national affiliation, cultural practices, and the Arabic language. Historically, Arab refers neither to a singular country nor to a geographic region. Instead, Arab is often used to designate countries or populations that speak Arabic, are national members of the Arab League, or share cultural and political histories.[15] Each classification can intersect with the next—Arabic is the language of the Quran and as such is used in Muslim communities that may or may not identify with Arab identity; regional differences in the spoken version of the Arabic language might render one Arabic speaker unintelligible to the next. The Arab League includes twenty-two separate nations: Algeria, Bahrain, Comoros, Djibouti, Egypt, Iraq, Jordan, Kuwait, Lebanon, Libya, Mauritania, Morocco, Oman, Palestine, Qatar, Saudi Arabia, Somalia, Sudan, Syria, Tunisia, United Arab Emirates, and Yemen. Each has its own complex, individual history; how can the moniker "Arab" account for their heterogeneity? Additionally, the Middle East and North Africa (MENA) region is a geopolitical designation that includes countries and communities not considered Arab (e.g., Iran, Kurdish peoples) despite their geographic proximity to Arab nations and their shared histories of Western colonialism.[16] Moreover, many scholars consider the term "the Middle East" a colonial nomenclature and prefer to describe the region as Southwest Asia and North Africa (SWANA).[17] Still, one might reject ethnic or geographic markers as too monolithic or sweeping altogether and opt instead to discuss national formations—such as Egyptian or Iraqi.[18] When im/migrant and refugee populations are factored in, one's relationship to Arab as an identifier might change altogether. Asylum seekers, refugees, and immigrants might all have different and complex relationships to either national or ethnic signifiers. Their own understanding of their identity is further mitigated by how they are hailed upon their arrival in a new place. For example, many who leave Arab nations and reside in the US diaspora are variably read as Arabs, Arab Americans, Muslims, and/or Muslim Americans; they might be classified as Black, Brown, or white.[19] Like others not born in the country in which they reside, their path to citizenship can be complicated by anti-Arab and anti-Muslim sentiment.[20] All these factors make "Arab" an ambiguous and difficult term to apply to a community or body of literature in general.

I find the overlaps and antagonisms within Arabness useful to demonstrate that Arabness is produced not only in one location or another, but in the movement, tension, and in between. I take a transnational approach to thinking Arab identity, one that is committed to unseating Orientalist and nationalist renditions of Arab identity that produce essential, authentic Arab subjects. *Between Banat* looks at Arabness not only in relation to non-Arab nations, but Arabness as it is produced between Arab national constructs. An emphasis on Arabness as a between, produced in relation and exchange, begins a slow process of detaching Arab identity from national or state identities and encourages us to consider how we understand an Arab cultural identity for its many stateless subjects. My positioning of Arab as a moving, transnational configuration builds on Arab and Arab American feminist thought. In *Arab and Arab American Feminisms*, the editors note that for many Arabs, both in Arab nations and diasporas, home exists on a continuum.[21] They describe their choice to use "Arab and Arab American" simultaneously to demonstrate the discomfort their writers and interlocutors feel with either/or formations of identity and experience. I too locate Arabness neither in Arab home nations nor in their diasporas, where diaspora can refer to Arabs outside Arab nations but can also refer to Arabs displaced to other Arab nations. In *Contemporary Arab-American Literature*, Carol Fadda-Conrey argues that Arab Americans' transnational circuits are central to their configuration of Arab identity. Like Fadda-Conrey, I employ Arabness as relational and transnational in order to demonstrate the agential ways Arabs negotiate and imagine their cultures and communities amid the violence that surrounds them.[22] Arabness is relational between Arabs and non-Arabs, but betwixt as well. It is transnational insofar as Arabness crosses, circulates, and changes within Arab nations. I further suggest that the transnational circuits do not only impact Arabs in the diaspora, but that the circuitry informs construction of Arabness in Arab nations. It is not only Arab Americans that are formed in the transnational circuit: Arabness itself is in the shifting current, the ongoing dialectic between here and there, between discourses. Thinking about Arabness as a transnational relation allows us to think about the significance of multiple nationalities for Arabs. It similarly describes the cultural and social ways that Arab life takes place across and through multiple kinds of borders. Thus "transnational relation" describes not only a national multiplicity in Arab histories, but the multiplicity of Arab cultural experiences. In this, I aim to evade some of the traps of transnational formations elucidated by critics like Leela Fernandes that illustrate how the transnational might sometimes reify a US-centric project.[23]

Additionally, foregrounding Arab as a transnational relation and formation allows us to recognize the uneven and imperialist ways racialization has impacted Arab identities. I work here, especially in chapters 1 and 3, to show how Arabs themselves engage in processes of racialization that uphold white supremacy via anti-Blackness. In her work on 1920s Syrian Americans, Sarah Gualtieri highlights the ways Arabs are ambiguously racialized and how that racialization impacts their citizenship.[24] This articulation is explored for contemporary subjects in *Race and Arab Americans Before and After 9/11*, where the editors and essays attend to anti-Arabness as a racialized formation.[25] At the same time, I am conscious of how Arabness often disappears Black Arabs, or forms Arabness via opposition to Blackness in order to come closer to whiteness.[26] This is the case for diaspora Arabs, but also for Arabs in their Arab nations. Safia Elhillo writes, "So much of the thinking behind the horrific treatment of South Sudanese by the 'Arab' Arabophone North stems from the false binary of Blackness/Arabness that aspires to pursue an Arab identity by erasing the Black one. So much of the thinking behind the flourishing industry of skin-lightening creams in Sudan, so much of the thinking behind the derogatory term '3irig,' meaning Black blood or African blood—it all comes from this legacy of anti-blackness tied up in the word 'Arab.'"[27] Rayya El Zein notes in the introduction to a special forum on cultural constructions of race and racism in MENA/SWANA regions that many non-Black MENA/SWANA communities are "grappling with the historical legacies of European colonial violence and neo-imperialism in the shape of the global war on terror, [and] have struggled to also recognize the local and regional lineages of empire and colonialism that continue to dispossess and discriminate racially in the region."[28] Both Elhillo and El Zein highlight how we must continue to interrogate and unsettle our understanding of the word "Arab" and of Arabness. *Between Banat* insists on a relational Arabness to foreground racialization and to consider Arabness without reifying anti-Blackness.

Arab is not a fixed category that describes sedimented cultural practices or peoples, but rather a relationship between people and their shared cultures. Queer Arab subjects, particularly women, index the circuitry of Arabness itself, revealing how notions of Arab identity in multiple locations are impacted by Orientalism, coloniality, nationalism, and heteronormativity. Within these meta-narratives emerge distinct strands, such as anti-Blackness, authenticity politics, homonormativity, and respectability politics. Queer Arab critique foregrounds that Arabness is constructed through gender and sexuality. Queer Arab subjects are discursively overwritten and invisibilized via the multiple discourses of race, gender, sexuality, and nation that surround them.

Queer Arab Critique

This book employs queerness as a method, a practice, and a subject position one occupies with regard to normative sexual power structures. Queer Arab critique is the method and practice by which we reveal queer Arab subjects. Through it, I argue that queer subject formation in Arab contexts is distinct from precolonial renditions of Arab homoeroticism and Western articulations of sexuality. Queer Arab critique helps undermine the centrality of Western nation-states in queer of color discourses, challenges Arab nationalist paradigms that erase queer subjects, and brings women to the center of queer Arab studies.

Studies of nonnormative sexualities in Arab communities are few. Many are historically driven and emphasize sexuality in relation to Islam, for example, Khaled El-Rouayheb's *Before Homosexuality in the Arab Islamic World*. Others are regionally specific, like Sofian Merbet's *Queer Beirut* or Jarrod Hayes's *Queer Nations: Marginal Sexualities in the Maghreb*. Few focus explicitly on women. There are Samar Habib's two projects: *Female Homosexuality in the Middle East* and *Arabo-Islamic Texts on Female Homosexuality: 850–1780 A.D.* We might also look to Sahar Amer's *Crossing Borders: Love between Women in Medieval French and Arabic Literature*.[29] While useful grounding for this study, all three use a historical approach and only speculate on current iterations of same-sex desire between women. *Between Banat* picks up the thread of these studies by shifting to a contemporary focus, by invoking transnational Arab positioning, and by emphasizing women. The use of diverse language in these titles (homosexuality, queer, love between women) also hints at a concern across all our studies: How do we name or narrate same-sex desire, practices, or identities in Arab contexts?

Recent scholarship on the topic, in queer studies broadly and in Arab critique specifically, is concerned with how queer subjects might be caught between difficult binaries that foreclose their possibility: first, the sexual binary of heterosexual and homosexual, and second, the Orientalist constructions of East and West. While some Arabs do claim identity categories like gay or lesbian, many more organize their sexual desires and practices in ways that are not readily legible in either frameworks of gay and lesbian identity or Arab nationalist articulations of sexuality. What I mean by this is that nonnormative gendered and sexual practices are part of Arabs' lives, but the people practicing them might not claim the identities available and associated with such practices, such as lesbian, gay, sahaqiya, or shaatha. The latter terms, "sahaqiya" (a word some translate as "lesbian") and "shaatha" (a word that some translate as "abnormal"), might be overwritten with negative connotations. For the former, queer Arab subjects might not check off benchmarks of LGBT identity common in Western cultures. Lisa Duggan describes the normative trajectory and narrative for Western LGBT subjects as homonormativity.[30] Many Arab subjects are not homonormative—they might not be "out" or have a "coming out story." Many might be in same-sex relationships without naming them lesbian or gay. For these reasons, I avoid using lesbian, gay, or homosexual to describe same-sex practices in Arab contexts.

Tensions around the heterosexual and homosexual binary are complicated by the prescription of moral, political, and social values to Arab sexualities by Orientalism and by Arab responses to it. Numerous discourses circulate about Arab sexualities that make it difficult to locate same-sex desires, practices, and identities. Hanadi Al-Samman and Tarek El-Ariss write that there is a standstill in current studies of Arab sexualities that turns "into a premodern Eastern versus modern Western-oriented division. While the East is studied as a repository of tradition with an identifiable sexual and amorous nomenclature, the West is often presented as a fixed hegemonic structure distinct from the East . . . this division has generated a set of binaries pertaining to the applicability of terms (gay, lesbian, homosexual) and theoretical frameworks (queer theory) to Middle Eastern literary and cultural contexts."[31] Accordingly, some scholars consider the use of identity categories like lesbian or homosexual out of line for Arab subjects because of their association with the West. Jasbir Puar uses the term "homonationalism" to describe how homonormativity becomes an object of imperial and Orientalist activity in SWANA regions.[32] Homonationalism also describes how homophobic and heteronormative nations like the United States are framed as exceptionally free and democratic because of their sexual liberation. Joseph Massad names the apparatus of homonationalism—Western imperialism and exceptionalism around gay subjects—the "Gay International." The Gay International includes both the discourses about it and the structures that mobilize those discourses. Massad also suggests that LGBTQ identities could be inappropriate for Arab subjects precisely because of their historical inaccuracy and association with colonialism and imperialism.[33]

At the same time, Arab nationalist paradigms often disavow nonnormative sexualities as inauthentic to Arab culture. We can look to national crackdowns on queer life in Egypt, Lebanon, and other Arab nations as examples. LGBTQ activism and scholarship on it has evidenced how Arab national projects champion normative sexual and gendered identities, desires, and practices as one means by which to establish an "authentic" Arab subject. For example, Liat Kozma argues that the late nineteenth-century anticolonial nationalist project in Egypt defined itself against Orientalist discourses via articulation of specific gendered and sexual politics.[34] Deniz Kandiyoti suggests Arab reformers refashion the nation via recourse to "traditional" cultures.[35] Nadine Naber studies this practice in the United States via Arab Americans, who articulate normative gendered and sexual scripts as one way to resist assimilation in the diaspora. Naber calls this the politics of cultural authenticity.[36] In both instances, a rejection of queerness is thus an assertion of "traditional" Arab culture as the basis for anti-Orientalist Arab identity. To highlight how the cultural politics of authenticity operate in the Arab nations as well as in their diasporas, I use the shorthand "heteronational." Heteronational refers to normative sexual and gendered discourses based on allegedly precolonial values that emerge as responses to colonialism and Orientalism, in an attempt to restore an authentic Arab subject fit for the postcolonial Arab nation. While these concepts—homonormativity, homonationalism, Gay International, heteronational—are useful to name Orientalist discourses that inform Arab sexualities, they also make it difficult to imagine or make space for Arab subjects who are indeed engaged in homoeroticism or same-sex behaviors.

Recent scholarship turns to queer and queer of color critique to manage this discursive logjam. Queer of color critique elaborates a model of theorizing that actively attends how sexuality is informed by other facets of difference. In *Aberrations in Black*, Roderick Ferguson suggests that queer of color critique "interrogates social formations as the intersections of race, gender, class with particular interest in how those formations correspond with and diverge from nationalist ideals and practices."[37] Amal Amireh notes that using "queer" in relationship to Arab culture is often framed in one of two ways—as a capitulation of Arab cultures to neoliberal identity politics or as a means to discuss organizations and performances of same-sex eroticism that are significant to and emergent within local cultures and histories.[38] Routing queer through transnational feminist and queer of color engagements undermines the insinuation of the former and grounds us in the latter. The history of colonization and Orientalism alongside the ongoing globalization of economies and cultures makes imagining an Arab subject hermetically sealed from the influence of the West impossible. Queerness in Arab contexts is always about local cultures and histories at the same time that it is about the global location of these cultures. I follow precedent set by recent scholarship on this topic and use queer, first, "not as a field with a delimited object of study (such as homosexuality or even sexuality), but as an analytic, a methodology, a critical sensibility, a conceptual strategy, or a reading practice."[39] Second, queer names modes of gendered and sexual interactions that resist or challenge heteronormative ideals but are (usually) not codified through a sexual identity.[40] I include under this articulation of queerness displays of homoeroticism, nonnormative gender performance, ambiguously oriented lust, and more.

Thinking about queerness as a relation to power is indebted to Cathy Cohen's "Punks, Bulldaggers, and Welfare Queens: The Real Radical Potential of Queer Politics?"[41] In the essay, Cohen resists structures that recommit queerness as a binary opposition to heterosexuality and instead asks us to think about how nonnormative subject positions can be the basis for progressive coalitional politics. This is especially salient for Black, Indigenous, and people of color who might not identify with queer and/or LGBT identities and who might be perceived as heterosexual, but are very rarely heteronormative. Building on this necessary reframe of queerness, I use queerness to denote that which resists and subverts heteronormative Arab cultures, rather than looking for categorical LGBT identities.

Between Banat uses queer of color critique couched in transnational feminist frames. As noted earlier, current examples of queer of color critique in Arab contexts tend to study men and desire between men. As Rodríguez notes, heteronormativity and misogyny often evacuate desire from female subjects, or dismiss it as insignificant.[42] When desire happens between women, it is easily disappeared or overlooked because it fails to manifest in homonormative iterations. Though many texts can attest to the minimization of Arab women's lives and (same-sex) desires, I offer here some anecdotal evidence: as of this writing, each time I have presented my work an audience member has asked why I study Arab women and not Arab men and has implied the study lacked rigor because of its focus. Others have suggested that the book would not have an audience or gain interest because it examined only desire between women. As such, one of the primary feminist gestures of queer Arab critique is its investment in what happens between women and an unwillingness to disregard the femme and feminine as always already hegemonic.

My thinking in this book is guided by other queer of color and transnational feminist projects. In order to make possible women's seemingly *Impossible Desires*, Gayatri Gopinath brings together "postcolonial feminist scholarship on the gendering of colonialism, nationalism, and globalization, with a queer critique of the heteronormativity of cultural and state nationalist formations."[43] In her introduction to *Thieving Sugar*, Omise'eke Natasha

Tinsley considers the many kinds of names that one might use to understand homoeroticism between women in the Caribbean, including queer by way of transnational queer critique, and settles on women who love women, in order to avoid the culturally specific examples (like lesbian) as well the identity politics that attend to such identities.[44] Though they arrive at different names, both Gopinath and Tinsley center women's bodies, desires, and practices to bring gender to the foreground as a significant axis in the formation and articulation of sexual subjects.

Queer Arab critique holds Arab women's bodies, desires, and practices at its center. Via the study of Arab women, I emphasize queerness's mutability, shape-shifting, and diffuse operations. Focusing on women reveals different kinds of queer forms, queer practices, queer ways of being. It requires different kinds of queer archives. To locate desire between women, Rodríguez, Tinsley, and Gopinath all turn to other kinds of evidence—gestures, homosocial spaces, homoeroticism between seemingly heterosexual subjects. They also perform different kinds of readings: gestural, ephemeral, affective. In short, centering women necessitates alternate queer archives and queer methods, alternate stories and alternate tellings. Queer Arab critique begins with women as the catalyst and develops archives and methods accordingly.

Women and Femininity

Between Banat disrupts the oversignified category of "Arab woman" through use of the transliterated Arabic term "banat" (بنات) to refer to its subjects. It also challenges stereotypical modes of representation for Arab women and considers how Arab femininity is normatively rendered and how queer subjects can use femininity to reject heteropatriarchy.

As I have argued, how we name and articulate gender and sexual nonnormativity offers us an opportunity to rend power from Orientalist and heteronational scripts and prioritize the voices of queer Arab subjects. Through attention to language and narrative, queer Arab critique positions queer Arab sexuality as neither a derivative or assimilationist version of the West, nor a failed Arab subjectivity. The ambivalence around naming gender identity, while not as central to the book as a similar ambivalence around naming sexuality, certainly haunts it. Though "Arab woman" seems like a simple enough label, I was struck in my research by how many queer subjects expressed discomfort with it. This was similar but not collapsible to their uneasy experience with various names for sexual identities. Sometimes this discomfort was evident not in exposition wherein a writer or character considered their gender identity, but in the ways they narrated women at large: in their proximity or distance to the idea of women, in their articulation of what and who constituted womanhood. Many of the texts under consideration in this book feature writers or subjects who identify in varying degrees with the category "Arab woman," insofar as it describes their gender identity, and use multiple terms to name that experience. This includes cis and trans women writers and/or characters depicted. It includes those who express feelings of gender nonconformity or nonbinary gender identity. It includes young women, girls, and elders. For example, in chapter 4, many collections devoted to Arab women's voices feature writers that reject the identity "woman" to describe their experience but find value in understanding their position within society as people presumed to be women or forcibly policed into hegemonic femininity. This is to say, they narrate their experiences of sexism through the analytic category of woman. Some subjects in this book find use in gathering under the sign of woman even as it fails them.

In Arabic, many of the words that describe "woman" hold different connotative meanings. For example, بنت (bint) is the Arabic word for girl, daughter, or feminine child, but it is used in many texts to signify infants to adolescents, young Arab women, and adult Arab women, or to describe normative discourses about Arab femininity (e.g., in Christina Atik's "مش حلو لبنت" / "It's Not Nice for a Girl" discussed in chapter 5). Bint occurs more frequently in representations of Arab femininity than its formal and older counterparts نساء (nisa') or امرأة (imra'a), and certainly more than classed سيّدة (sayyida/lady). I use bint (and the plural banat) precisely because of its frequent invocation and multiple significations. The choice to use bint and banat is also indebted to Evelyn Shakir's groundbreaking ethnography of Arab and Arab American women, *Bint Arab*. Shakir's project centers Arab and Arab American women's voices in order to unsettle Orientalist visions of them. Finally, banat finds ancestry in the collection وقفت بنات (*Waqfet Banat*), an anthology about queer Palestinian women produced by أصوات (Aswat), a queer and women's activist organization in Palestine. *Waqfet Banat* was the first time I had tactile, permanent evidence that other queer Palestinian women existed, and that I could hold their stories. I discuss *Waqfet Banat* at length in chapter 4. Like Shakir and Aswat, I use banat to call my familiars; I sustain its use to emphasize the different kind of story/telling the book performs. Banat Arab are kin, and this work amplifies our creative and powerful stories of survival.

I also use banat because "Arab women" is at once an overfull signifier and an empty one. It is mutually constructed by Orientalist paradigms and anti-Arab sentiment, and Arab heteronationalisms. In Orientalist constructions, Arab women occupy one of three types: the silent and veiled Muslima; her hypererotic, "revealed" counterpart in the form of the harem girl or belly dancer; and lastly, the female terrorist.[45] As *Orientalism* tells us, the first two characters are a production of colonial fantasies: the former is the oppressed subject who necessitates imperial intervention; the latter is the stage on which imperial desires play out.[46] The first figure contributes to the construction of white saviorism and demonization of Arab culture that Gayatri Chakravorty Spivak describes as "white men saving brown women from brown men."[47] The veiled woman is, notably, silent. Lila Abu-Lughod notes that the physical object of the veil and opinions about it—is it freeing? is it oppressive?—become the central focus of conversations about Muslim women, and subsequently the actual lived realities and voices of those subjects disappear.[48] Alsultany notes how anti-Arab racism post-9/11 mobilized this figure anew and produced her as a sympathetic yet still silent object.[49] The second figure, the belly dancer or harem girl, constructs the Orient as a sexually deviant space where women's bodies are available for consumption. At the same time, the hypersexual Arab woman's availability is not a product of the woman's desires, but, as Amira Jarmakani notes in *Imagining Arab Womanhood*, a figure that bolsters the construction of Arabs as exotic and erotic others.[50] The hypersexual Arab woman is simultaneously a testament to Arab men's hypersexuality; their savage lust requires a harem of sexually available women. In both cases, the silent and the sexual, Arab women are not subjects but objects. They are capable of manifesting neither voice nor desire. These two figures exist alongside a third: the female terrorist in the form of hijacker or suicide bomber. The trope emerged primarily in the 1980s and into the 2000s, when plane hijackings and suicide bombings became strategies for armed resistance in Palestine and elsewhere. Though seemingly agential, Amireh argues that this figure is also coopted into the Orientalist clash of civilizations and reveals both the lack of Arab women's agency (they are allegedly duped into participation) and the inhumanity of Arab cultures that communicate through violence and martyrdom.[51]

At the same time, Arab femininities are mobilized by Arab nationalist paradigms that are responding to colonialism and attempting to construct an independent Arab state that rejects, overcomes, or disregards such Orientalist typification. Therese Saliba writes that although some nationalist struggles have offered women a platform to challenge normative practices within their communities, the use of women's liberation as a justification for imperial activity often produces a reactive response that sees women and femininity as spaces in which Arabs might "return" to an authentic, precolonial culture, the process I named earlier as heteronational.[52] As Minoo Moallem notes, in both Orientalist and nationalist responses, women's bodies become flat signifiers rather than agential subjects.[53] *Between Banat* rejects both the Orientalist framing and the heteronational response to articulations of Arab femininity and sexuality by centering Arab women's texts, lives, and voices. Though I use my first chapter to further outline how queer Arab women's stories are foreclosed by competing discourses, the remaining chapters emphasize how queer subjects exist and resist in expansive ways. Each subsequent chapter reckons with how queer subjects interrogate and challenge femininity and womanhood via their sexual desires, practices, and identities.

Significantly, *Between Banat* challenges the construction of femininity as always already a capitulation to heteropatriarchal constructions of gender and sexuality. In both Arabic and English texts, femininity is collapsed onto women's bodies through its normative compulsions. In many examples femininity functions to inform and help police the category of woman; in these examples femininity refers to a position in patriarchy, circumscribed by heteronormativity, binaristically defined against masculinity—what Raewyn Connell calls "emphasized femininity."[54] Karen Pyke and Denise Johnson offer a recalibration of Connell's formulation to attend to hierarchal organizations within femininity that are informed by intersections of race, sexuality, class, ability, and so forth.[55] Mimi Schippers defines "hegemonic femininity" as "the characteristics defined as womanly that establish and legitimate a hierarchical and complementary relationship to hegemonic masculinity and that, by doing so, guarantee the dominant position of men and the subordination of women."[56] Where hegemonic forms exist, so too do counterhegemonic forms. In my first chapter, I take care to unpack the hegemonic form of Arab femininity as modeled in Scheherazade, a femininity that prescribes heterosexuality and precludes queer subjects from representation. In later chapters, however, many characters and writers lay claim to femininity, deploying and embodying it in ways that resist normative gender and sexuality. By this I mean that either their performance of femininity is imagined independently of a masculine binary, or that the feminine desires, practices, and politics that are produced position femininity as a mobilization against heteropatriarchy rather than against men or masculinity. In *Between Banat*, many subjects occupy femininity as a subject position in order to reject and resist heteronormativity. I attend especially to instances where femininity becomes a foil for queer potential to flourish: where femininity and homosociality pair and produce space for intimacy, homoerotic desires, and nonnormative sexual practices. I borrow this strategy from Gopinath's *Impossible Desires*, where she argues that homosocial and home spaces were sites for women's desires.[57] The femininities discussed in *Between Banat* do not uphold heteronormativity as much as they are embodied in sensual acts against it. In the book, I ask that we consider and reconsider our understanding of femininity as a counter to masculinity that reifies the gender binary and suggest instead that it is a dynamic concept produced and appropriated by multiple kinds of subjects. Inasmuch as *Between Banat* makes and unmakes queer archives, it calls us to make and unmake femininity.

The book also attends to femme figures in Arab contexts. In queer critique, femme refers to performances of femininity by queer subjects. As Rhea Hoskin and Allison Taylor write: "Beyond an identity, femme is an enactment (Maltry and Tucker, 2002), a politic (Serano, 2013), an erotic (Nestle, 1992), an adjunctive or noun (Bergman, 2006) and a critical analytic, which requires bringing the multiplicities of femininities into focus (Dahl, 2017; Hoskin, 2017b, 2018, 2019). As such, femme potential ought not to be reduced to an aesthetic—or, perhaps, even an identity."[58] Hoskin and Taylor define femme in a similar fashion to how I define queer: as a potential identity and an analytic that allows us to see how gendered and sexual normativities are challenged. Femme can also usefully name how some subjects perform femininity but do not identify with or desire to be understood as women. In this way femme, like banat, offers us a means to mark subjects who evade the oversignification and evacuation of "queer Arab women."

The hyperpositionality of the subject "queer Arab women" is undone by attention to subjects who challenge each of these positions: who are not considered "properly queer" because they don't claim a lesbian or gay identity, who perform Arabness without recourse to authenticity politics, and who perform femininity and womanhood in provocative, nonnormative ways. Arab femininities and women's subjectivities are also constituted in the between: between various ethnic, racial, and national discourses; between the various physical sites and virtual texts of the book; between the temporal landscape that begins with thirteenth-century Scheherazade and ends with contemporary transnational artists; and last, but not least, between the multiple performances and rejections of femininity and sexuality discussed. *Between Banat* chooses to look beyond heteronormative surfaces for gestures, intimacies, and ephemeras that occur within femininity and enable other kinds of femininities and sexualities to emerge. By attending to the lives, loves, and traces of banat, women, and femmes, I create a new kind of queer archive. At the same time, the ambiguity and ambivalence that undergirds these subjects unmakes the archive in favor of imagining new ways of existing for queer Arab futures.

Languages, Genres, Mediums

As the previous sections articulate, this study has the tricky work of discussing several contested subjects (queer, Arab, women) whose contestations are central to it. In this section, I discuss how the selection of terms used and the objects studied are part of the argument of the book itself. Namely, language selections reflect the relationality I emphasize in the construction of queerness and Arabness; they also mark the particularity of queer Arab critique. Moreover, the multiplicity of languages, genres, and mediums in this book undergird the book's commitment to producing fluid, relational, and productive queer Arab archives.

I use queer to refer to subjects who perform nonnormative femininities and sexualities, and as an analytic to consider a subject's relationship to heteronormativity. When I say "Arab queers" I am referring to trans and cis Arab women, femmes, and those Arabs who identify with femininity or the social subject position of woman, if not the identity of "woman" per se. In deference to how many subjects name and understand themselves, I also use the transliterated term banat. I believe the visual and sonic disruption of banat on the page reminds us that Arab womanhood is produced in constant tension with colonial and national discourses about Arab women. In the case where a writer or character is explicitly named or identified by markers of cis, trans, nonbinary, or femme, I use the language the text provides. I acknowledge my own failure to be more explicitly inclusive and articulate regarding moments of trans and nonbinary representation, while at the same time respecting how some trans and nonbinary subjects in Arab communities prefer their gender, like their sexuality, to operate without definitive naming.

Between Banat thus offers multiple configurations of queer Arab subjectivity and uses multiple modes of reference to represent the diversity and fluidity of its subjects. I have chosen not to produce or select a single word to account for the superfluity or resolve the tension these words conjure. I cannot, nor do I politically desire to, identify with certainty each writer or character's gender or sexual identity. I choose to work with the sticky languages that exist; I stick with sticky language for several reasons. Neither "queer" nor "women" nor "femininity" captures the complexity of operations happening under their sign. Arabic versions of these terms similarly fail. The choice to work within the limited language available rather than engage in neologisms is about protecting obfuscation as a strategy and rejecting the impetus of categorization itself. New terms will not make those operations transparent, because it is impossible to ever make the intersections of such words clear without creating new exclusions. At the same time, by maintaining signifiers like queer and femme, those who have some attachment to or intrigue regarding such signifiers might find themselves in these pages.

In addition to mining language's failure, *Between Banat* chooses to allow obfuscation and refusal, to resist naming, translating, or making concrete queerness or women or femininity. The right of refusal and defiance and the right to privacy are often denied Arab subjects, particularly in an Orientalist colonial project, which demands unveiling and discovery. Some Indigenous scholars suggest Indigenous communities resist absorption into settler states through practices of refusal or defiance.[59] Here, refusal narrates some of the ways this book and the subjects therein reject Orientalist, colonial, and assimilationist narrations of Arab gender and sexuality. There are refusals in the specific texts studied, and in the book in general, to scopophilic Orientalism, to unveiling, to men as subject and center, and to the discursive oversignification of religion in Arab cultures. *Between Banat* and many of its subjects refuse a tidy narration of their identities and, in so doing, resist assimilation to Orientalist and heteronational paradigms. There will not emerge from this book "an Arab lesbian history" or a singular narrative about "what it's like to be an Arab lesbian" or a common set of tropes with which to simplify queer Arab identities. Instead, my goal is to present works that resist easy categorization, works that produce rupture in the very categories they seek to represent. As Muñoz writes in "Thinking Beyond Antirelationality and Antiutopianism in Queer Critique," refusal can be a productive gesture that animates queer horizons.[60] By diverting our focus from expected, singular representational tropes, *Between Banat* brings to bear new ways of living.

Since "between" is the central location of this book, I study subjects and objects that feature relationality as a primary ethos, and I toggle between many kinds of texts. By invoking multiple genres, mediums, and languages, I foreground a relational articulation of queerness and Arabness rather than one anchored in a singular "authentic" cultural practice, text, or geographic location. The breadth of texts and their linguistic, national, and generic diversity requires constant stitching and illustrates the relational nature of queerness in Arab cultures. Through stitching, I suggest Arabness is itself a relational quality or subject position. The texts surveyed here travel back and forth in time and across Arab geographies and diasporas. They do so because Arab peoples travel, and because our understanding of Arabness, of Arab people, is formulated in tension with the many ways Arabs have been understood and understand their identities in history, particularly in their interactions with imperialism and their resistance toward it. I tread across language and genre because queerness takes all kinds and appears everywhere. In so far as I configure Arab as a transnational identity, I also consider queerness in Arab cultures to be produced at a transnational intersection in which Arab and non-Arab iterations of Arab gender and sexuality are created and contested, usually with specific political aims. Exploring the discursive restraints on queer representation reveals how representations of gender and sexuality are configured via racial and national discourses. The transnational and queer frame of this project pushes against those limiting discourses and makes space to see and consider gender and sexual nonnormativity in Arab cultures.

In the chapters that follow I attend to work in Arabic, English, and Arabish, the language between Arabic and English. I include literary work in multiple genres: fiction, poetry, creative nonfiction, and autobiographical essays. I analyze Arabic language films as well as prints and graphic novels. I have surveyed texts that are considered mainstream and widely accessible, like Golden Era Egyptian films, alongside works that are more intimate and written for small audiences, like essay collections by a queer women's activist group in Palestine. I have considered texts that are widely translated and available, like *The Thousand and One Nights*, as well as texts that operate outside a linguistic medium, like contemporary prints and graphic novels published by diasporic art collectives. By including multiple genres and languages, I aim to expand the field of signification and provide the most opportunities for queer Arab women, femmes, and banat to emerge.

Another strategy of this work is to employ multiple mediums in the construction of queer Arab critique and in the production of its archive. As I noted earlier, the field of representation for Arab subjects, and women especially, is densely oversaturated and simultaneously evacuated of content. I oscillate between the linguistic and the visual because in some cases the visual relieves the pressure to name, a pressure that haunts the linguistic. In some film and art, facial expressions, gestures, or moments make known what the verbal language fails to adequately capture. As earlier, I turn to queer of color critique's emphasis on the ephemeral and gestural as sites of queer becoming. At the same time, the visual is not exclusively freeing. As the earlier discussion regarding Arab women archetypes attests, visual registers can essentialize and bind. Neither is language only a realm of restriction. Language can shift and surprise us, as chapter 4 demonstrates.

Between Banat produces queer Arab critique and pursues queer Arab archives through different kinds of story/telling. The diversity of texts in this book offers multiple opportunities to consider and imagine queer Arab subjects. The textual diversity also invites comparison, an opportunity to emphasize the relational as the central location of the book. I demonstrate how multiple texts exist and converse in relation to one another. The analysis oscillates between verbal and visual registers, and it does so intentionally to escape the discursive restrictions of each medium. Its focus on queer subjects foregrounds how Arabness and queerness are formed in relation and offers us new models for analyzing both. Finally, *Between Banat* is primarily written to study texts by queer Arab subjects rather than texts produced about them by others. It emphasizes women's, femmes', and banat's voices.

Toward Queer Arab Critique and Queer Arab Archives

In their introduction to *Arab and Arab American Feminisms* the editors ask, "What would analyses of race, gender, sexuality and nation look like if we were to center Arab and Arab American women, queer, and transgender experiences?"[61] *Between Banat* takes this question to the heart of its inquiry and argues that by centering queer women, we articulate Arabness as a transnational relation, we produce a mode of queer of color critique that is appropriate to transnational Arab subjects and resists reification of colonial or heteronational modes of queer subjectivity, and finally, we locate strategies to make possible queer presence and futures.

The procession of my analysis unfolds over five chapters. While the book proceeds in a mostly linear fashion regarding time, it moves constantly through language and location. It also resists a teleological trajectory and instead emphasizes the ambivalence in the subject's articulation of their sexualities, and the ambivalence of the archive at large. Chapter 1 is the only chapter that I consider pessimistic in nature; it details the obstacles and discursive foreclosures to seeing and imagining queer Arab subjects. Chapter 2 outlines strategies for locating queer Arab desire amid mainstream, hegemonic texts and provides the operational strategies of queer Arab critique. Chapters 3 and 4 examine contemporary articulations of queer Arab life by Arab writers that defy queer erasure and demonstrate how queer critique challenges the

many normativities, violences, and manifestations of imperialism and heteronationalism in Arab cultures. Chapter 5 studies visual mediums and film
to outline three strategies for queer futures—a practice I call sahq. Sahq uses
the methods of queer Arab critique and the record of its archives to think
about the necessary conditions for a queer future.

Chapter 1, "A Thousand and One Scheherazades," names the discourses
that limit the production and visibility of a queer Arab archive through a
study of normative Arab femininities as translated in the figure of Scheherazade. The study of Scheherazade illustrates how Arabs are transnational
subjects, how gender and sexuality become sites of racial and ethnic nego-
tiation for Arabs, and how Arab femininity is over- and underwritten by
Orientalism, heteronormativity, and heteronationalism. To do this, I offer a
literary history of the pan-Arab storyteller Scheherazade. I analyze the figure
of Scheherazade within the frame story of *The Thousand and One Nights* and
in contemporary Arab American literature to articulate how Arab femininities are manipulated to serve the interests of Arab national programs as well
as Orientalist and anti-Arab immigrant paradigms. At the same time, the
chapter reveals how writers reckoning with Scheherazade's troubled legacy
attempt to reclaim and reorient her narratives. This chapter is grounded in
literary theories regarding minority canon formation and critical ethnic studies, and uses close readings of the literature to outline the limiting discourses
that inform and frame depictions of femininity and women's sexualities in
transnational Arab cultural production.

Despite the limitations outlined in chapter 1, there are ways to locate and
read queer Arab subjects in normative Arab cultural productions. My second
chapter, "Between Women," develops queer Arab critique as a methodology
and toolkit for locating queer women's desires. To read queerness in texts
that are not explicitly or transparently queer, I argue that we must attend
to queer spectatorship; queer space and time; homoerotic triangulation; and
queer containment. These four strategies of queer Arab critique are the methodological foundation upon which the remainder of the book is predicated.
In the chapter, I examine two films from the Golden Era of Egyptian cinema,
a nostalgic and celebrated site of Arab cultural production. I read the popular films against their heteronormative grain to reveal how even mainstream
texts allowed alternate femininities and homoeroticism between women to
emerge. Queer Arab critique refutes the discourse that queerness comes from
Western colonization and is therefore inauthentic to Arab culture. Instead,
the films function as archival evidence of same-sex desire and eroticism
between Arab women. I draw on queer of color critique and transnational

feminist scholarship from the SWANA region to decenter the United States in queer of color critique and to prioritize an Arab and specifically in this case Egyptian cultural context. At the same time, I attempt to ground my critique against Orientalist sensationalism by articulating the many cultural levels and references within which the films operate.

While chapter 2 examines mainstream texts where queerness moved in ephemeral, gestural, and unnamed ways, chapter 3, "Longing in Arabic," studies three Arabic-language novels where characters and their same-sex desires are explicitly named with known identity categories like "lesbian." Through their direct representations, I argue that the novels produce a queer story/telling more expansive than the identities named suggest. I show how the novels narrate a community history of queer Arab women, banat, and femmes; how they reject essentialist articulation of queer Arab identities; and how they produce robust criticisms of Arab heteropatriarchy and heteronormativity. Specifically, the texts ask us to consider the significance of ableism, anti-Blackness, socioeconomic status, and imperial and state violence as intersecting concerns for queer Arab subjects. The chapter discusses how an explicit naming of sexual identities unfolds for the characters, and how the characters in the novels respond to their overwritten sexualities. The regional specificity of the novels (which take place in Lebanon, Saudi Arabia, and Syria) allows us to explore how local and national normativities impact queer Arab life. At the same time, by considering the role of genre and the novels' multiple audiences, I suggest that the works have a broader transnational readership. The chapter thus makes and unmakes a queer Arab archive by insisting on the history and presence of queer Arab women in Arab cultures and rejecting a categorical representation of banat's loves and lives. A secondary argument of this chapter is that Arabic novels are a potentially queer and feminist literary form.

Chapter 4 builds on the ambivalent archive of the previous two chapters by examining three collections of autobiographical writing by queer Arabs, collected and published by two queer activist organizations in Palestine and Lebanon. While the previous chapter examined how the genre of the Arabic novel made space for queer women's intimacies and interiorities, "Love Letters" challenges the notion that the Arabic language itself forbids or erases queer sexuality. I argue that writers in these collections manipulate Arabic and English to offer new ways of seeing and thinking queer life. I offer a close reading of the naming practices writers use in these texts to move us toward a contemporary vocabulary for queer Arab subjects, one that evades, challenges, and upturns the restrictive discourses from chapter 1. As in the previous chapter, chapter 4 argues that we can look to our own communities for strident and intersectional critiques of Arab heteropatriarchy, imperialism, and occupation. Taken together, chapters 3 and 4 look toward how Arab cultural formations and the Arabic language both empower and foreclose queer Arab subjectivity. From queer stories, Arabs can locate useful critiques and interventions into heteropatriarchy, respectability, and nationalist paradigms. Chapter 4 thus makes evident that queer Arab life is not only present and possible but begins to imagine what must be undone to ensure queer futures.

My concluding chapter, "Sahq," discusses film, prints, and graphic novels that imagine otherwise. It asks: What do we need for Arabs to be queer and OK? In it, I argue that queer Arab futurity necessitates a rejection of respectability and authenticity politics and relies on the formation of transnational collective communities to resist imperialism and violence. To describe these measures, I recruit the Arabic term سحق (sahq). I define sahq as an embodied form of queer Arab action and world-making that holds at its center the tenets of transnational collective organizing, rejection of respectability politics, and refusal of cultural authenticity as the central metric of Arab identity. Sahq serves queer subjects and eases the pain heteropatriarchy and normativity visits on all bodies. The texts in this chapter use sahq to create moments of pleasure and joy in the representations of queer life. The texts directly challenge normative representations of gender and sexuality in Arab culture and attempt to disrupt and educate Arab communities against homophobia and misogyny. Through the texts in the chapter, I suggest that the creative and political labor of banat and femmes—their sahq—offers transnational Arab subjects a guide map for a free and joyful queer future.

☾

In *Between Banat*, queer Arab women, banat, and femmes are not only a part of Arab history, active voices in the Arab present, but they are the visionaries of joyful Arab futures. The journey of this book is thus threefold: First, to outline the multiple discourses and obstacles that obfuscate queer Arab subjects, particularly for banat. For queer Arab women and femmes, the horizon of possibility is egregiously eclipsed by essentialisms and nationalisms that abject queerness from Arab culture, by ongoing Orientalist erasure of a mobile and shifting Arab culture, and by blatant anti-Arab, misogynist, and homophobic sentiment in the Arab world and its diaspora. Yet despite the discursive and material threats to queer Arab life, it persists. As such, the second aim of this book is to demonstrate the presence of queer Arab life in heteronormative spaces and catalogue how queer Arabs animate and narrate themselves. I establish queer Arab critique as the mode by which we can archive queer histories and presents. Queer Arab critique is located in the between; I define both Arabness and queerness as relational concepts in constant movement between transnational, diasporic, and Arab national circuits. Queer Arab critique centers banat and emerges from the between of transnational feminist thought and queer of color critique. Finally, drawing on artists and creators who are both aware of the limiting discourses that frame queer Arab life and committed to representing it with joy and pleasure, the book discusses the strategies and activisms necessary to hold and create queer Arab futures, with banat at the center.

a thousand and one scheherazades

1

Arab Femininities and Foreclosing Discourses

In the tales of *The Thousand and One Nights*, Scheherazade escapes death by spinning stories for a murderous king.[1] King Shahryar took a virgin as his wife each night and had her executed in the morning. Scheherazade volunteers for this fate but arranges for her sister, Dinarzad, to request one story as a goodbye. Scheherazade tells a long tale, one that extends beyond the dawn of morning. So intrigued is the king by her story, he lets her live to tell the ending the following night. Scheherazade completes the first and begins another, repeating the pattern a thousand and one times over a thousand and one nights. By this time she has borne the king's children, and he has come to respect and trust her. The king pardons her and they rule together ever after.

This uncommon fairytale where the heroine rescues herself from destruction has served as an inspirational metaphor for Arab and Arab American writers, who recognize that Scheherazade's ability to narrate is a matter of life and death. Despite her emergence in the tenth century, Scheherazade remains a compelling figure in Arab and Arab American literature and culture. As a storyteller and state queen, she evades the three typical representations of Arab femininity outlined in the introduction: silent veiled Muslima, hypersexual dancer or harem girl, and female terrorist. Scheherazade is hailed as ancestor, muse, and icon for many Arab and Arab American writers. The sheer volume and variety of texts in which she's invoked is a testament to her versatility and centrality to an Arab literary canon. Tracing Scheherazade's appearance across multiple texts offers a long view of transnational Arab literatures. Examining her meaning and function in those texts across time offers insight into the formation of and expectations for Arab femininity.

In this chapter, I identify and discuss the discourses that limit the emergence of queer Arab subjects in order to begin to identify, articulate, and represent those subjects in later chapters. I argue Scheherazade is in an index of multiple discourses that influence and at times preclude representations of Arab femininity. These discourses include the heteronormativity within Orientalism and heteronationalism, elitism and anti-Blackness, and anti-Arab racism and Arab reactions thereto. While citing Scheherazade can productively join Arab creators to a legacy of Arab literary production, it comes at the cost of reifying hegemonic femininity. Studying Scheherazade avails us to the normative and hegemonic archive of Arab femininity, one that can overwrite or eclipse that of a queer feminine subject.

Scheherazade's original frame story in *The Nights* and her appearance in Arab American literature makes visible the demands on Arab femininity and its transnational shape.[2] *The Nights* and their heroine operate as an ur-text of Arab culture in the larger world. As a transnational Arab icon, Scheherazade is well suited to indexing a broad understanding of Arab femininity, one that takes into account how Arab and non-Arab writers convey feminine subjects. Studying Scheherazade can reveal how representations of Arab women and femininity change given the cultural and political context in which they emerge. Her versatility opens her up to a number of political maneuvers. Her hyper-referentiality makes Scheherazade a living figure, an index of perceptions of Arab women and Arab cultures, both from Orientalist and racist perspectives, as well as from Arab writers and artists who seek to reclaim her. Because of the dominance of heteronormativity and heteropatriarchy in these scripts, imagining and representing queer Arab subjects, especially women, is quite difficult. This is offered not necessarily as a critique of cultural producers who cite Scheherazade, but rather as an explanation of why queer subjects are exceptionally difficult to name and locate in Arab cultural products.

To outline the discourses that inform normative Arab femininity and foreclose representations of queer subjects, I study Scheherazade as she appears in five contexts: two translations of *The Nights* and three contemporary retellings. First, I analyze Scheherazade's depiction and frame story in two translations of *The Nights*: Richard Burton's (1855) and Husain Haddawy's (1995).[3] Here I argue that femininity is a crucial site of racial negotiation in Orientalist depictions of Arabs and in Arab responses to Orientalism. As

Naber argues in *Arab America*, Arab Americans often negotiate their racial belonging/abjection from the US state via recourse to respectability and normative gendered and sexual expectations, what she calls the "cultural politics of authenticity."[4] It is this formation that underlines the construction of what I call heteronationalism, which accounts for a similar phenomenon in Arab nations alongside the diaspora. Heteronationalism describes how many Arab national projects champion normative sexual and gendered identities, desires, and practices as one means by which to establish an "authentic" Arab subject that harkens back to a "precolonial" Arab culture as the basis for a "postcolonial" Arab national identity. Using translations of Scheherazade and her frame story, I outline Orientalist visions of Arab femininity as well as Arab reactions to it, which rely on heteronationalism, elitism, and anti-Blackness.

Next, I discuss three contemporary invocations of Scheherazade that illustrate how Arab femininity is still shaped by the same discourses that animate translations: Orientalism, heteronationalism, elitism, and anti-Blackness. The three texts under discussion—*Scheherazade's Legacy: Arab and Arab American Women on Writing* edited by Susan Muaddi Darraj; *E-mails from Scheherazad* by Mohja Kahf; and *The Night Counter: A Novel* by Alia Yunis—also reveal how anti-Arab discrimination in the United States factors into the formation of Arab femininity. These texts often engage in the cultural politics of authenticity at the same time as they attempt to interrogate anti-Arab racism and respond to Orientalism. As such, this chapter reveals how Arab femininity is produced in the "between" of colonial and imperial negotiations of Arab culture, and how Arabness is constituted relationally between multiple stakeholders. I will discuss the translations in the following section and the three contemporary retellings in the subsequent sections.

Using Scheherazade to Outline Orientalist and Heteronational Discourses of Arab Femininity

In this section, I analyze two translations of *The Nights'* frame story that feature Scheherazade prominently in order to articulate normative discourses of Arab femininity. Though one of the translations is considered an example of Orientalism (Burton's) and the other attempts to respond to Orientalism (Haddawy's), both use femininity as the site of racial and ethnic negotiations of Arab identity. Scheherazade's idealized femininity thus tells us both about normative gender and sexual roles for Arab subjects and about how "authentic" Arabness is defined through its gendered and sexual norms. Through

Scheherazade we learn that ideal Arab femininity is patriotic, reproductive, elitist, and anti-Black.

To understand the significance of Scheherazade it is useful to discuss briefly *The Nights* and its multiple translations. The historical legacy of *The Nights* refutes the idea of Arab culture as lacking or underdeveloped as suggested by colonial and Orientalist discourse. As *The Nights'* revered and accomplished orator, Scheherazade becomes a representative of the genealogy of Arab literature and its lyricism. For contemporary writers, Scheherazade and *The Nights* offer legacy and the points of departure for new literature. *The Thousand and One Nights*, better known in English as *The Arabian Nights*, is a collection with diffuse origins, namely Persian, Arab, Indian, and Asian. Historians have found reference to the existence of the stories in partial form as early as the tenth century, particularly in the now lost Persian story Hazār Afsān, from whence Scheherazade's story hails. The ambiguous origins of *The Nights* add to Scheherazade's allure—since she belongs to no clear, codified nation, she offers a generic legacy to the region, available for citation by any and all writers who understand *The Nights* as part of their literary history. *The Nights* began as an oral tradition and started appearing in written form in the second half of the thirteenth century. From that point forward, multiple versions of the collection proliferated. With transcription, Arabic versions of *The Nights* became historic archives of the changes in the Arabic language and literature.

However, *The Nights'* and Scheherazade's literary legacy is troubled by the history of Orientalist translations into other languages. Translations of *The Nights* essentialize and otherize Arab men and cultures, while women other than Scheherazade are treated to hypersexualization à la the harem girl. In most translations, Scheherazade becomes the ideal feminine foil to the exotic, morally destitute Orient. With lurid descriptions and hyperbolic representations, translations of *The Nights*, most notably Burton's 1885 English travelogue version, began to signify the Arab world to non-Arabs. *The Nights'* English translation coincides with rise of the British Empire through colonial endeavors in the East and North Africa. As Edward Said has noted, the fascination with *The Nights* and the characterization of the Arab world therein are part of the colonizing project. Orientalism created the East as a discreet object in need of guidance: moral, political, and economic. During this period of colonization and imperial conquest, Western European nations (particularly England and France as dominant colonial powers in the Middle East) produced travelogues, scholarly journals, photographs, scientific findings, literature, and more to document and penetrate "the mysteries of the lush orient." This, of course, is part of the fascination with *The Nights*—their spectacularization of the barbarity and sensuality of the East. Said documents this phenomenon extensively in *Orientalism*, citing the problematic framing of the East by the West through discourses of knowledge.[5] Through invoking harems, the sexual lasciviousness of the Arab world, and thinly disguised racial politics, Burton's translation of *The Nights* provided fodder for why the East needed the West to rule it.[6]

In translations of *The Nights,* Scheherazade's femininity becomes crucial to both Orientalist representations of Arabs and Arab responses to Orientalism. Scheherazade is the body upon which Arabs' racial and ethnic identity is cast in both Orientalist translations like Burton's and translations that seek to respond to Orientalism like Haddawy's. Despite various changes across translated versions and new editions of *The Nights,* Scheherazade is consistently positioned as an exemplary and ideal feminine figure. Scheherazade is serving of family, husband, and kingdom. She is faithful and feminine and educated. Though she has some access to power, her power is never complete and always under threat of retribution. Scheherazade, the woman who saves a man and a nation, is inevitably a consumable figure, poised to offer a glimpse into the East (as in Orientalist renditions) while maintaining its respectable face (as in reclamations and responses). Across translations and editions, the frame story depicts Scheherazade as a model feminine subject.

To fully illustrate the gendered and sexual normativity that Scheherazade encompasses, I will offer a brief analysis of Scheherazade and *The Nights'* frame story as they appear in the two translations already mentioned, Burton and Haddawy. I use these translations of the frame story because Burton's translation outlines Orientalist discourses while Haddawy's constitutes a response to Orientalism, which manifests in discourses of respectability.[7] In these texts, there are surprising moments of consistency and deviation in Scheherazade's character. The moments of difference and continuity reveal the demands placed on Scheherazade's femininity by both colonization and anti-Orientalism. Similarities in the translations of the frame story speak to shared heteropatriarchal values. Both texts use Scheherazade to offer a very particular vision of virtuous Arab womanhood, treat patriarchal state violence as du jur, and invoke anti-Black rhetoric. Her position within *The Nights* as the daughter of the vizier, her learnedness, her management of the king, her fertility, her engagement in normative gender and sexual paradigms, and her investment in the heteropatriarchal nation make her a model Arab woman and feminine subject.

Sexuality is a key site of Scheherazade's normativity. In the frame story of *The Nights*, two other characters are depicted as ravenous, hypersexual women and serve as counterpoints to Scheherazade: King Shahryar's first wife, the queen, and a jinni's captive bride. The former's sexual appetite causes her to cuckold the king with his own servants, while the latter responds to her imprisonment by using the jinni's power to force men to have sex with her. These "bad women" are marked by their sexual appetites. Unlike the queen and the jinni's wife, Scheherazade enters into a relationship with the king not for sex, but to save other women and the nation. While the jinni's bride and the king's first wife both sought sex for satisfaction, Scheherazade's sexual experience with the king is in service of her greater mission of saving the king and kingdom. Scheherazade is a literal virgin next to the other women, who are presented as whores. Indeed, there are no descriptions of sex between the king and Scheherazade, allowing her to remain unsullied and exceptional against the crude and voyeuristic depictions of sex in which the other women feature. Here we learn that sex for pleasure is not an appropriate or acceptable mode of feminine sexuality, and as such, is not one in which Scheherazade is seen to participate.

Scheherazade is also configured as exceptional through her relationship to the nation. As many scholars have noted, women are often considered a critical symbol for constructing the nation. Constructions of womanhood in the nation are reliant on patriarchal values.[8] Mrinalini Sinha suggests national ideologies often yoke women to motherhood, both symbolically and explicitly through the act of reproduction.[9] Scheherazade is produced as an exceptional national figure through her sacrificial femininity and reproduction. In the frame story, Scheherazade chooses to marry because she believes she can convince the king to stop murdering young women. If she succeeds, this will also save the nation, which is becoming restless with the king's murders. Scheherazade is confident in her decision, exclaiming, "Either I shall live or else I should be a ransom for the children of the Moslems and the cause of their deliverance from his hands and thine."[10] In the Haddawy translation, Scheherazade informs her father, "I would like you to marry me to King Shahryar, so that I may either succeed in saving the people or perish and die like the rest."[11] Thus, Scheherazade is distinct from the other women of the story. Willing to die to save others, Scheherazade strikes the reader as potentially naïve but also brave, patriotic, and especially pious in the Burton. Furthermore, she places the needs of the nation and her future husband over the needs of her father and family, and in so doing, fulfills the heteronormative as a national imperative. Scheherazade becomes a good woman by identifying and pledging allegiance to the political system in play, and attempting to civilize the king.

In the frame story, femininity and appropriate feminine sexuality are systems that buttress not only the masculine figure of the king, but the kingdom itself. The frame story of *The Nights* employs the heteropatriarchal trope wherein the nation is the normative family unit: the king is father and figurehead; Scheherazade is the mother who upholds the morality and cohesiveness of the royal unit. Sinha and Kandiyoti suggest that the nation operates as a heteropatriarchal institution that upholds binaristic and limiting gender roles through and with normative and procreative prescriptions for sexuality.[12] Scheherazade fulfills this heteropatriarchal national function in many ways: she stops the king from murdering more citizens, thereby saving the nation. She bears the king's children, insuring their continued reign. Finally, Scheherazade's faithfulness to the king is further rewarded when the king bestows a castle upon her father, making her success a reflection of her father's reputation. Thus, we learn from *The Nights* that normative sexuality for women is the absence of sexual drive and the patriarchal reproduction of the kingdom.

The third way Scheherazade's idealized femininity is differentiated from others is through her superior class standing, which enables her education. Najmabadi discusses how educational regimes were central to the production of womanhood in modern Iran.[13] Similarly, Mary Ann Tétreault and Haya al-Mughni explore how education contributed to and helped construct class stratification in Kuwait.[14] Both Haddawy's and Burton's translations underscore Scheherazade's exceptionalism with regard to her education and her intelligence. In the frame story, Scheherazade is described first and foremost as well read and learned. She is reported to have "read the books of literature, philosophy, and medicine." She has memorized poetry, has studied history, and is familiar with political ideologies. She is the daughter of the king's vizier, and thus occupies a higher socioeconomic position than many of the other women who appear in *The Nights*. Her elite status in both education and class foregrounds her request to marry the king, and her ability to survive said marriage. Scheherazade's access to education and her relationship to a high-ranking official within the kingdom offer her two survivalist strategies unavailable to the other women in *The Nights*: she draws on her education and familiarity with history to entertain the king later in *The Nights*, and her social status has thus far protected her from the effects of the king's wrath. Here then, Scheherazade's femininity is made exceptional through its access to education and its elite class standing.

Scheherazade's ideal femininity is not only marked via class, it is also developed via its distance from Blackness. Scholarship on anti-Blackness in

Arab nations has grown in recent years, though Yasmine El-Geressi suggests anti-Blackness has long operated as an open secret, evident in linguistic choices, beauty standards, the common practice of blackface, and numerous other forms of violence.[15] In addition to cultural representations, Bina Fernandez, Burcu Ozcelik, and Yasin Kakande reference the kafala system, a migrant sponsorship program, to concretize contemporary forms of Black enslavement in Arab states.[16] These studies focus primarily on racialization in Arab cultures, but Scheherazade makes clear how idealized Arab femininity is constructed against and away from Blackness. The frame story relies on anti-Black tropes to identify and idealize Scheherazade. In *The Nights*, both the queen and the jinni's wife have sex with Black men (the slaves and the jinni). The slaves' racial identity is explicitly marked as such, while the other major players in the frame story (Scheherazade, queen, wife, king) are not. The Black lovers are used to further condemn the queen and the jinni's wife and affirm their voracious sexual appetites. The emphasis on the race of the men produces Blackness as outside of Arabness, which Leila Tayeb argues is a consistent feature in constructions of Arabness.[17] Further, the use of race to mark hypersexuality reveals how anti-Blackness is structured into both normative gender and sexuality, as well as into the social fabric of *The Nights*. The derision lobbed at Black bodies in both translations of *The Nights* indicates for readers (and indeed the original listeners) how questions of colorism and racism were in play in Arab society well before the experience of Western colonization. In the text, the hypersexualization of Black men and their inferior class status alerts us to how Arabs also engage in racial hierarchization, which separates Blackness out from Arab identity. It is also notable that because the frame stories reference the slaves as cross-dressing men, Black women are absent entirely from the narrative. This subjugation and abjection of Blackness is a troubling consideration not only for Black Arabs, but for thinking about Arab subject formation at large, particularly after Western colonization, where anti-Blackness will be further reified as a stepping stone to whiteness.

Despite their difference in intent, both translations produce normative versions of Arab femininity that rely on heteronormativity, elitism, and anti-Blackness. Indeed, Scheherazade cannot be understood outside of her position between Orientalism and heteronationalism. As the ideal Arab woman, Scheherazade teaches us that Arab femininity is produced in a necessarily transnational set of exchanges between countries within the Arab world, as well as between Arab nations and those who sought to colonize or understand them. To continue to trace Scheherazade's movement and index her discursive functions, I turn now to contemporary mobilizations of Scheherazade in Arab American literature.

Using Scheherazade to Resist Orientalism and Assimilation in Contemporary Arab American Literature

In the second half of this chapter, I argue that recourse to Scheherazade in Arab American literature attempts to mobilize her normative femininity and sexuality to mitigate the increased queerness of the Arab body in the transnational imaginary. My analysis of Scheherazade in *Scheherazade's Legacy*, *E-mails from Scheherazad*, and *The Night Counter* demonstrates how some Arabs seeking acceptance or belonging in the United States do so through recourse to the colonial and racial regimentation of gender and sexuality. In the three contemporary examples, Scheherazade performs a model of Arab femininity that relies on heteronormative and heteronational iterations of Arab identity. The reconstruction of idealized Arab femininities and sexualities preclude nonnormative subjects from emerging and reify anti-Blackness and authenticity politics as structures of Arabness. In these texts Arab inclusion can rely on the exclusion and displacement of nonnormative, often queer, Arab bodies. *Scheherazade's Legacy* foregrounds women's writing to respond to Arab American racialization while erasing (queer) sexuality; *E-mails from Scheherazad* resists Orientalist representations of Arab and Muslim American women as sexually repressed while presenting an Orientalist treatment of Arab masculinity and queer sexual difference; and, finally, *The Night Counter*'s narrative exposes the effects and affects of state-sanctioned violence on Arab Americans while never fully recognizing or including Amir, the queer character, in the novel.

I investigate *Scheherazade's Legacy*, *E-mails from Scheherazad*, and *The Night Counter* for several reasons. First, each features Scheherazade explicitly, as opposed to generically referencing *The Thousand and One Nights*. Second, they are written in English and by authors understood as Arab American writers, via both their location in the United States and the contexts from which their texts emerge. I use these Arab American texts to continue to trace Scheherazade's border crossings and transnational subjectivity and to foreground how anti-Arab racism and ongoing Western imperialism foreclose possibilities for representing queer Arab subjects. Third, they encapsulate the generic diversity of Arab American literature, including autobiography, poetry, and fiction, respectively.[18] They are thus representative of some of the larger themes of the Arab American literary project—a project through and against which I am seeking queer Arab archives.

Notably, many texts that invoke Scheherazade in the United States emerged in the early 2000s. The timing is significant for two reasons. First, Scheherazade arrived in the wake of 1990s literary and liberal multiculturalism. The 1990s witnessed a flourishing of the Arab American literary scene in the form of numerous collections that sought to establish Arab Americans through the creation of an ethnic literary canon. These anthologies, such as *Food for Our Grandmothers: Writings by Arab-American and Arab-Canadian Feminists* and *Post-Gibran: Anthology of New Arab American Writing,* attempted to situate Arabs alongside other minority groups in the United States. These collections produced Arab American literature as an ethnic literature, one that could be incorporated alongside other minor canons in a multicultural frame. At the same time, Arab American writers negotiated their ambiguous racial assignation in the United States with literary projects that demonstrated their assimilation to the national culture through language mastery. Finally, as in other minor literatures, Arab American writing needed to appear authentically "Arab" in order to maintain its difference and be included in the multicultural spectrum. As Arab Americans struggled to craft their image within the discursive frames of difference and assimilation, Scheherazade offered a connection to an Arab literary history while inviting new narratives; drawing on her rhetorical role in *The Thousand and One Nights* as a framing device, she offers an opening for Arab Americans to tell more stories.

Second, the Arab American texts that feature Scheherazade explicitly were published in and after 2001.[19] These texts are marked by their proximity to 9/11. Regarding this marker, Arabs' experience of racialization is more accurately understood as a historical continuum along which 9/11 serves as a plot point—both in the United States and more transnationally. Especially surrounding 9/11, Arab Americans' experience of racialization has been marked by a simultaneous invisibility and hypervisibility.[20] As such, Scheherazade offered respectability through access to an Arab literary genealogy and her successful negotiation of Orientalism. She invites the American reader into the difference of the East with none of its threats. However, Scheherazade's exceptional capacity to represent Arab Americans in literature is inextricably linked to her gender and sexuality. Her gendered and sexual normativity is crucial since 9/11, which rendered the Arab body queer in a more explicit way than it had been rendered before.[21] While Said noted as early as 1978 that Arabs and the Arab world function as "a tableau of queerness" against which European normativity is defined,[22] the many graphic sexual threats issued to Bin Laden after 9/11 and to Saddam Hussein in the Second Gulf War, and the use of sexual torture against the bodies imprisoned at Abu Ghraib, all demonstrate how Arab bodies continue to invoke a sexually queer ontology. Beyond these incidents, the generic Orientalist discourse on Arab love and sexuality renders it simultaneously perverse and homophobic. For example, the notion that many Arabs, through their relationship to Islam, believe in polygamy, in heaven awarding virgins, and in women covering themselves insinuate a non-Western and thereby nonnormative practice of sexuality in Orientalist versions of Arab culture. Via Orientalism, the men are insatiable sexual addicts whose sexuality is repressed, and the women's sexuality is so repressed that women's bodies disappear in public. Meanwhile, the homosociality of Arab culture—along with the sometimes real, sometimes perceived homoeroticism of gender-segregated spaces—further distances "Arab culture" from "American" or "Western" ideologies, which present the United States and the West as sexually free and primarily heterosocial.

As such, Scheherazade is a site of contested meaning for Arab writers negotiating the politics of representation and their cultural citizenship in the diaspora. Through the analysis of Scheherazade, I articulate the discourses that form and inform representations of gender and sexuality in contemporary Arab culture, discourses that ultimately obfuscate queer women and make locating or creating a queer Arab archive difficult. Though these texts use Scheherazade to resist Orientalism and respond to racism, they often produce visions of Arab femininity and Arab cultures that erase or abject queerness. In the next three sections, I explore how the foreclosing discourses of Orientalism, heteronationalism, and anti-Blackness operate in three contemporary Arab American texts that employ the figure of Scheherazade. The following sections explore *Scheherazade's Legacy*, *E-mails from Scheherazad*, and *The Night Counter* in turn.

Using Scheherazade to Substantiate an Arab American Literary Canon

Scheherazade's Legacy uses Scheherazade to construct a vision of "Arab American" ethnic literature as one response to Orientalism and anti-Arab racism. The process of anthologization of Arab American voices attempts to produce the ideal Arab American subject. Unfortunately, the text's construction of Arabness invisibilizes or erases queer subjects. In *Legacy*, Scheherazade is used to create similarity between Arab Americans and other ethnic communities; she offers a means of substantiating Arab belonging to an American literary tradition and nation. She allows the authors to authenticate themselves as

Arab speakers and to respond to anti-Arab and Orientalist sentiment in the United States. Her presence foregrounds the centrality of gender and sexuality in discussions of what constitutes an authentic or assimilable Arab subject in the United States.

Legacy profiles the writerly lives of twelve Arab American women. The women, such as Lisa Suhair Majaj, Etel Ednan, and Diana Abu-Jaber, are recognizable names in Arab and Arab American literature, and their works include novels, poetry collections, and memoirs. *Scheherazade's Legacy* includes a preface by Barbara Nimri Aziz and an introduction by the editor, Darraj. As a collection, *Legacy* positions itself alongside other minority and ethnic literature canons. We can see this alignment in the publishing press for the collection, Praeger, a company committed to "Multiple cultures. Multiple tongues. Multiple ways of viewing the world." According to its mission, "Praeger opens the window to the rich world around us."[23] This language of liberal multiculturalism has been criticized by literary scholars and queer of color theorists. In *The Ethnic Canon*, David Palumbo-Liu argues against the additive nature of diversity programming in higher education while detailing the means by which that inclusion has and has not affected the minority subject's inclusion in the democratic process.[24] In *Aberrations in Black*, Ferguson examines how authors use literature to represent the subject's participation in national ideals of equality, unity, and diversity.[25] The imagining of a fully included subject by minoritarian authors signals an agreement with the ideals they mimic. Literature can thus deliver what the nation cannot: belonging. The pursuit of an Arab literary legacy is thus also the pursuit of Arab inclusion in the nation whose ideals their writing mimics. To be a good writer is to be a good citizen. In *The Nights* Scheherazade performs this citizenship for a direct representation of the state: the king. In *Scheherazade's Legacy* she navigates more cultural citizenship.

This is most readily illustrated in Aziz's preface remarks on becoming a writer. In order to speak for oneself, Aziz suggests that a writer must "master the language. Yet, craft is not the foremost issue. Honesty and intimacy, often accompanied by some pain, face us when we really examine our truths."[26] The remark regarding mastery suggests that the collection may have a hand in creating the identity it represents, but it also has a hand in evaluating that identity. By collecting a certain group of writers or kinds of writing, those writers and texts are validated as valuable contributors and contributions to the literature. To master literary aesthetic practices has frequently been a hallmark of American belonging.[27] Each author who appears in the collection does so with degrees of critical acclaim, cementing the Arab voice as capable. Aziz confirms their virtuosity when she articulates that it is through "art, not nostalgia" that she is moved by authors such as Naomi Shihab Nye.[28]

Far from objective, this emphasis on aesthetic beauty indicates a concern with being understood as capable writers, assimilable subjects, and modern citizens. This struggle is especially relevant for Arab American women; as we've discussed, representations of Arab women default to three categories: oppressed veiled victims, militant political terrorists, and exotic harem dwellers. None are considered credible speakers. Jarmakani argues that writing itself requires subjectivity that Western culture has deemed impossible for Arab and Muslim women.[29] David Lloyd explicates the ways aestheticism becomes racialized and entangled with ethics. In order to be canonized, Lloyd argues, one must produce work that is familiar to audiences insofar as it adheres to the aesthetic guidelines they accept. Recognition relies on similarity and emulation of normative ways of writing oneself. The subject's ability to measure up aesthetically is also a measure of the subject's modernity and her civilization. Ultimately, then, the efforts of the subject toward canon are no less than an assertion of the subject's humanity.[30]

Scheherazade's Legacy is in line with Jarmakani's and Lloyd's analyses. Aziz names three tasks for the Arab American writer: respond to stereotypes, overcome her colonization, and represent the self honestly.[31] According to Aziz, Arab American writers may not have matured to the third step in that process, although they are on track to do so. They may still struggle to "expose little of the real conflicts we face"; they are stuck figuring out how "to tolerate, to cleanse our image, to move on."[32] She calls for an "intimate" experience of Arab American life that is not entirely focused on politicization or assimilation into American society. This is indicated by her use of "real," which suggests that what is currently written is not "real" or dissociates the "real" from the political. She offers Suheir Hammad's work as exemplary in its realness, positioning Hammad as a writer with "face-to-face maturity of what it is to be Arab and American" via her poem "first writing since," which conveys Hammad's fear for her brothers and the men that look like them after 9/11. The piece draws attention to the moment where the personal (Hammad's brothers) and the political (the discrimination against Arabs and Muslims in the United States) meet.[33] Aziz "elevates" Hammad out of the political by arguing that Hammad's concern for her brother is a universal human response. Aziz thus pushes for a more relatable and palatable experience of Arab Americanness that does not rely on critiques of the foster nation, connectivity to the nation of origin, or politicization. The writer's trajectory is also *Legacy*'s challenge: to forge the "Arab American Woman Writer" out of the fire. However, who is this woman? Who is the inheritor of *Scheherazade's Legacy*?

Darraj's introduction explicates the title and provides a second frame story for the pieces in the collection. The following passage indicates Darraj's concern for her foremother and her desire to recuperate her from Orientalist imaginings: "Scheherazade, the heroine of the *The Thousand and One Nights*, had suffered terribly at the hands of the translators. . . . Scheherazade became nothing more than a harem sex kitten . . . reduced to an erotic, shallow, sex-crazed body behind a veil."[34] Thus, the misrepresentation of Scheherazade and minimization of Arab women is one legacy to which the collection refers and which Darraj wants to repair. Arab American women inherit with Scheherazade a Western public that reads Arab women as victims and against which they must struggle to articulate themselves. Darraj notes, "What I needed was the voice of an Arab woman to speak the truth without the filter of translation, without the influence of others sliding in to corrupt her story, because her story was possibly mine as well."[35]

As in Aziz, the language of authenticity deployed here is troubling, as is the suggestion that any speech could be unmediated. Darraj suggests that Scheherazade is lost in translation and insinuates that by speaking for themselves the authors can offer true versions of Arab American womanhood. Darraj eventually finds a voice that speaks without the translation or corruption of others in a novel by Ahdaf Soueif. She claims Soueif offered her an insider view and led her to find other Arab American writers, creating a genealogy of authorship necessary in the production of a canon. From that journey comes *Scheherazade's Legacy*. Like Scheherazade, the authors in the collection are "inspired by their Eastern connections, their writing and their themes touch a global audience while reclaiming Scheherazade as a woman who wove a marvelous tapestry of tales."[36] Darraj elaborates the parameters of the Arab American voice by pointing out themes of convergence across her relatively small sample group of Arab American women writers. These themes include consideration of Scheherazade as "common ancestor, the storyteller who saved a nation and healed its king"; matrilineal and patrilineal connectivity; affiliation with Arab culture through language and custom; and politicization around Palestine.[37] The list does double duty: it is a list of themes in Arab American women's writing, but it is also a checklist for authenticating Arab women's voices. In short, *Legacy* creates the authenticity it claims to seek.

In this collection we begin to see the discourses that impact Arab American subject formation via the example of Scheherazade: the attempt to become a visible and viable US subject via field-building, canonization, and securing minority status. If Arab Americans, through cultural production, can be recognized as national citizens, they can then access the material and discursive benefits of citizenship. Without such access, the Arab American subject becomes an object, treated outside the realm of law or made expendable.[38] Of course, this is a fraught procedure. The process of ethnic canon formation renders that same subject still inferior to the "American" it tries to become. For Arab identity to become legible, it is immediately juxtaposed with American and named for its difference. The minority literature collection is a curious place to make a claim about oneself, precisely because it necessitates multiple and varied voices at the same time that it commands unification of these voices.[39] Thus, *Scheherazade's Legacy* has a difficult double task: present unity without eliding diversity. In this way, too, Scheherazade is a perfect medium, offering a collective framework to host multitudes. In *Scheherazade's Legacy*, the multiple literary genres and authors underline the diversity of Arab culture that the collection attempts to establish while characterization of the content as Arab American reflects a limited definition of Arab American identity. This double process of difference and sameness is not unique to Arab American culture but rather symptomatic of immigrant identity; indeed, the hyphenization of minority groups simultaneously reveals their inclusion in American identity and the ways they are separate from it.

Despite attention to how racism and sexism challenge "authentic" Arab American representation, *Scheherazade's Legacy* takes for granted Arab Americans' (hetero)sexuality and presumes a non-Black identity for Arabs. It implicitly excludes LGBTQ representation and Black writers from its vision of Arab American identity. Many queer of color critiques make a case that heterosexuality is one means of marking oneself as belonging to the dominant community.[40] Siobhan B. Somerville argues that nineteenth-century discourses of race and sex underwrote one another. Normative sexuality was ascribed to white bodies while sexual deviance was ascribed to Others.[41] From Somerville, we learn that membership in the dominant class might not be accessed racially, but adopting heteronormative stances on sexuality can bring people of color closer to white hegemonic ideals, and simultaneously move them away from Blackness. This is especially important in the Arab context since Arab culture has been represented in Western media, as discussed earlier, as both queer and homophobic, and thus in need of redemption. Arabs are also frequently imagined as non-Black people of color. We see the effects of this racialization in minimal inclusions of Black writers in the anthology. We see the effect of heteronormativity both in the emphasis on familial modes of inheritance and in the invisibility of nonnormative sexuality in the anthology. An idealized femininity and an idealized notion of family, argues Naber, are components to a politic of cultural authenticity practiced by immigrant communities in an effort to maintain their cultural heritage in the face of annihilation in the West and, at the same time, participate in whiteness and white middle-class acceptability.[42] Heteronormativity, via Somerville and Naber, is a politics of cultural authenticity and one means of marking oneself as a member of the dominant community.

Queer visibility is not the central aim in *Scheherazade's Legacy*. Nor is it the case that the inclusion of a writer who spoke explicitly to queerness or the inclusion of a queer-identified writer would be satisfactory. In fact, the collection does include at least one queer writer. Rather, in an otherwise thoughtful collection about the ramifications of gender, race, class, and nation on the lives of Arab American women, sexuality is not discussed—as though it is not a force that affects life, or that it is self-evident. By the same "token" (pun intended), the inclusion of many Black writers would not assuage this erasure. Blackness is referenced as a comparable minoritarian position, but not one held within Arabness.[43] One of the ways the Arab American voice is recuperated in the collection is in its assumed heterosexuality and non-Blackness. If *Scheherazade's Legacy* is about the creation of Arab American identity, the identity put forward is unmarked by sexuality and thus defaults to the heterosexual, and it erases Black Arabs from the story.

For those seeking queer subjects, the silence around nonnormative sexualities in multicultural and minority literature projects, such as *Scheherazade's Legacy*, that attempt to offer a composite and authentic vision of Arab Americans can result in denial or abjection (intentional or otherwise). If queer Arab women exist, they do not fit within the paradigm of authenticity being offered. In *Legacy*, the citation of Scheherazade demonstrates how attempts at inclusion into US cultural citizenship amid anti-Arab racism and Orientalism require shifting the boundaries of acceptable subjects in the community, often to nonnormative gendered and sexual subjects' exclusion. Like *Scheherazade's Legacy*, *E-mails from Scheherazad* attempts to respond to anti-Arab and Orientalist representations of Arab and Muslim women, but often does so at the expense of nonnormative subjects. While heterosexuality is assumed in *Scheherazade's Legacy*, it is foregrounded in *E-mails from Scheherazad* as a measure of Arab women's normalcy.

Using Scheherazade to Normalize Arab and Muslim Women's (Hetero)Sexuality

E-mails from Scheherazad demonstrates a double bind for Arab writers: they are writing from within a binary where Arab women must be both authentically Arab *and* show they are "liberated" in response to Orientalist and anti-Arab sentiment. In attempting to circumvent this binary, the poems sometimes create new gendered and sexual binaries. *E-mails* challenges mainstream representations of Arabs by citing and critiquing Orientalism. The poems effectively refuse an Orientalist logic that simultaneously desexualizes or hypersexualizes Arab and Muslim women's bodies. However, they do so at the expense of other marginal subjects within and outside the Arab American community, including Arab men, Arab queers, and other minorities. I offer critical comments on the text's negotiation of gender and sexuality to reveal how representations of Arab women are limited by cultural logics of race. My comments are not intended to demarcate the author as homophobic or problematic; rather, my analysis illustrates how resistance to Orientalist and sexist representations of Arabs can implicitly affirm heteronormative expectations. In this case, heteronormativity also essentializes Arab men and creates new marginal groups.

E-mails from Scheherazad collects over fifty poems produced over the course of twenty years in Mohja Kahf's writing career. The earliest was written in 1983 and the latest in 2002. Kahf's poems reflect the politicization of Arab American identity around the First Gulf War and its aftermath. In "E-mail from Scheherazad," Kahf reintroduces Scheherazade as narrator, arrived in the new millennium to pursue a career in writing. She is living in New Jersey following her divorce from Shahryar. This geographic relocation positions Scheherazade as a diasporic subject who no longer lives in her homeland. The transposition of Scheherazade to the American context allows Kahf to go beyond calling on Scheherazade as an ancestor, as *Scheherazade's Legacy* had, by instead hailing her as a contemporary—allowing that an Arab might come to the United States and still be read as Arab or that Scheherazade can come to the United States and become "American." In the poem, Scheherazade manages this displacement by asserting her placement in the economic and social fabric of the United States: "I teach creative writing at Montclair State, / And I'm on my seventh novel and book tour."[44] Her success in the United States implies Scheherazade's seamless integration into the country, erasing the actual struggle most Arab immigrants have in finding and maintaining gainful employment, especially when their work relies on communication and when we can safely assume that English is not Scheherazade's first language. At the same time, publication as success echoes *Legacy*'s emphasis that language mastery is one way that Arabs become proper US subjects.

Likewise, Kahf's Scheherazade refutes stereotypical configurations of Arab culture that deem divorce impossible or dismiss women's potential for individualism. Gendered paradigms are refused for Scheherazade's calling as an artist. Meanwhile, she describes her split with Shahryar as amicable—Shahryar wanted a traditional marriage while Scheherazade desired publication. Kahf's Scheherazade differs from the usual depictions of her in that she has personal desires beyond the needs of her nation. The desire for publication suggests that her "calling" for artistry is only valid through recognition by a reading public. At the same time, Shahryar is working with Dunyazad, Scheherazade's sister, to offer workshops "On art & conflict resolution."[45] They share custody of their daughter, another divergence from the original story, wherein Scheherazade gives birth to three boys rather than one girl. These small changes from *The Thousand and One Nights* have broad significance.

First, the decision to bring Shahryar into the future alongside Dunyazad, and place them in contexts that emphasize narrative as triumph over conflict, reinforces the "write or die" mentality of minority literature wherein survival is predicated on the author's ability to not only compose a narrative but to have that narrative received. Second, the decision to change Scheherazade's offspring from three boys to one girl proposes a disavowal of patriarchal lineages in favor of matriarchal ones. This change attests to an Arab culture that is not misogynist or oppressive to women, where Kahf relies on a version of the liberal feminist woman, raising her child while having her dream job, to modernize the Orientalist vision of the Arab woman. Rather than being silenced in her marriage, Scheherazade finds her personhood there. Rather than being trapped by Shahryar, she is liberated. If Scheherazade, riddled by centuries of Orientalist imaginings, can acclimate and become successful in this modern life, so too can contemporary Arab American women.

Many of the other poems in the collection also explore how Arab Americans navigate inclusion via their gendered and sexual subjectivity. In "Thawrah," Kahf constructs a fantasy in which all the Odalisques walk out of Matisse's paintings. In response to their massive evacuation, some are offered photo shoots with *Playboy* and book and movie deals. Some don hijabs and are shunned by Western feminist organizations such as the National Organization for Women (NOW), which still "wanted [them] up on their dais as tokens of diversity" but wouldn't let them speak at rallies.[46] This particular reference hails NOW's refusal to condemn Israel's invasion of Lebanon in 1982 and references the colonial feminist rhetoric of many Western organizations.[47]

Here Arab American women are caught between two sets of cultural expectations that limit their agency, both of which emerge in tandem with Orientalism and Arab cultural authenticity.[48] In "Thawrah," Kahf criticizes this false binary that circumscribes representations of women: if they are in hijab, they are oppressed. They can only be "feminist" or "liberated" from oppression if they cede to a Western definition of feminism wherein women are allegedly allowed to wear whatever they want. In this way, E-mails foreshadows a similar process for Arab queers where their alleged sexual liberation will rest on rejection of Arab patriarchal norms and investment in Western sexual paradigms.

While the poem attempts to reject this binary regarding what is acceptable bodily adornment for Arab women, it finds itself in another binary regarding how to situate sexism in Arab culture. Orientalism represents Arab women as oppressed by religion and by men; it further frames Islam as inherently sexist. While the poem rejects Islam as a source of sexism and champions Arab and Muslim women's strength and sexuality, it depicts Arab men as backward and oppressive, unable to follow the Odalisques out of the Orient and into the liberated present. In the tenth stanza, "someone spread conspiracy rumors about [the Odalisques]. . . . Like why had we hung around so long? . . . With our legs so open?" (lines 84–86, 66). The narrator later attributes the critique to "Narrow-minded bastards . . . even though they are [her] Arab brothers" (lines 92–93, 67). The narrator's indictment of men is troubling in that it reinscribes Arab culture with sexism and repressed sexuality even as the previous stanza argues for a liberated notion of Muslim womanhood. Does it suggest that Arabs are backward but Islam is not? Or is the speaker attempting to divorce Islam from Arab conceptions of femininity and sexuality? The tension between her exoneration of Muslim women and defamation of Arab men reveals the slippage between Arabs and Islam as well as the tension feminists face in exposing sexism in the Arab world while fearing reification of Orientalist ideas about Arabs. Since the sexual binary is the grounds on which the battle for women's "liberation" is fought, and Eurocentric or Western sources define oppression and freedom, the speakers in the poem cannot help but contradict one another. The discrimination faced by men is brought up and dropped, complicating the anti-Orientalist position of the piece and collection: Are the women saved because they are able to take up the discourse of rights in the West? Or are they saved because they abject Arab men from their rights discourse?

While E-mails from Scheherazad challenges the Orientalist notion of Arab women's sexuality as impossible, repressed, or subordinate, it sometimes does so by inadvertently inferring a virile sexuality for Arab men. Amal Talaat

Abdelrazek applauds "Thawrah" as an achievement of Arab American feminism: "This new Arab American woman will have her own feminist theories that fit her place in the third space."[49] However, such a celebration is disingenuous for Arab American women, whose struggle with discrimination at the hands of the West is contained in a false binary of oppression and liberation, where liberation is only achieved through rejecting the oppressions of Islam and "breaking silence" about Arab men's sexism. The poem's speaker reveals how Muslim women's choices are too complex to be about only veiling or unveiling. Yet the poem does not offer a similar possibility for Arab men, that perhaps they too are trapped between Orientalism and Eurocentric feminism.

E-mails from Scheherazad's treatment of Arab masculinity and Arab men is one example of how responding to the Orientalist binary by exalting a certain kind of normative sexuality creates new binaries. Its emphasis on reworking the category of "Arab woman" relies repeatedly on the sedimentation of opposing groups' "otherness." In "I Can Scent an Arab Man a Mile Away," the narrator calls Arab men "macho, patriarchal, sexist, egotistical, parochial."[50] The narrator loves these sexist Arab men anyway, as opposed to, say, loving the men who are Arab but not all of these things, or loving the Arab men who also feel strongly about respecting Arab women's sexuality. This move normalizes Arab men as sexist, reifying the Orientalist interpretation of Arab masculinity, and normalizes desire as heterosexual. Again, here, the women are capable of growth, but the men are unchanged, essential sexists. Given that Orientalism, Western liberalism, and cultural authenticity are all structured around sexuality, the possibility for a redemptive and untroubled representation of Arab American women is almost impossible—we are much more likely to witness, as we do here, an unrelievable tension between subverting stereotype and inscribing and reinscribing normative ideals for other Others. This tension will haunt queer subjects as well.

In *E-mails*, it is not only Arab men who become foils for the gendered and sexual liberation of Arab and Muslim women. The poems' responses to Orientalism and anti-Arab sentiment can also create other Others. "Hijab Scene #1" and "Hijab Scene #2" juxtapose the "strangeness" of the Muslim woman's hijab with the strangeness of presumably white characters in the United States. In "Hijab Scene #1" a tenth-grade boy with blue hair and a tongue ring tells a hijabi girl, "You dress strange."[51] The implication is that the boy has little room to talk about being strange given his blue hair and tongue piercing. We might argue that the poem tries to highlight the hypocrisy of the boy's statement, but it also relegates the boy to outsider status. Rather than finding points of solidarity with this other Other, the poem implies that his weirdness trumps the hijabi girl's. This labeling process creates new divisions between the stylized boy and the hijabi girl. What the poem fails to mention is that the boy's markers of strangeness, like the girl's, are also associated with certain social expectations and likely render him a social outcast.

In "Hijab Scene #2," a "pink-collar" temporary employee wearing three-inch heels and panty hose tells a (presumably) hijab-wearing woman, "You people have such restrictive dress for women."[52] This poem, like the previous one, attempts to draw attention to the hypocrisy of the woman's statement regarding hijab. It proposes that wearing high heels and tight clothing is just as, if not more, restrictive than the hijab itself. The hypocrisy the poem intends is readily apparent. Yet within that hypocrisy is another element: distaste for or belittling of the woman in her heels and hose. Her dress is correlated with her work in what is likely an office setting, since the speaker calls it "pink collar."[53] The woman is a temp, which indicates she lacks consistent employment. In other words, this woman also struggles for respectability within the American workforce, but the speaker jettisons the means by which the pink-collar worker is similarly subject to patriarchal and class dominance. The speakers in the poems throughout the collection make the case for their normativity by pointing out the strangeness of other Others who are in reality occupying a comparable position with regard to dominant power.[54] The fracturing of communities in similar positions with regard to power is one of the ways that empire functions: like Somerville's citizens from earlier, these speakers gain respectability by aligning with the normative ideals they can access, ideals that are not equally accessible to all Others.

The normalcy of the speakers in "Hijab Scenes" denaturalizes other communities through comparison of their position on another axis of difference; the same norm that naturalizes the speaker, here appropriate gender expression, outcasts the new Other. The speakers are naturalized through recourse to ideals of gender—boys who do not have dyed hair or pierced tongues, women in work-appropriate heels. Kahf's "Hijab Scenes" model the means by which nonnormative gender and sexuality become sacrificial axes of difference. We see how gender and sexuality are determinants for communal, cultural, and, eventually, national belonging. In *E-mails from Scheherazad,* Scheherazade becomes a symbol of the "modern" Arab woman in the West. She brings enough of her Eastern heritage, through narrative, to remain of the East but assimilates enough to succeed in the West. She assimilates by aligning herself with a heteronormative center and accenting the difference of other Others such as Arab men and queers. A study of Scheherazade in *E-mails* illuminates more clearly how Arab femininity is shaped by heteronormative discourses, which are themselves shaped by, and give shape to, Orientalism, anti-Arab racism, and gendered/sexual modernity. These discourses foreclose nonnormative gender and sexuality and contribute to the difficulty of articulating queer Arab subjects, both in representation and, as we will see in later chapters, in real life.

E-mails from Scheherazad helps us to understand that Arab American writing is always already situated between the discursive frames of the colonizer and the discursive response of the colonized. What Arab Americans can say about Arab men and Arab women is also affected by how the Arab world has already responded to Orientalism and colonization, often rejecting "liberated" Western logics of race and sex in favor of remaining "authentic" Arabs.[55] Thus, Arab American representations are overdetermined by anti-Arab demands for assimilation on the one hand and heteronational demands for maintaining cultural authenticity and independence on the other. Like sati debates in India or veiling in Iran, writing sex and sexuality about Arab and Arab American women is the terrain of a "semiotic war"—the women and their bodies become representational proxies that determine who is moral and capable of subjectivity.[56] This creates impossibility for Arab women, and especially for those who occupy nonnormative gender and sexual subjectivities. Morality and subjectivity are then measures of rule and independence. If the United States is the moral determinant, it can continue to disappear Arab men on behalf of Arab women, and, eventually, other minorities (for example, queers) in the Arab world. If morality falls to the masculinist and nationalist response of the Arab world to colonization, women are relegated to patriarchal gender roles, which include compulsory heterosexuality. Those whose gendered and sexual practices or preferences fall outside such roles are cast out.

The poems illustrate how communities disparaged by the dominant power begin to negotiate their survival by drawing lines of acceptable and unacceptable difference. In this collection, as in *Scheherazade's Legacy*, acceptable difference takes the form of normative femininity and sexuality. Rescuing Muslim women through recourse to classed and often conservative gender norms excludes those without class privilege or those who cannot and do not perform appropriate gender roles. Responding to the false binary constructed to marginalize Arab and Muslim women results in the construction of new binaries. More than *Legacy* or *The Night Counter*, *E-mails* stages the encounter between Orientalism, anti-Arab racism, Western feminism, and heteronationalism that animates conversations about queer Arab subjects. *The Night*

Counter, however, allows us to better understand the impact of imperial state violence on Arabs, violence that necessarily limits queer life.

Using Scheherazade to Understand and Mitigate State Violence

The Night Counter explores the relationship between narrative and state violence that Scheherazade's frame story represents. By exposing the heightened surveillance of Arabs after 9/11, *The Night Counter* witnesses the state interrupting Arab American life in particularly affective ways. Scheherazade has many uses in the novel: a champion of narrative, a producer and critic of gender and sexual norms and of Orientalism, and, combining the first two functions, the catalyst and means by which the protagonist and her family find redemption in one another. *The Night Counter* draws on Scheherazade's diverse themes and demonstrates the impossibility of Arab inclusion in the US nation-state, and, ultimately, some of the limits of representational politics for queer subjects. Though *The Night Counter* includes a representation of a queer Arab subject, he is never fully incorporated into the family and construction of Arabness the novel presents.

As in *E-mails from Scheherazad* and *Scheherazade's Legacy*, in *The Night Counter* Scheherazade is used to respond to anti-Arab and Orientalist discourses, specifically representations of gender and sexuality. As in *The Thousand and One Nights*, Yunis's Scheherazade weaves together disparate stories into a cohesive narrative. In *The Night Counter*, Scheherazade's capacity for presenting the whole story, a seeming omnipotence, allows readers to witness fractures within the lives of the characters that are perpetuated by systems beyond their control. *The Night Counter* combines the approaches of the previous two works by making Scheherazade an immortal ancestor visiting the contemporary world. As such, she offers both an authenticating link to the homeland and a diasporic Arab perspective.

The Night Counter follows eighty-five-year-old Fatima, a Lebanese transplant, from the suburbs of Detroit to Los Angeles, where she has moved to live with her gay grandson, Amir, following her divorce from Ibrahim, the father of her ten children. Since moving to Los Angeles, Fatima has been visited by the immortal storyteller Scheherazade. Every night Scheherazade visits Fatima for a tale, and Fatima obliges, telling stories of her home in Lebanon. We meet both on the 992nd night of their relationship, when Scheherazade is pushing Fatima to tell her love stories and Fatima is anxiously planning her death, which she assumes will occur on the 1001st night of Scheherazade's visit. The novel proceeds in a series of small section headings, using multiple narrators, with each section told from the perspective of the chapter's titular character.

The Night Counter uses Scheherazade as a frame to tell the story of Arab Americans as they navigate the obstacles of being Arab in the United States. Thus, Scheherazade enacts her classic function in *The Thousand and One Nights* and sets the stage for storytelling. Scheherazade extracts the story of Fatima's survival in the diaspora and elicits the details of her many, often self-perceived, failures. Scheherazade enables the narrators' multiple perspectives to emerge when she visits them on behalf of Fatima. As she learns about Fatima's life, she becomes curious about the people therein and begins traveling to see them, scattered across the United States, and, in one instance, Beirut. During the day she flies on a magic carpet to see Fatima's children, trying to piece together the frayed story Fatima tells her. Scheherazade stitches the disparate aspects of the story together through her visits and allows us glimpses into multiple worlds we would not have seen from Fatima's limited perspective. The relationship between Fatima and Scheherazade parallels the relationship between Shahryar and Scheherazade, although the roles of narrator and listener are reversed. Scheherazade becomes the listener and, through seeking stories, enables Fatima to find a kind of peace with her children's lives and her marriage to Ibrahim. However, in both tales, whether Scheherazade is the listener or the teller, the outcome is similar: narrative offers redemption from violence and loneliness. Scheherazade's presence enables a cohesive narrative to emerge and contributes to the possibility of the Abdullah family's redemption.

Scheherazade's second, now familiar, function in the novel involves responding to and representing notions of femininity and sexuality that are salient for Arab women, particularly multiple generations of Arab immigrant women in the United States. Scheherazade does this in a number of ways: she models good femininity and sexuality to Fatima; she reveals the significance of family in the novel; and she responds, quite explicitly, to Orientalist visions of her character. Scheherazade has clear impressions of what is appropriate femininity and sexuality for women, demonstrated by her self-care and her care for Fatima. Scheherazade proposes several common themes around femininity for Fatima: the importance of grooming; beauty as a necessary aspect of one's personality; and the responsibility of women to "shine" or keep up their appearance in order to sustain a husband's interest and the passion in a relationship.[57] In this way, Scheherazade links appropriate feminine behavior with heterosexual practices.

In regard to sexuality, Fatima often catches Scheherazade ogling men when they are out together in public.[58] Fatima finds this overt sexual gaze troubling, while Scheherazade justifies it: "Sexy is not an ugly thing. . . . Vulgar though, is another matter."[59] She laments: "Why do they always have to make me look so vulgar?" Here, Scheherazade points to the double bind in Arab American femininity: ideal Arab femininity is threatened by Americanness when Arab women "let themselves go" and fail to become appropriately feminine.[60] Then, in a pendulum swing, these same women might confuse femininity with hypersexuality and thereby debase their femininity once more. Any rendition of Arab women's sexuality becomes subject to Orientalist tropes about it. By contrast, Scheherazade is both feminine and sexy. In the novel, Scheherazade renders herself in the image highlighted earlier: exotic but not alien, sexy but not vulgar, feminine but powerful. As in the previous texts, Scheherazade's femininity, or the Arab femininity she idealizes, is the discursive terrain for negotiating Orientalism and Arab authenticity. As in E-mails, the fraught position of gender in the novel, always already yoked to sexuality, foreshadows how nonnormative sexuality will become a site for further tensions between the dual and dueling discourses of Orientalism and authenticity.

The novel's engagement with sexuality and gender is also apparent in its emphasis on love and family, which I will discuss in the treatment of two characters: Amir, the gay grandson, and Decimal, a newly discovered great-granddaughter. Although the novel itself is saturated with love, love's expression as sexual is only enacted through Scheherazade. Fatima, meanwhile, is exceedingly obsessed with matchmaking. Her attention is fixated on her gay grandson, Amir, despite his protests, because she wants to leave her mother's house in Deir Zeitoon to him, but only if he is married and can thus carry on the family name. Amir represents an engagement with sexuality we have not yet seen in the texts under discussion. Namely, Amir's nonnormative sexuality challenges both Scheherazade's and Fatima's heteronormativity. Because they do not express enough interest, Fatima cannot justify leaving her home in Lebanon to her children and other grandchildren despite the fact that many are in successful heterosexual unions. So even for Fatima, there is recognition that heterosexuality does not ensure that her love of her home in Lebanon is passed along. Her home functions as a symbol of her diasporic longing and her Arab identity. She fixates on the house as Amir's inheritance to ensure that her family and their lives remain sutured to Lebanon.

Although Fatima does not question Amir's place in her family, she sidesteps his sexuality by refusing to use the word "gay," ignoring his uses of it, and pushing for his engagement to a number of eligible women she selects. Fatima only ceases her attempts to marry off Amir after he lands a role as Jesus in a feature film: "Those who were chosen to play a divine prophet do not inherit earthly possessions. Nor do they marry. [Amir] belonged to the world, not just one woman."[61] Fatima includes Amir in her life and in her family but sanitized from sexuality in each moment. While the novel successfully represents a gay Arab character and includes him in the family, his inclusion is tempered by the muting of his sexual identity. Amir's openness and assertiveness about his sexuality suggests he understands it as central to his subjectivity and thus makes Fatima's pointed avoidance of it painful. Fatima's partial inclusion of Amir leaves the question of his sexuality unresolved in the novel. While he is not excluded from the family, his sexuality is ignored and dismissed by Fatima, the heart of the novel and of the Abdullah family. The novel features familiar and unproductive liberal strategies for dealing with nonnormativity: the silence around his sexuality is a version of "don't ask, don't tell," and the push toward exalting his character without allowing him human desire is a version of "love the sinner, hate the sin." Both are examples of tolerance; both leave Amir simultaneously outside and inside the vision of Arab American culture the novel creates.[62]

Decimal functions as a second ambiguous example of how heteronormativity is fashioned and resisted in the novel, and how heteronormativity is racialized. Aisha "Decimal" Jackson is Fatima's great-granddaughter. Decimal's mother, Brenda Wang, is Hala's daughter, and Hala, a gynecologist in Minneapolis, is Fatima's daughter. Decimal's father is Tyrone Jackson. Brenda and Tyrone have Decimal when Brenda is seventeen, and are briefly married to avoid "the cliché of unwed African American teenage Dad."[63] Though their marriage ends quickly, they coparent Decimal amicably. Decimal writes to Fatima after becoming pregnant at seventeen herself, and her letter is Fatima's first knowledge of the child. Decimal casually and candidly discusses family history. Fatima doesn't like the Wangs because they are not "from her village." The Wangs don't like Hala because she is not Chinese. Dr. Wang does not like Tyrone because he is Black, and she resents Decimal for diverting Brenda's future from education to child-rearing.[64] Decimal ponders her mixed race identity with little judgment—commenting that she does not feel she looks Arab, Chinese, or Black, and she does not feel she understands or fits in with any one of the categories. Her ambivalent rumination stands in contrast with Fatima's reaction to Decimal's existence—which is marked by shame and anxiety. Decimal represents to Fatima another failure of her parenting and confirms her suspicions that Hala was wrong to marry outside her culture. She explains this sentiment by suggesting that it is already too hard to be an outsider in the United States, and marrying an outsider to one's own culture makes peace and comfort intangible. Fatima is also shamed by Decimal's disruption of a heteronormative timeline: both Brenda and Decimal are nonnormative sexual subjects because their pregnancy and childbirths occur outside marriage. When coupled with Decimal's mixed racial identity, Somerville's point becomes doubly useful. Fatima, having internalized assimilation norms of both Arab and US white culture, sees Decimal as sexually deviant via her sexual activity and her Black and Asian heritage.

While Scheherazade suggests Fatima leave the home in Beirut to Decimal, Fatima refuses it immediately, wondering what people would say at such an inheritor. Eventually Decimal travels to see Fatima, and their relationship, though stunted, is surprisingly warm. Decimal is eager to learn about Fatima and her life and her heritage, and Fatima finds in Decimal someone besides Scheherazade interested in hearing her speak. In "Modern Family," Therí Pickens suggests that Decimal and Fatima's relationship disrupts some of the anti-Blackness that marks white assimilation, which has been demonstrated elsewhere in this chapter. At the same time, Pickens suggests that Decimal's presence in the novel complicates how acculturation and inheritance are experienced for Arab immigrants and yokes "an Arab and Black past to a possible future."[65] I would add here that the novel works to repair and confront the anti-Asian sentiment possible and present in Arab cultures. We see Fatima's rejection of the Wang family, even though they are all doctors, as one way that migrant communities fracture against one another in order to shore up against whiteness. Decimal's presence and articulation of similarities between the Wangs and the Abdullahs challenges this fracture and suggests instead points of communion.[66] At the same time, however, Decimal, like Amir, is never fully accepted by Fatima. Fatima is unable to cede her rigid internalization of white and Arab heteronormativity to articulate an unconditional love, kinship, and inheritance structure for the only two members of her family actively interested and concerned with her on a day-to-day basis.

Scheherazade's third function in The Night Counter is to reveal how state violence disrupts and affects Arab American life. While this may seem like a novel use, recall how the frame story positions Scheherazade to intervene in state violence by marrying Shahryar and stopping him from killing women in his kingdom. In The Night Counter we meet "Sherri Hazzad," an FBI agent tipped off to the Abdullah family by one of Amir's former lovers. There are two notable aspects of this story arc: first, the phonetic duplication of Scheherazade in the FBI agent's name, and second, that the surveillance the Abdullahs undergo is prompted by a failed queer relationship. Like Scheherazade, Sherri Hazzad questions Fatima about her family, particularly Amir, and, like Scheherazade in *The Thousand and One Nights*, her conversations are an attempt to mitigate potential violence—Shahryar's in the first instance and the alleged violence of Amir in the second.

Both Scheherazade and Sherri Hazzad reveal the arbitrariness of state violence and the precarity of personal security, particularly for Arabs, in the state. They do so in their capacity as listeners, drawing out the stories of heartache from Fatima and the Abdullah family. Sherri Hazzad, an FBI representative, does so additionally as an agent of state violence. The violence of arbitrary surveillance on Arab bodies results in an incredible heartbreak in the novel. The FBI tap on Amir's phone creates static on the line every time Ibrahim calls Fatima after their divorce. Ibrahim is attempting to call to explain how he has preserved her memory of her home in Lebanon, an act that Fatima will later recognize as an act of love, proving Ibrahim loved her all along and that their divorce was a mistake. Before he can reach her, he dies alone on a bus in Detroit on his way to watch arrivals from Lebanon at the airport. While Ibrahim and Fatima's separation is linked to a different family tragedy, their reconciliation is prohibited by the FBI's surveillance. The couple's inability to reach one another and Ibrahim's death alone are two profoundly affective moments in the novel and are experienced as violence against the characters. This violence is enabled by Sherri Hazzad's state-sponsored intervention and visible to the reader through Scheherazade's narration and witness.

State-sponsored violence disrupts the possibility for human connection and leaves Ibrahim unable to resolve the disjointedness in his family. Ibrahim's habit of visiting the airport during international arrivals speaks of his longing. His death alone, away from his wife and children, exposes one terror of the diaspora—the inability to create a home and the fracture of connection to the home one used to have. Ibrahim's death alone is a result of state violence, enacted by the wiretapping and unnecessary surveillance Arabs are subject to in the United States. Had Ibrahim been able to reach Fatima in the days before his death, they may have reconciled, and he might not have been alone at the time of his death. The psychic violence inflicted on Ibrahim and his family through his solitary death creates an emotional disruption for the reader: yes, we will all die, but no one deserves to die alone. The devastation at Ibrahim's death and the impossibility of Fatima and Ibrahim's reconciliation are the means by which the couple is rendered human first and

Arab second. As characters who have experienced love and a number of tragic losses, they are relatable and sympathetic subjects. The reader's sympathy and sense of injustice is further activated by the discriminatory treatment the Abdullah family faces from the state, especially because the FBI's unnecessary surveillance results in the couple's sustained separation and Ibrahim's solitary death. In other words, their "relatable" humanity is disserviced by the racialized treatment they receive from the FBI. As Scheherazade's namesake, Sherri Hazzad's presence in the novel as an agent of state violence ties the violence to Scheherazade, even as Scheherazade's omnipresence in the novel allows us to see how that violence comes about.

By framing state violence as violence to heterosexual love and family, through Ibrahim's death, the novel argues for the incorporation of Arabs into the American milieu as subjects that have prioritized family and love above all else. Importantly, the state prevents a satisfying heteronormative resolution to the central love story of the novel. Fatima and Ibrahim can never fix their marriage, and their family can never be "complete" without its patriarch. The novel's emphasis on (mostly heteronormative) love and family marks them as desirable citizens and subjects. At the same time, a seamless incorporation of Arabs into America is resisted through the presence of Scheherazade and the Abdullahs, whose humanity is undermined by the state's discrimination. Both have been subject to material and discursive violence at the hands of the state and broader American culture. The only belonging either can secure is to family and to one another, not to the state or to the United States.

At the same time, *The Night Counter* critiques the racist and Orientalist representations of Arabs that deem them homophobic and sexually backward through the presence of a queer character and through the critique of Amir's inability to be cast as an "authentic" Arab while queer. Yet, it is the failure of another relationship that helps lead to the FBI investigation of the Abdullah family. Amir's decision to end a relationship causes a vindictive ex to report Amir to the FBI as a suspicious character. While it might be easy to assume this turnabout as evidence in the novel against Amir's queerness and the enactment of his sexuality, it is only because Arabs are already assumed to be suspicious characters worthy of surveillance that the ex's tactics gain traction. The representation of Arabs as homophobic or the invisibility of queer Arabs in the dominant culture ensures that no one questions the ex's motives. Yunis concretizes that invisibility on the advice of Amir's agent regarding casting calls, wherein she insists Amir downplay his sexuality because he certainly cannot get roles as a terrorist or cab driver if he is perceived to be gay.[67]

While *The Night Counter* represents nonnormative sexuality through Amir's character, and even critiques anti-Arab and Orientalist views of Arab sexuality, the place of queer love or queer lives in the "family-oriented" Arab culture is precarious and seemingly conditional. Though Amir's representation critiques Orientalist notions about sexuality in Arab culture, Fatima's treatment of Amir's sexuality is not particularly inclusive or radical. In Amir's first block of exposition, he reveals that his breakup with his fellow actor and next-door neighbor is due to Fatima's decision to visit and eventually live in Amir's home.[68] Amir, although out to his grandmother, cannot imagine hosting both in the same home. Later in the chapter, he notes that his ex would not have been welcoming of his grandmother either and feels secure in his decision to end the relationship. In this way, Amir reiterates the novel's insistence on family and love above other commitments, and the novel again presents Arab family and queer love as inconsistent with one another.

Ultimately, the novel has many uses for Scheherazade, but forecloses the possibility of full inclusion of Arabs into US culture and queerness into Arab culture. In *The Night Counter*, Scheherazade proposes modes of femininity and sexuality and models responses to Orientalism but cannot redeem Fatima's family from its losses, which are perpetuated by diasporic and state violence. It neither excludes queer bodies nor fully incorporates them, in the case of Amir. The novel challenges the possibility of assimilation through Fatima's and Ibrahim's outsider status and questions the happiness that assimilation is capable of bringing through their children. In *The Night Counter*, Scheherazade helps illuminate several significant discourses that inform representations of Arab femininity: heteronormativity, state violence, and assimilation. As we shall see in later chapters, the violence of heteronormativity and imperialism will shadow queer Arab representations and subjects and intersect with the other discourses Scheherazade alerts us to (e.g., Orientalism, heteronationalism) in foreclosing and painful ways.

After the violence enacted upon her in translation and interpretation, Scheherazade is recuperated by Arab Americans as a symbol of immigrant desires: to be understood as capable producers of knowledge and artistry, as in *Scheherazade's Legacy*; to be free, to be sexual, to be persons and not stereotypes, as in *E-mails from Scheherazad*; to be loved, to have family, to die peacefully, as in *The Night Counter*. At the same time, these invocations reveal to us the many discourses that circulate around Arab femininity: Orientalism and anti-Arab racism, authenticity and assimilation, heteronormativity from within and without Arab communities, and finally, state violence. Given these forces, it is no wonder Arab femininities, particularly queer ones, seem entangled in an ever-receding horizon of possibility.

☾

In this chapter, I have offered a literary biography of Scheherazade in order to articulate the multiple discourses that frame representation and formation of Arab femininity and that will impede and haunt queer Arab representations and lives. By tracing her exposition in the frame story of *The Nights*, I delineated how Arab femininity is informed by Orientalism, respectability politics, and anti-Blackness. In contemporary Arab American literature, representations of Scheherazade give insight into how transnational Arab subjects, here Arab Americans, are minority ethnic subjects that must navigate questions of authenticity and assimilation, heteronormativity, and state violence. Just as the frame story evidences some of *The Nights'* anti-Black and heteropatriarchal aspects, so too the contemporary works find themselves buttressing heteronormativity and Arab exceptionalism to stabilize their subjects. In all the works discussed, some useful takeaways emerge and will continue to operate within the book: for Arab and Arab Americans, gender and sexuality are sites of racial and ethnic negotiation; within Arab nations or outside them, Arabs are transnational subjects; Arab femininity is deeply over- and underwritten by Orientalism, elitism, anti-Blackness, anti-Arab racism, the cultural politics of authenticity, heteronationalism, heteronormativity, and heteropatriarchal state violence. In combination, these factors foreclose queer Arab cultural production and make discerning a queer Arab feminine subject incredibly difficult. In the next chapter, I discuss strategies we might use in spite of these limiting discourses and propose queer Arab critique as a means for circumventing these discursive foreclosures.

between women

2

Homoeroticism in Golden Era Egyptian Cinema

In order to construct a queer Arab archive or imagine a queer Arab subject, one must maneuver around, against, and through the gendered and sexual discourses in Arab cultures that the previous chapter outlines. To read Scheherazade queerly, for example, would necessitate a reading strategy that acknowledges the heteronormativity that abounds within her frame story while at the same time seeking moments of rupture within which nonnormative iterations of gender and sexuality might form. We might comment on the strangeness of Scheherazade inviting her sister Dinarzad into her marital bedroom each night to hear the stories she weaves for King Shahryar. While this has a narrative function—Dinarzad solicits the first of Scheherazade's tales—Dinarzad does not disappear from the bedroom and, in one case, sleeps under the couple's bed during the night. While I don't mean to suggest incest, I remember Dinarzad's presence in the room as one way that we might disrupt the heteronormativity of the frame story. Another possibility is available in the romantic entanglements of the previous queen, whose lovers' presence in her quarters is enabled by cross-dressing. Despite the overwhelming heteronormative arc of the texts, looking under the straight bed allows the reader a moment of curiosity and "what if" that provides an opening to tell another kind of story. This chapter is devoted to the moments of curiosity and "what if" within mainstream Arab texts that provide an opening to tell queer Arab stories; here I outline a mode of queer Arab critique that animates the remainder of the book.

Because of the forbidding discourses outlined in the previous chapter, I suggest that locating queer Arab subjects and especially banat, women, and femmes requires an alternate reading practice, queer Arab critique. Queer Arab critique looks to Arab cultural productions to establish what is normative for banat Arab, and then locates nonnormative and counterhegemonic performances of femininity and sexuality. Queer Arab critique employs four central concepts—queer spectatorship, queer space and time, flipped homoerotic triangulation, and queer containment—in order to read around and against heteronormative Orientalist and heteronational discourses that preclude queer subjects. Employing queer Arab critique avails us to instances of homoerotic desires in mainstream Arab texts and contributes to the construction of queer Arab archives, albeit ambivalent ones. Queer Arab critique allows us to see the traces of queer desire in mainstream Arab cultures and undermines the erasure of queer people from Arab histories. Queer Arab critique also reveals how queerness and Arabness are constructed relationally, between many locations, texts, and times.

My study of homoeroticism between women in Golden Era films intervenes in two significant bodies of literature: Arab film studies and queer of color critiques. First, studies of nonnormative sexuality in Egyptian film have often focused on independent film, and within that on the work of men and on work featuring same-sex desire between men.[1] Texts that focus explicitly on mainstream and Golden Era work also tend to center men, masculinity, and male homoeroticism.[2] Some work, notably Viola Shafik's, offers a sustained feminist analysis of gender in popular cinema.[3] This chapter explores homoeroticism between women as portrayed in mainstream Arab film and contributes to queering Arab film studies. Second, it brings Arab women to the center of queer of color critique and through attention to them develops queer Arab critique as an alternate methodology by which to discuss queer Arab histories and archives. As I noted in the introduction, same-sex desires between banat are virtually unstudied—most notable exceptions focus on medieval and precolonial time periods. I am interested in rejecting the narrative that queerness is either precolonial or impossible for Arab subjects, and I make that rebuttal by focusing on the rich Golden Era, where Arabs are negotiating their subjectivity amid Orientalism, colonialism, and heteronationalism. I argue that Golden Era films, especially those that featured belly dance, made considerable space for homoerotic exchanges amid women.

Golden Era belly dance films reveal a rich gender and sexual diversity, one that troubles the Orientalist representation of an explicitly homophobic "traditional" or authentic Egyptian culture. I aim here not to offer an analysis of belly dance as a form, but rather to point to how belly dance, a particularly intimate feminine performance, allows eroticism between women to emerge. As such, the chapter recovers women's nonnormative and queer legacies within popular Egyptian texts. I locate moments of queerness that are overlooked in dominant and hegemonic readings of the text. In so doing, I demonstrate an ongoing queer Arab subject that is not sacrificed in either colonial or heteronational constructions of Arabness.

I focus on the Golden Era for three reasons: first, it is a prime location to document norms around gender and sexuality in Arab cultures. Second, the Golden Era operates as a synecdoche for broader constructions of Arabness. Third, the Golden Era offers a prime example of how Arabness is constructed in the between: between Arab nations, between Arab nations and diasporas, and between text and reader. To the first point: in Egypt, colonial film standards started in 1947 and ended in 1976, replaced by anticolonial governance that enacted new taboos against sex, politics, and religion.[4] Much of the Golden Era work, then, preceded the regulation now placed on Arab film. Its films, featuring men and women kissing, women undressing women, women drinking and fighting, and cross-dressing, would likely not pass today's stringent censorship standards. I use the Golden Era's relative representational freedom to train a lens on how gender and sexuality were being discussed in mainstream Arab culture via the silver screen.

Second, Egyptian Golden Era texts function as a synecdoche for transnational Arab cultures. Given the Golden Era's significance to transnational Arab audiences, I suggest that trends within Golden Era films are salient to the many Arab communities that follow and consume them. The continued significance of Golden Era films to audiences in and outside Egypt is a result of that particular era's centrality in Arab film and media history. Egypt experienced rapid and expansive film production from the 1940s to the 1960s. It was the only Arab country to develop an industry during the colonial period, with the first company emerging in 1917 in Alexandria; by 1948 the country had produced 345 feature-length films.[5] Two-thirds of the films distributed in Arab countries were from Europe and America, while the final third were almost entirely from Egypt—making the latter the dominant mode of self-representation for Arabs during the Golden Era.[6] Additionally, film stars' appeal exceeded regional affiliations, and their films found pan-Arab audiences.[7] Many Golden Era works became vehicles for favorite performers. The actors and actresses in the films discussed in this chapter had and have established fan bases that ensured the films' success at the time, as well as their ongoing relevance. For example, Farid al Atrash, a Golden Era star, continues to be celebrated and listened to by Arabs around the globe. He was even honored with a Google Doodle on the anniversary of his 110th birthday in 2020. Consider, too, these comments by Said in his eulogy for Tahia Carioca, the renowned belly dancer:

> Most Eastern Arabs, I believe, would concede impressionistically that the dour Syrians and Jordanians, the quick-witted Lebanese, the rough-hewn Gulf Arabs, the ever-so-serious Iraqis never have stood a chance next to the entertainers, clowns, singers and dancers that Egypt and its people have provided on so vast a scale for the past several centuries. Even the most damaging political accusations against Egypt's governments by Palestinians or Iraqis are leveled grudgingly, always with a trace of how likeable and charming Egypt—especially its clipped, lilting dialect—as a whole is.[8]

The dominance and significance of Egyptian Golden Era texts and stars in Arab cultures connects to the third point: Golden Era texts index how Arabness is formed between multiple circuits. With its mass appeal, the Golden Era expands the gendered and sexual dialogues of the films and extends the dialogue beyond the bounds of the nation and the Arab world and well into its diaspora. Egypt as the center of Arab cultural production and the circulation of Egypt's exports function to create three viewing audiences for Golden Era work: Egypt, other Arab nations, and the diasporic Arab world. If Arabs left Arab nations during the Golden Era, the Arab films they could access were most likely Egyptian. Even today, movie houses that distribute Arab films rely heavily on Egypt's classic cinema, perhaps even more so than on contemporary work. A cursory exploration of Arab satellite television demonstrates the primacy of Egypt's cultural production as well as the lingering attachment to Golden Era work. Of Dish Network's Arabic Elite Super package, a primary provider of Arab television in the United States, five of the twenty-nine channels feature Egyptian content exclusively. One, Nile Drama, touts itself as the viewer's choice for classic Egyptian film. Moreover, the channels that are not regionally affiliated, those channels understood as pan-Arab (e.g., Al Arabiya), all explicitly name Egyptian content in their programming descriptions. These same channels populate televisions in homes across the Middle East as satellite television provides the primary mode of broadcast in the region. Online, the Golden

Era has its own robust afterlife on Pinterest, YouTube, and numerous other locations.

Golden Era texts are thus available to many kinds of viewers, including queer ones. The contemporary life of the Golden Era as a queer archive is traced, much as queerness is in the films, in ephemeral and gestural ways. In queer Arab dance parties from Beirut to Berlin to Brooklyn, footage of song and dance routines from Golden Era works plays in the background. Arab drag queens perform as Asmahan or dance the routines of Naima Akef. Whispers and gossip about her sexuality trail Umm Kulthum's biography. In contemporary Arab Anglophone novels like *A Map of Home* or *Guapa*, self-proclaimed queer Arab characters make reference to their viewing history of Golden Era films, their familiarity with Golden Era singers (who often featured in films), and their general knowledge of Egyptian cultural production. The playfulness of the Golden Era, its queer potential, reaches queer audiences within and without the location of its production. As such, it offers a queer history or genealogy within the culture to its queer subjects and viewers. The two films discussed in this chapter demonstrate flexible engagements with sexual paradigms. In both films, and in the Golden Era in general, we see diversity and nonnormativity in performances of desire that today are uncommon or seemingly impossible.

This chapter also elaborates how queer Arab formations are produced relationally. Queerness here is not exclusively or inherently intentional in the production of the film but is found within the reception and interpretation of the spectator. I locate queer possibility in these seemingly normative representations of Arab women. In the process, I offer a method for reading Arab culture queerly, a mode of queer Arab critique that is useful for circumnavigating the many Orientalist and heteronormative tropes that would erase queer sexuality from Arab cultural production and Arab history.

Using queer Arab critique on mainstream Arab texts resists the erasure of queer subjects from national and transnational Arab culture, challenges the notion that queerness threatens "authentic" iterations of Arab cultures, and asserts that queer subjects are neither alien to nor outside Arab cultures.[9] Queerness in Arab culture, as the introduction outlined, has been considered an assimilatory gesture influenced by colonization and thus inauthentic to Arab cultures, or relegated to a romanticized precolonial Arab culture. In *Impossible Desires*, Gopinath studies Bollywood and other South Asian cultural products to refute such queer elisions. I follow this trajectory in the Arab context and show how characters in these two films repudiate the elision of queerness from national and transnational memory.

While the characters and their nonnormativity are central to the world the films construct, as subjects of the queer Arab archive, they are also ambivalent. They simultaneously challenge the family and heteronormative sexual order through homoerotic and nonnormative behaviors while buttressing that normative model. To articulate and demonstrate queer Arab critique, I turn to Golden Era Egyptian cinema as a site of queer Arab potential and an ambivalent queer archive. I argue via analysis of two popular Golden Era films that mainstream film in Egypt simultaneously enabled and disciplined nonnormative gendered and sexual behavior, specifically between women.

From the rich archive of Golden Era production, I focus on the films حبيبي الأسمر (*Habibi al Asmar*) and سيجارة و كاس (*Sigara wa Kass*) for several reasons. First, both are belly dance films about belly dancers. The films use belly dance, which fosters women's homosociality, to comment on expected norms for Egyptian women, sometimes refusing and at other times reinforcing those norms within the films' overall plots. Second, both films feature multiple popular Egyptian performers: *Habibi al Asmar* places iconic Golden Era dancers Tahia Carioca and Samia Gamal in their only film together, while *Sigara wa Kass* features Gamal alongside singers Kouka and Dalida. The combined star power in each film guarantees the films' popularity at the time of production. Third, both are still in circulation within and outside Egypt. As noted earlier, Golden Era work is still played routinely on Arabic channels in the Middle East and via satellite outside it; these films are also available on YouTube and from online retailers, increasing their circulation. Finally, the stars of the film, particularly Gamal, Carioca, and Dalida, remain transnational favorites with afterlives online in and outside Egypt.

Drawing on queer of color critique, I articulate how and to what end the films *Sigara wa Kass* (A Cigarette and a Glass) and *Habibi al Asmar* (My Dark Darling) portrayed nonnormative gendered and sexual behaviors. The queer possibilities I uncover indicate that on- and off-screen, Egyptian culture was engaged in discussions about sexual behaviors and desires, which may or may not be legible under Western categories of lesbian, gay, bisexual, or transgender identity (LGBT). In other words, queer desires, practices, and subjects were present in Arab cultures despite Orientalist and heteronationalist erasures. The chapter employs queer Arab critique in the films to demonstrate the long-term presence of nonnormative gendered and sexual subjects within Arab cultures and how locating queer Arab archives necessitates a new way of thinking and reading, one that deviates from Western frames of LGBT identity politics and practices and allegedly precolonial narrations of Arab culture.

Queer Arab Critique

I have said throughout that queer Arab archives require a different kind of story/telling. To tell the story of homoeroticism between banat, I use queer Arab critique—a practice for reading around and against Orientalist and heteronational scripts that preclude queer subjects. Queer Arab critique is, as Cohen reminds us, grounded in the ways subjects resist and relate to normative power structures. Following Rodríguez, Gopinath, and Tinsley, it offers queerness not as a fixed identity but as a set of relations, of affects, gestures, and ephemera that occur between subjects. Queer Arab critique employs four central concepts: queer spectatorship, queer space and time, flipped homoerotic triangulation, and queer containment.

Queer spectatorship or queer reading is first about locating homoeroticism on-screen that may be explicitly integrated into the story as a comedic or cautionary plot point.[10] It also entails reading queerly, wherein the viewer's position as a queer subject produces points of identification, recognition, desire, or connection that might be otherwise unavailable to nonqueer subjects.[11] For example, in *Impossible Desires* Gopinath recovers a seemingly "impossible" queer female subject through a queer diasporic reading of Bollywood film.[12] In such practices of queer spectatorship, the viewer reads the film against the heteronormative central plot and actively refuses the dominant narrative in favor of fleeting moments and ephemeral gestures that are by definition insignificant or secondary within the overall film. In the book of the same name, Muñoz dubs this process "disidentification" and understands it as a means of queer world-making and survival for subjects rejected by the dominant culture.[13] In conversation with theories of spectatorship, Najmabadi articulates that women often enter and enjoy productions that seem to explicitly disempower or forbid them: they may do so through a fragmentary engagement in which they take in only the positives and discard the negative; women locate in such work a surplus of pleasure, wherein they can be both the object of desire and the desiring subject, and they use the films' fraught depiction of women to navigate their own anxiety.[14] In the two films I discuss, I underscore the on-screen homoerotic desire between women and the intimacies women share as a form of queer spectatorship and queer disidentification, above and against the heteronormative plot. On the whole, the process of queer spectatorship acknowledges the censor of queer content in heteronormative and culturally reauthenticating texts as only one layer of gendered and sexual representation in any text and offers readers and viewers a more agential relationship to the text as meaning makers and consumers.

Second, queer Arab critique uses the concepts of queer time and space to recognize queer kinships. Jack Halberstam uses queer time to refer to how queer people's social and sexual developments occur against or outside heteronormative time. Heteronormative time refers to how heterosexuals are expected to meet benchmarks of "normal" development (e.g., young love in high school, serious relationships in college, marriage proposals and children before thirty-five).[15] The concept of queer time is useful for thinking about how some heterosexual subjects are not heteronormative when they fail to meet these benchmarks—spinsters, childless women, women who marry multiple times, and so on. In *The Feeling of Kinship*, David Eng uses queer time to locate kinship patterns in queer communities, wherein the lack of adherence to a heteronormative timeline means that queer people develop alternate family and relationship structures suitable to life outside normative marriage and reproduction patterns.[16] As I discuss during close readings of the films, queer time and kinship are salient concepts for reading the relationship between dancer Hoda and singer Azza in *Sigara wa Kass*.

Queer space describes how subjects othered from normative culture and publics create subcultures and counterpublics. It also refers to spaces that actively disrupt normative sexual paradigms or foster nonnormative subjects and behaviors. Such spaces allow queer cultures and kinships to flourish. For example, Gopinath argues that homosocial home spaces foster homoeroticism between women.[17] Building on this thinking, I argue that in both films nightclubs and belly dance are nonnormative spaces that foster queer kinship and intimacy, especially for women. For Arabs who do not always adhere to Western markers of queer identity like "coming out," articulating a concept of queer time and space that is read against Arabs' own markers of heteronormativity makes visible challenges to normative gender and sexuality that are coming from within the culture rather than seeking out preestablished markers (e.g., naming an identity lesbian, coming out, cruising).

Third, queer Arab critique uses flipped homoerotic triangulation to read for intimacies between women. To do so, I offer a flipped reading of Eve Kosofsky Sedgwick's concept of triangulation from *Between Men*.[18] Sedgwick describes the triangulated tension in American literature and film between two men competing for a woman as one means by which men can negotiate homoerotic desires in a socially sanctioned manner. In this formation, women's bodies are both incidental and central: any woman might function as a proxy for men's desires, and it must be a woman, to avoid any allegations of eroticism between the men. The presence of the woman substantiates a heterosexual narrative. Writing on the "wiles of women," Najmabadi asserts the agency of women rather than their flat presence as foils for men's homoeroticism.[19] Women cast out boys and men from female homosocial spaces as part of an Oedipal psychoanalytic development, and in so doing actively encourage male homosociality and the by-product, homoeroticism. Moreover, the spaces from which they cast out men are domains of female power that "[mobilize] to combat male power."[20] I combine Najmabadi's and Sedgwick's approaches to articulate how women's actions might substantiate or create eroticism between women. I argue that we can "flip" Sedgwick's triangle of eroticism between men to a triangle between women. In these films a triangle of eroticism exists between two women and one man; the women's actions in these triangles serve more than male sexuality. In the flipped triangle, when two women compete for the affections of a man, as Samra and Zakia do in *Habibi al Asmar* and as Hoda and Yolanda do in *Sigara wa Kass*, they also negotiate homoerotic tension between women. The man for whom they compete is both incidental and central: it could be any man, and it must be a man to substantiate the heterosexual plot. I make this argument by attending to the dynamics between women in the films. In these triangles, as well as in the friendship dynamic between Hoda and Azza, the intimacy between women is primary and continually supersedes the women's relationships with men. As with queer space and time, attending to the primacy of women's relationships allows us to upend heteronormative and Orientalist readings of Arab culture that deem it masculinist at its core and categorize women in relationship only to men via the tropes of veiled woman, harem girl, and suicide bomber.

Finally, queer Arab critique traces processes of queer containment to locate nonnormative sexualities and subjects. Queer containment refers to how we might locate evidence of queerness in the existence of punitive and disciplinary measures against it. In other words, the need to discipline the nonnormative characters in the films evidences their nonnormativity. In the films studied, two strategies of containment are employed to discipline queer subjects: marriage and madness. Many histories of sexuality have sought evidence of nonnormative gendered and sexual behavior in disciplinary records.[21] In film, subjects might flirt with nonnormative or immoral behavior eventually deemed as such and discarded through the narrative resolution of the plot. As Elizabeth Freeman suggests, in the case of queer erotic potential, the normative gendered and sexual order is secured through marriage and heterosexual coupling.[22] Gopinath also notes this process in her analysis of *Bend It Like Beckham*.[23] In *Crip Theory*, Robert McRuer demonstrates that queerness and disability are often yoked together and that queer and disabled characters are used to advance the story's major heteronormative plot.[24]

In both films, processes of queer containment reveal the presence of queerness that requires containment. I suggest the disciplining of women in the films both shores up the heterosexual narrative and reveals that it requires shoring up. In *Sigara wa Kass* a "crazy" stage manager is the primary site of queer containment, and in *Habibi al Asmar* two nonnormative characters die to make way for the appropriate heterosexual union. By attending to the flirtations with nonnormativity, those moments—ephemeral, marginal, and gestural though they may be—are valuable to a queer reading, and to queer spectators, beyond and against their heteronormative resolution. In other words, by directly confronting discourses that seek to erase queerness, we find evidence of its existence. I suggest this holds true not only for heteronormative plots, but can be useful for thinking about those discourses that particularly foreclose queer representation in Arab culture, like Orientalism and heteronationalism.

In the following sections, I use queer Arab critique to read mainstream texts for queer traces and locate within the films characters that exist ambivalently in the queer Arab archive. Throughout my analysis of *Habibi* and *Sigara* I point toward scenes, exchanges, and narrative arcs within both films that feature queer time and space, flipped homoerotic triangulation, and queer containment. These concepts are enabled by and are examples of a reading practice or spectatorship explicitly engaged in reading against the heteronormative narrative in favor of developing points of dis/identification, desire, connection, or recognition for queer audiences. Using queer spectatorship and disidentification, I offer comments in the subsequent sections on how both films invoke queer space and time, triangulation, and containment respectively. Before this close reading, I offer a brief plot synopsis of each film.

Sigara wa Kass follows dancer Hoda (Samia Gamal), who leaves dance to marry a doctor, Mamdouh (Nabil al Alfi), whom she meets while performing. Hoda becomes jealous of Mamdouh's head nurse, Yolanda (Dalida), and turns to alcohol for comfort. With the help of her best friend, fellow performer, and former roommate Azza (Kouka), Hoda narrowly escapes dying and losing her husband and child in a house fire she has caused. A secondary plot is Azza's attempt to marry, first a failed attempt to her and Hoda's former stage manager (no name given) and then successfully to a friend of Mamdouh's, Omara (Seraj Munir).

Habibi al Asmar follows two women, Samra (Samia Gamal) and Zakia (Tahia Carioca), as they negotiate love and money in 1950s Egypt. Samra is بنت بلديّة (bint baladia/country girl) living in her father's home and engaged to her childhood sweetheart, Ahmed. She dreams of dancing onstage with Zakia, her next-door neighbor, an older single woman who works in Zamalek. Under Zakia's influence, Samra meets and marries a wealthy businessman, Rostom, ending her long courtship with Ahmed and cutting ties with her birth family. With Zakia's help, Ahmed seeks revenge. Ahmed, Zakia, and Samra eventually uncover Rostom's illegal activities, and Rostom commits suicide to avoid capture by the police; Zakia suffers a fatal gunshot wound protecting Ahmed. Ahmed and Samra are reunited at the end of the film.

Queer Space and Time: Dance as a Conduit for Queer Kinship and Homoerotic Desire between Women

In this section, I argue that belly dance and belly dance venues operate as queer spaces for women performers. The emotional excess of song and dance sequences in film offers opportunities for multiple kinds of desire to emerge. The homosocial expectations and norms around belly dance performance in Arab culture create forms of intimacy between women performers. Belly dance and belly dance venues foster queer kinship as well as provide opportunities for lust and desire between women. Attending to dance is a form of queer Arab critique because it creates queer space and time and because dance is an embodied form that is simultaneously ephemeral and gestural in its perpetual movement. Queer Arab critique highlights the fleeting, relational ruptures of desire in belly dance films to envision queer subjects.

Song and dance sequences are sites of affective excess in film; I argue that part of the excess rendered in song and dance scenes in these films is a non-normative, homoerotic tension between women. Dance is a central site of conflict and conflict resolution in the two films under discussion. In musicals, song and dance numbers are often scenes that address excess emotion and conflict not easily integrated into the narrative.[25] Gopinath writes that within Bollywood, song and dance numbers are opportunities for queer viewers to enter and disrupt heteronormative narrative arcs. In *Popular Egyptian Cinema*, Shafik theorizes that women's dancing bodies in particular are locations at which moral, cultural, and gender conflict is raised and resolved.[26] Drawing on their theorizations, I suggest that song and belly dance sequences in Arab films, especially those taking place within nightclubs, are opportunities for queer kinship and homoerotic desire between women.

Belly dance is a richly signified practice in Arab cultures, and where one performs speaks to how the performer is perceived in the culture. In her study of women's performance in Egypt, Karin van Nieuwkerk traces how singers and dancers understand and experience gender expectations. Van Nieuwkerk's ethnographic research revealed that women's social status rested largely on the kind of performance, for whom, and where they performed.[27] Public opinion designated musicians most respectable, followed by singers, actors, folk dancers, and lastly, belly dancers. The venue of women's performance was also significant: wedding singers were more reputable than nightclub performers. The nightclub, catering to men alone rather than families, serving alcohol, and inviting intimacy between patrons, placed performers in an already nonnormative space with regard to gender and sexuality: it threatened heteronormative family and religious values. Both films feature actresses who are also dancers and singers outside the film industry: dancers Gamal and Carioca and singers Kouka and Dalida. As such, all four well-known actresses are already considered somewhat disruptive of normative and respectable femininity.

As dancers in nightclubs, Hoda and Zakia, in *Sigara* and *Habibi*, respectively, are already considered nonnormative with regard to their performance of hegemonic Arab femininity. The position of dance and the nightclub as antithetical to heteronormative time is rendered explicit in *Sigara*. Hoda works at Casino al-Galaaʾ. In it she meets Mamdouh; Mamdouh proposes but will marry her only if she gives up dancing and her stardom. Thus the space of performance is read as incompatible and mutually exclusive to family and respectable marriage.

At the same time, the nightclub fosters queer intimacies that replace biological or patrilineal kin structures: Hoda has no birth family in the film, and we know nothing of her life prior to the stage. The only person with whom Hoda is family or familiar is Azza, who sings during Hoda's performances, and they live together. Casino al-Galaaʾ brings the women together and offers a venue for homosocial kinship between them. Their kinship occurs within and against the nightclub as a space of heteroerotic fulfillment in which women dance and sing for audiences of men. Obviously, dance and performance lend themselves to a more readily available reading involving men's spectatorship as the central purpose of the nightclub. My argument has no need to dispense with this reading. The nightclub may have as its purpose men's heteroerotic fulfillment and simultaneously foster intimacy between the women providing it. In short, normative and queer modes of kinship and spectatorship coexist.

In *Habibi*, dance and performance in nightclubs is rendered nonnormative ad hominem: figures that emerge from the world of dance are of questionable moral character, and their failures are duly punished. Zakia opines a position of sexual freedom that risks corrupting the hero of the film; she is also responsible for corrupting Samra by introducing her to the nightclub scene against Samra's parents' and fiancé's wishes. Rostom meets Samra at the nightclub during one of Zakia's performances. Rostom is a criminal who interrupts Samra's baladia story line when he marries her, ending her engagement to her longtime fiancé, alienating her from her birth family, and removing her from her neighborhood and country. That Zakia and Rostom are corruptors of the sexual order—by and through their rejection of cultural norms for femininity, masculinity, and heterosexual romance—is further emphasized by the disciplining of the figures in the resolution of the film's conflict (a queer containment we will return to later). Both characters die, and they must, to reunite Samra with her erstwhile fiancé and the film's heteronational hero, Ahmed.

Finally, the mise-en-scène of the nightclub underscores its capacity for nonnormativity. Unlike the well-lit scenes of Samra and Ahmed's neighborhood of flowers and smiling food vendors, the nightclub is dark and hazy. We rarely see characters' faces; they are turned toward the stage and obscured by cigarette smoke and drinking glasses. Characters in these spaces also dress in typical Western attire, while those in the neighborhood wear thowbs and abayas. The nightclub thus gives way, especially for women, to more flesh and more visible figures. This styling challenges the performance venue and performers' respectability, much as van Nieuwkerk described. The visual rhetoric of the club, and who is found in it, is positioned against conservative and heteronormative arcs.

I will now demonstrate how song and belly dance performances themselves are moments of queer space and time in the films. As noted earlier, song and dance sequences are already considered spaces of affective surplus, which lends them to readings of queer desire. I suggest fantasy song and dance sequences amplify both the excess and its possibility; each fantasy dance sequence ruptures the heteronormative order established in the rest of the film. Both films use fantasy sequences to imagine alternative timelines for the characters of Hoda and Samra. In *Sigara* Hoda has two fantasy sequences: the first is at the time of her departure from the Casino al-Galaaʾ; the second after Hoda and Mamdouh's relationship has floundered. In both sequences, dance is the vehicle and the object of fantasy against the rather mundane action happening in real time. I will discuss her second fantasy sequence now and her first in a later section.

At the time of her second fantasy arc, Hoda is drunk and mourning her rejection by producers and directors unwilling to bring her back as a dancer. They have rejected her on the advice of her friend, Azza, who is certain that Hoda's return to dance will end her marriage. Hoda stumbles into the Casino al-Galaa' and witnesses Azza singing. As the camera captures Azza singing, Hoda imagines herself the object of Azza's song and fantasizes that she is dancing onstage with her. Hoda is transformed from her pedestrian clothing into dance costuming. The camera then repositions us to view Hoda through Azza, repeating shot reverse shots of previous song and dance scenes between the two. The use of shot reverse shot in this scene sequence establishes the primary relationship of the scene between Azza and Hoda; at the same time, the shot distance decreases as the scene continues, until Azza and Hoda are together in the frame. During the scene Hoda's dance backdrop fluctuates from the nightclub to a Spanish flamenco hall, to a desert with cacti, to a balcony with other Egyptian-style dancers, and finally back to the nightclub. The multiple backgrounds speak to Hoda's longing for life beyond her marriage to Mamdouh, to the difference and richness her performance career could bring. Through dance and fantasy, Hoda transcends space and time and her heteronormative life. Hoda's love of dance, her desire for more, leads her outside the appropriate model of feminine and heterosexual behavior and into immoral territory (alcoholism, potentially leaving her child and marriage).

Like *Sigara*, *Habibi* features two fantasy sequences. The first is between Samra and Zakia; the second occurs after Samra has learned that her husband, Rostom, is a jewel smuggler. I will discuss the second here and the first shortly. The second fantasy sequence uses a long shot of a hallway with a domed ceiling and open windows along the left and right sides. It is a dark shot, lit just enough for us to see Samra enter from the left, thus creating a rather narrow and ominous frame. In the scene Samra wears a fitted ball gown, elbow-length gloves, two sheer scarves draped over her shoulders like a cape, and a small tiara. The camera remains long while Samra begins dancing forward and back. At first she is alone, but when she reaches the end of the hallway for the second time, men in black suits start appearing at the open windows and attempt to grab her as she walks by. Each time she advances in the frame, new men appear, until there are six of them pawing at her from all directions. When she tries to flee the hallway entirely, the men step into it from the windows and stop her movement. Eventually they surround her, and she twirls between them looking for an escape route until she passes out with a complete fade to black.

When she awakes, she is back in her childhood neighborhood. The scene is markedly different: there are stone steps, potted plants, and a rustic water fountain. Samra is in a new dance costume. Rather than the sleek evening wear of the previous long shot, she is wearing a belly dance costume. Here she is smiling, and her movements are light and fluid instead of sharp and frenetic. Similarly, the lighting of the scene is significantly brighter and the camera wider, creating a sense of relief and freedom comparatively. Around her, several men are wearing عبايات (abayas). They are playing instruments instead of smoking, their presence encouraging rather than threatening. After Samra dances for a bit, Ahmed, her former fiancé, enters the scene wearing his suit. She dances for him and to him, and they embrace. Just as he puts his hands around her face as though to kiss her, we hear a gunshot and he crumples. The scene cuts back to Samra in the present, waking up with a start.

In both halves of the dream sequence, dance signals Samra's moral conflict. In Rostom's world of evening gowns and tiaras, dance signifies danger. The longer she remains in the scene, the more ominous it becomes and the more the men encroach on her space. In Ahmed's world of abayas, dance brings her close to kissing a man to whom she is not married, despite their history. A man she has betrayed. Indeed, her betrayal causes her to imagine Ahmed's death in the dream—a death he suffers in proximity to Samra's dancing form. In both halves of the dream, dance plays up the anxiety and danger between Samra and the men in the film, and in both, her relationships distinctly fail to achieve a heteronormative ideal.

So far this section has articulated how dance and performance spaces create opportunities for queering time, space, and relationships by virtue of dance and performance's antithetical positioning against heteronormative time, space, and intimacy. Now I pursue this argument by examining how dance enables a homoerotic exchange between women. There are three scenes in *Sigara* where homoerotic exchanges occur between Hoda and Azza. The first is the first performance sequence between Hoda and Azza at the Casino al-Galaa'. In it Azza is already onstage, softly chiming finger bells as Hoda emerges to instrumental music. When Hoda appears in the foreground, Azza follows her first with her gaze and then physically, singing a song whose lyrics praise Hoda's beauty and grace. Azza sings that her heart belongs to Hoda: "My heart is hers alone . . ." During these lines the camera moves to a close-up of Azza's face, and she gazes adoringly at Hoda. Although men

2.1 Azza sings while Hoda dances in *Sigara wa Kass.*

are onstage and in the audience, Hoda's body is positioned in the frame to repeatedly meet Azza's gaze. Hoda turns her body to Azza as she undulates her hips and moves her arms.

In many Arab musicals, men usually sing alongside women belly dancing. Instead, in *Sigara,* Azza replaces the male lead and usual love interest. This queering is enabled in part by their performances of femininity. Both women are ornately dressed, wearing makeup and hair extensions. Azza's femininity enables her to touch Hoda during the dance, which would be in poor taste if a male singer did it. While Hoda performs for a roomful of men, on a stage with some male performers, only Azza touches her. In the space of performance the women's performance to, with, and against each other can be read erotically. Azza's attention to Hoda's features, her testament to her in music, and the intimate touch she gives Hoda—standing behind her, resting her hand on Hoda's hip—produce Azza as the desiring subject and Hoda as the object.

The camera work in this first scene reinforces its homoeroticism. The introductory shot reverse shot sequence culminates with the pair together in frame, with moments of close-ups of each before widening back to the pair. Usually both women are in frame simultaneously, indicating that the performance happens between them first and to the cabaret audience second. Indeed, the only interaction we have with the cabaret audience, in a four-minute song and dance sequence, is a three-second long shot of Mamdouh, whose gaze rests on Hoda. We see him just before Hoda dances to a musical interlude in the song. I suggest that the temporary recession of Azza's singing allows Mamdouh to make an appearance, but that again, his desire is secondary to Azza's in order and scope. The stage and cinematography not only enable but also necessitate Hoda and Azza's performance of desire for each other. Mamdouh's presence, despite the seemingly heteroerotic cabaret scene, takes a secondary position to the interplay between the women. At best, his desire and the desire of the other patrons are enabled and enacted through the female presence of Azza. Still, the primary dialectic is Azza and Hoda.

The second moment that stages homoeroticism in the film is Hoda's farewell performance for the Casino al-Galaa'. The scene directly follows a conversation Hoda and Azza have had at their apartment before bed, in which Hoda agonizes over leaving show business for a man. This scene ends with Azza's face pressed against a pillow, praying that God will send her love. In the scene that follows, Azza watches Hoda perform her farewell dance from the wings. The stage manager follows Azza and gives her tokens of his affection. Undistracted, Azza rejects them. Instead, she watches Hoda. Because Azza's dream of love is followed immediately by Azza watching Hoda dance, the audience can read Hoda as Azza's wish fulfillment; this reading is affirmed by Azza's response to the stage manager's come-on (a brush-off).

The audience of the cabaret appears only when the performance is over; during the dance, the camera vacillates between Azza watching from the wings and Hoda dancing on stage. The choice to focus on Azza's viewership asserts her primacy in the film. As film viewers, we are more often treated to viewing Hoda from the perspective of Azza than of the audience. As such, the person with whom the viewer identifies is Azza. She becomes the conduit of desire for Hoda; like Azza, film viewers are enchanted with Hoda. The fact that Azza is Hoda's actual and only audience for the dance further queers this fantasy scene: desire is conducted homoerotically through the filter of Azza; thus the scopophilic gaze is arrested from men. Azza is not here, nor has she been rendered as the masculine subject, however. She remains as hyperbolic in her femininity as Hoda, and her longing for her fellow performer does not come from occupying a man's social position or affect. In fact, femininity is centered in the appearance of both women and is the means by which Azza cares for and interacts with Hoda. Their shared femininity is what allows for their intimacy. Their similarities enable the enactment of desire.

The third scene that fosters an unusual erotic encounter in *Sigara* is Hoda's first fantasy sequence, her farewell dance before she leaves to marry Mamdouh. It is unlike previous dance scenes that emphasize eroticism between women or the refusal of heteronormative arcs. Instead, it fosters the eroticism of Hoda to herself. Hoda's farewell dance is steeped in fantasy. She is in an unfamiliar room full of ornate chandeliers and mirrors. She is wearing a rather plain costume, akin to dresses she wears later. She pauses in front of a mirror and the screen blacks out. When the lighting is restored, Hoda's wardrobe changes and she wears a provocative costume with multiple scarves that elongate and exaggerate her movements. As usual, the only visible audience for Hoda's phantasmic performance is Azza. In Hoda's fantasy there

2.2 Hoda's first fantasy dance sequence in *Sigara wa Kass.*

is no audience; indeed, she seems unaware of Azza. For Hoda, there is only dance and the pleasures of dance. The scene is almost narcissistic as she revels in herself. Hoda's attention to herself renders her performance nonnormative insofar as the production of desire is aimed at herself, rather than for men. I stress the narcissism of the moment not to mark narcissism as a queer attribute but to note the ways that the performance space again has allowed alternate geographies of desire to emerge, geographies that disrupt the map of heterosexual desire and reiterate dance and the nightclub as spaces that challenge heteronormativity. Moreover, this sequence offers a vision of the dancers that has not yet been noted—the pleasure in dance as dancers, rather than as a means to an end, an index of female corruption, or whatever else may be written on the dancer's body.

In *Habibi*, dance similarly fosters erotic exchange between Samra and Zakia. Two scenes illustrate this argument. In the first, Samra, dressed for bed in her room, gazes longingly at her record player. As she watches the record spin, a small figure appears on the player and begins to dance. The figure is Zakia, and she is wearing a belly dance costume that sits low on her hips and wraps around her breasts in halter-top fashion; Samra watches her intently. Then a second figure appears. This one is Samra herself, also dressed in a belly dance costume, wearing her hair cropped shortly against her neck rather than in braids. In a previous fantasy sequence Samra danced with her braids and nightgown. But in her fantasy with Zakia, she undergoes a haircut and costume change. The two apparitions dance with each other while Samra watches. At first they take turns, one dancing while the other watches; then they simply dance together. The camera zooms in on each apparition's face so we can see the look of admiration for the movement of the other; then it pans to Samra's face a couple times while she continues to watch, sighing with pleasure and smiling slightly. Finally, the two figures disappear, and Samra is left staring at the record player, which has started to skip. But Samra, enchanted by something only she sees, does not notice.

In this scene the object of Samra's desire initially appears to be Zakia; her pleasure at Zakia's presence is not intuitively around Zakia's dancing but around Zakia herself, performing for her eyes alone. Even Fantasy Samra is taken with Zakia's movement, shaking her head in disbelief at Zakia's virtuosity.[28] Then the fantasy becomes about the camaraderie and kinship between the two women as they dance together. This reading underscores the female homoeroticism in the film, where Zakia and Samra perform and dance for each other before their bodies turn outward for the other spectators. That the primary spectator, Samra, conjures this fantasy is evidence

2.3 Samra watches an apparition of herself and Zakia dance on the record player in *Habibi al Asmar.*

that her desires are somewhat unruly and nonnormative. This evidence is corroborated by her mother, who admonishes her for wanting to see Zakia, for wanting to dance in public, and for dancing in her room to her music in the first place.

The second scene occurs at Zakia's nightclub, where Samra has accompanied Zakia against Samra's parents' and fiancé's wishes. Zakia first appears onstage in the shadows, her arms raised and draped with scarves. The lights come up, and she begins to dance. The camera pans between her performance and Samra watching from between two curtains in the wings, similar to scenes in *Sigara* between Azza and Hoda. Samra's pleasure at Zakia is physical; she executes a couple of her own dance moves with glee. When the number ends, Zakia exits to find Samra and kisses her not on the cheek but, unusually, on the mouth. This is not a common mode of greeting between women or between men. Between friends or relatives of the same sex, kisses are restricted to cheeks. Lip kisses are restricted to committed, romantic

2.4 Samra and Zakia share a kiss after Zakia's performance in *Habibi al Asmar*.

relationships. This exchange positions Zakia and Samra in homoerotic tension with each other, physically staked through dance.

I have suggested that belly dance and nightclubs both queer time and space. In both films, belly dance and the venue in which it's performed offer opportunities to rupture heteronormativity. The club is a place in which the heteronormative order is threatened and new modes of kinship between women emerge. Belly dance, an ephemeral and intimate physical act performed between women, allows homoerotic desires and tensions to emerge. In the following section I take up flipped homoerotic triangulation, the third facet of queer Arab critique, to argue that despite their heteronormative narrative arc, the films' central and primary intimacy occurs between women and not between the heterosexual couples. Using queer time and space, and flipped triangulation, queer Arab critique allows us to imagine desire between women as well as other challenges to heteronormativity. As such, the films can also be read as objects within a queer Arab archive.

Flipped Homoerotic Triangulation:
The Primacy of Women's Relationships to One Another

Though both films use love triangles (two women and one man) to develop narrative tension, I argue that the relationship between the two women in the triangle takes primacy over either's relationship with the man. The relationship between Hoda and Azza in *Sigara* and Samra and Zakia in *Habibi* take primacy over their relationships with Mamdouh, Omara, or Ahmed. Though the films end with heterosexual marriage plots firmly in place for Hoda and Samra, their respective intimacy with Azza and Zakia dominate the overall narratives. If anything, the men offer continued points of contact for the women to navigate their relationships with each other. I will offer comments on how each film prioritizes women's relationships.

In *Sigara*, Azza and Hoda are constructed in relation to one another, and their friendship is prioritized over Hoda's marriage to Mamdouh and Azza's interactions with potential heterosexual partners. *Sigara* opens by panning to the outside of the Casino al-Galaaʾ, where a sign features the two women facing each other. The image is captioned "Azza the Tunisian Singer" and "Hoda Gamal the Dancer."[29] Thus the establishing shot of the film places Hoda and Azza as the stars in relation to one another. Hoda and Azza gaze through the stage curtains to the audience at Mamdouh. Together, they reverse the male gaze, and Mamdouh appears as the scopophilic object of desire, even insofar as he is framed by the dark color of the curtain. Mamdouh offers a point of commonality that underpins their proximity. The stage manager disrupts their scene of camaraderie when he calls the banat to prepare for their performance. Unnamed throughout the film, the stage manager fawns over Azza, but she rejects him, closing her dressing-room door in his face. Her dismissal of him and her attention to Hoda are repeated throughout the film and underscore the primacy of the two women's relationship over the relationships of the women with men.

Hoda and Azza's intimacy is continually demonstrated in the film. Hoda gives birth to a little girl she names Azza (for clarity I will refer to her as Azza Jr., as the younger of the two Azzas in the film). I suggest her choice to name her daughter after her best friend, fellow performer, and former roommate establishes Azza's incredible significance to Hoda. This significance is borne out by the film's representation of time and allotted screen times. After their marriage, Hoda and Mamdouh's life is told through montage. I suggest this cinematic choice to shorten Mamdouh and Hoda's time together relegates Hoda's relationship to Mamdouh to a nonprimary position. Similar to the earlier fantasy sequence wherein Mamdouh appears only when Azza is not singing, much of Mamdouh and Hoda's relationship takes place off-screen or in montage. In fact, Hoda and Azza overall share more screen time than Mamdouh and Hoda. In this way Hoda's heteronormative role as wife and mother mostly happens off-screen, whereas her time as a dancer and with Azza is foregrounded. While it may certainly be the case that this choice is made due to the star power of Gamal (Hoda) and Kouka (Azza) as the film's headliners, I repeat my assertion from earlier: such a reading does not disperse mine, but rather sits in tension with it. Put another way: the impact of the film cannot be ascertained via its assumed intent.

In *Sigara*, the love triangle between Hoda and Yolanda (Mamdouh's head nurse) over Mamdouh becomes a vehicle for further intimacy between Hoda and Azza. In a moment of jealousy over Yolanda's proximity to Mamdouh, Hoda turns to alcohol. When Azza comes to check on her, Hoda is already drunk. Azza attempts to help Hoda into bed. When Hoda tries to remove her own clothes but becomes tangled in them, Azza intervenes, undressing her carefully. Eroticism and intimacy between Mamdouh and Hoda never occur on-screen. What eroticism the heterosexual couple lacks is supplanted with homoeroticism between Azza and Hoda. Hoda's body becomes a site of pleasure for the viewer, who watches her disrobe, and is enacted through Azza, who finishes removing Hoda's clothing. As in the dance scenes, Azza becomes the conduit for the viewer's desire of Hoda. She does so without assuming a masculine position; indeed, she can do so only from the safety of her femininity.

The primacy of the intimacy between Hoda and Azza is perhaps most readily evident in Azza's marriage plot. I suggest that Azza marries Omara to stay close to Hoda. Through the film Azza has bemoaned the lack of love in her life, despite repeatedly rejecting suitors. First she rejects the stage manager and then a friend of Mamdouh's, Omara. At a party Mamdouh throws for Hoda, Azza begins actively interviewing men to marry because her visa is about to expire, and she does not want to leave Egypt for three months to renew it. She goes from man to man, dismissing them when she realizes that they are not Egyptian and thus cannot solve the visa problem. In a bind, she tricks Omara into kissing her. By forcing intimacy, she manipulates him into doing the "honorable thing" and marrying her. Until this point, Azza has not worried about maintaining her visa and has rejected multiple Egyptian suitors, including Omara. The concern that finally compels Azza to marriage is to remain close to Hoda and to secure Hoda's happiness, which she is willing

2.5 Azza gives Hoda a playful swat on her bottom while undressing her in *Sigara wa Kass*.

to do by any means necessary: fixing Hoda's marriage to Mamdouh, marrying an Egyptian to stay in Egypt, and at one point physically assaulting Yolanda.

It should be clear how Azza's behavior could be read queerly in the context of the film. I want to pause on Hoda, who mostly serves as the object of Azza's desire, while Hoda's desire is most often geared toward the stage and the acclaim that it brings. There is one moment that disrupts this mapping. When Hoda wakes up the morning after the party, Mamdouh, Azza, and Azza Jr. are gone. She runs through the house screaming, "Azza, Azza!" but it is not clear if she is looking for her child or her faithful friend. We might be inclined to read this as concern for her daughter, but queer spectatorship invites us to indulge in the moment of confusion: Azza Jr. appears on-screen very little, perhaps three minutes total. Hoda has never spoken of her. The child is named for Hoda's former roommate and longtime friend. It is reasonable that Hoda would wake wanting her friend over her daughter. After all, what has the daughter done for her lately? Azza could easily inspire as much, if not more, longing.

As in *Sigara*, *Habibi* uses flipped homoerotic triangles to emphasize intimacy between women rather than between the heterosexual couple. Samra's interest in Zakia, fostered via her interest in dance, overrules Samra's other affective attachments. The first real-time interaction between Samra and Zakia occurs after the fantasy sequence we discussed earlier, in which Samra imagined Zakia dancing for her, herself dancing for Zakia, and themselves dancing together. After the sequence ends, Samra opens her bedroom window to find Zakia waiting for her in hers—her fantasy come to life. They converse about Zakia's night at the club, and Samra wishes that she could come to see Zakia dance. Zakia promises to sneak her out the following night and encourages Samra to take up dance herself. That is, Zakia promises a night on the town that will remain secret from Samra's family. Though their secret relationship is indicative of its unacceptable nature because of its proximity to dance, it is also marked by the framing of Zakia as an overall unsavory character with whom Samra is advised not to associate by her family and fiancé, though she does anyway. After Samra is disciplined by her father and argues with her fiancé about her interest in dance, she continues to sneak out of the house to see Zakia. Her desires to be with or like Zakia override her other normative kin and intimate obligations.

As in *Sigara*, dance scenes in *Habibi* displace men as the primary audience for dancers and place women in the role of enamored spectator, allowing queer desire to flourish. When Samra arrives at the club to watch Zakia dance, she is as entranced by her as Azza is by Hoda. As Samra watches Zakia, Rostom watches Samra. He asks the club's manager about her, and together they approach her. But Samra spurns their conversation and continues to watch Zakia; when they attempt to touch her and claim her attention, she snaps at them and puts further physical distance between them. Her disinterest in the men and her focus on Zakia are manifest in her words and body language. Though the scene portrays heterosexual desire from Rostom to Samra, Samra herself diminishes it and fixates on Zakia.

Samra's infatuation with Zakia subverts Samra's heteronormative relationships and prioritizes the intimacy between women over relationships with her biological family and her heterosexual betrothed. Samra repeatedly relies on Zakia's counsel and company over that of her established kin and romantic relationships. She goes to the club to watch Zakia against her father's and fiancé's wishes; she enjoys watching the other woman dance; she agrees to a ride home from Rostom only because Zakia will be there and because Zakia encourages her. Indeed, Samra overthrows her biological family and her fiancé on Zakia's counsel. She marries Rostom on Zakia's advice and ends her engagement to Ahmed. Whatever we imagine Zakia's motives to be, Samra's affection for her goes beyond neighbor, student, or friend. Here I am not arguing that Samra marries Rostom but loves Zakia. Rather, I draw our attention to the intense intimacy between the women and how it offers an alternate queer plot or narrative alongside the heteronormative one.

In both *Habibi* and *Sigara* the relationships between the women are fundamental not only to the plot, but also to the characters' development. In both, women display loyalty and affection to other women that precedes and supersedes their relationships to men. When we couple this primacy with the eroticism between women fostered in dance as discussed in the previous section, the queerness of the characters and films begins to emerge. Though I have suggested that these queer longings are available through a position of queer spectatorship, it is not only from a queer viewing position that we can understand the nonnormative intimacies erupting on-screen. In the next section, we will document queer eruptions by attending to how the films discipline them.

Queer Containment: Tracing Queerness
via Its Attempted Containment

The fourth aspect of queer Arab critique, containment, documents how we can locate queerness in the films by attending to moments where queerness is disciplined or disparaged. The need to police queer desires and subjects makes evident their existence. In both films, queer ruptures are contained via marriage, madness, and death to sustain the heteronormative plot. In *Habibi*, Zakia and Rostom die in order to enable Samra and Ahmed's reconciliation and marriage. In *Sigara*, the stage manager's queerness is made exceptional via madness. His madness/queerness is juxtaposed with Azza's and overshadows it to render Azza less queer. Azza's queerness is also "cured" through marriage.

In *Sigara*, Azza and the stage manager invoke a queer pathology insofar as their mental instability is conveyed through their gendered and sexual performances. It is only against and through their abjection that the heterosexual couple can survive. Azza's affected (alongside the stage manager's seemingly actual) madness is used as a tool to produce and buttress heteronormative relationships. As I noted earlier, Azza often discusses love but has routinely rejected Omara and the stage manager as suitors. However, Azza not only refuses Omara after his initial proposal but convinces him that she is "crazy" to put him off marrying her. Azza uses "insanity" to escape normative heterosexuality, and her person is thus doubly queered by her supposed madness and her avoidance of men. Even without the use of madness, the absence of heteroromantic relationships in Azza's life reads queerly: her refusal to pursue men and the absence of even one reasonable suitor in the years that the film spans (about five) highlight her unusual single status. Azza's queer potential thus is marked both by her onstage eroticism with Hoda and by her lack of heterosexual relationships. Until her decision to stay in Egypt with Hoda, she has no intention of marrying for love, desire, or even money. She only becomes concerned with her visa status as the requirement for staying with Hoda.

Azza's queerness in the film is partially contained by her marriage to Omara at the film's conclusion, but it is also managed via the undeniable queerness of the stage manager, who ends the film in a hospital, dressed as a woman. I suggest that the stage manager's drag has three functions: first, it makes heterosexuality a source of threat and madness. Second, it pathologizes queerness. Third, the explicit queerness of the stage manager renders Azza less deviant.

The stage manager's transformation originates in his terror at a heterosexual marriage to Azza. Azza's devotion to Hoda is such that she is willing to make the ultimate sacrifice: marry the stage manager who has loved her for years, the same stage manager she has routinely rejected. When she informs him that she will marry him, the manager is at first ecstatic. But when Azza leaves he becomes visibly anxious and faints. The next and final time we see him is in a hospital room in drag, dressed as a stereotypical older Arab woman. He is slapping his palms together in a gesture attributed to worrying women. His reaction suggests he finds a heterosexual union threatening; the stage manager is so overwhelmed by the prospect of marrying Azza that he "becomes" a woman. Alternately, his transformation can be read as a concession to Azza's queer configuration in the film: the stage manager occupies femininity because thus far in the film Azza's desire is geared toward femininity via Hoda. We might also read his transformation as a mode of identification with the object he desires; after all, it is the similarities between Azza and Hoda, their shared femininity and positions, that allow for their intimacy. Perhaps the actualization of the stage manager's desire is not a sexual union with Azza but an emulation of her gender performance. In any case, what is not desired is heterosexual coupling, and the stage manager's transformation underlines this.

Second, the scene reinscribes queerness as pathology. Azza has already done this throughout the film by avoiding marriage with "insane" behavior, and the presence of the stage manager in the hospital for the "mental illness" of cross-dressing solidifies it. The pathologization of the stage manager is linked to my third point: his queerness overshadows Azza's through its visibility, and she is partially recuperated through his blatant nonnormativity. In his work on homosexuality in Egyptian film, Garay Menicucci outlines two possible reasons for men cross-dressing as women, a recurring trend during the Golden Era. He argues that cross-dressing often introduced questions of class and was persistently and explicitly tied to homosexuality in men.[30] Under Menicucci's reading, the stage manager's transformation explicitly marks him as a homosexual. By constructing an obvious homosexual character, *Sigara* softens Azza's queerness. Her love for Hoda and reluctance to wed may be curious, but it is unremarkable next to the stage manager's obvious deviance. As McRuer theorizes, compulsory able-bodiedness is bound to compulsory heterosexuality in this moment: the queer disabled subject (the stage manager) operates in opposition to Azza. Because the stage manager occupies the homosexual space, Azza is shifted toward heterosexuality.[31] The undoing of Azza's queerness is completed through the film's conclusion: she helps secure Hoda and Mamdouh's marriage, and then marries Omara. This conclusion conveniently removes both women from the queer spaces of belly dance and the nightclub and places them on a heteronormative narrative arc toward marriage and family. So while the film contains its queer ruptures, queer Arab critique witnesses their possibility all the same.

In *Habibi*, queerness is contained via violence against nonnormative subjects.[32] In *Habibi*, Zakia dies in order to undo the chaos she creates in Samra's and Ahmed's lives.[33] Zakia is a central figure in the narrative; she is the pivot point on two love triangles, between Samra and Ahmed on the one hand, and Samra and Rostom on the other. Zakia is repeatedly marked as a nonnormative figure through her associations with Samra and Ahmed. When she is attempting to convince Samra to sneak out with her, Zakia suggests that dance will bring more into Samra's life: more fun, more worldliness, more money! Her framing of dance reflects the antinormative qualities of Zakia's own life: her independence as the independence of women from fathers and fiancés; her self-sufficiency as the agency of women earning their own keep;

her scorn for a heteronormative story as insistence that there is more to life than men in the old neighborhood. With Ahmed, Zakia articulates antinormative values about love and family and is subsequently punished for those views and concordant behaviors. In a conversation with Ahmed after Samra has left him, Zakia suggests: "The thing you're looking for? It doesn't exist. Loyalty is just words." When Ahmed responds, "So there isn't anything called love?" Zakia makes a pass at him: "Exactly . . . there is something in the world called 'passing time.' I, for example, am dying for you." She prefers passion and honesty to love and loyalty. Zakia's comments are easily interpreted as antinormative within the prevailing generic standards for dramas, comedies, and romances, all of which intersect in this film. That Zakia does not believe in love, that she believes only in making the most of the moment, stands not just outside the formulas prescribed by the film industry in its narratives but also outside heteronormative attitudes about love in the mid-twentieth century. Certainly, the attitude she has cultivated threatens monogamous, heterosexual marriage; her lack of belief in loyalty makes her betrayal of Samra (by hitting on her ex-fiancé) logical if not acceptable. It is this attitude of pleasure seeking that makes Zakia so dangerous to those around her: she threatens many of the foundations on which their social order relies. She advocates for Samra's independence, she flirts with Samra and her fiancé, and she chooses thrills and money over love and loyalty. Perhaps Zakia's insistence on pleasure and taking it where one can makes her the most antinormative and dangerous figure in the film.

As such, for a heteronormative narrative to triumph, Zakia's unruly desires are disciplined. Zakia dies while saving Ahmed. Her death is the correction and punishment for her errors and the means by which the heteronormative plot can reemerge. As she dies, she apologizes for her antinormative viewpoints, especially her advice to Samra and Ahmed, indicating her choices have been immoral. What dies with Zakia is precisely the antinormative, agential vision of women's lives that she embodied. For Zakia, it is too late to be saved. Her lesson is passed on to Ahmed and Samra, who return to their pure, marriage-driven, and loyal love in the wake of her death. Like the stage manager in *Sigara*, Zakia's extreme nonnormativity and moral failures make Samra and Ahmed recoverable. Like Azza, her queer potential is quieted through a common narrative trope. It is only in her complete abjection, like the stage manager's, that the correct couple can survive. The very regulation of queerness and nonnormativity in the film intimates how prevalent concerns around desire and sexuality were in the Golden Era, and via the Golden Era, in the larger Egyptian and Arab cultural scheme. As such, the films reveal a more diverse gender and sexual dialogue in transnational Arab production than Orientalism and anti-Arab racism deem possible.

☾

Queer Arab critique invites viewers to locate queerness and potentially queer subjects in the film through attention to queer time and space, flipped homoerotic triangulation, and queer containment. In this chapter, I used queer Arab critique to demonstrate how dance fostered homosociality and homoerotic desire between women, how women's intimacy with one another challenged heteronormativity, and how the rupture of homoerotic intimacy on-screen required a narrative resolution that guarded against leaving the film with an "untoward" message. In the films, queer desire takes up as much space as, if not more than, heteronormative desire. While heterosexuality is ultimately restored in the conclusion of the stories, the presence of nonnormative bodies and desires makes space in the culture of the film and the culture of the viewer for alternate geographies of kinship, coupling, and intimacy to assert themselves.

There is in the films, and in the performances, an ephemeral and gestural quality that categorizes queer spectatorship and is in some way characteristic of desire itself—communicated more often through languishing looks and trace contacts, elaborated off-screen and behind closed doors. I'm drawn to the films and the expressions of desire located here not only because they imagine queer bodies and intimacies in the plain and popular sight of the Golden Era, but because they eschew Orientalist and heteronational gazes that would otherwise fetishize or erase them through their ephemerality. There is something withheld from the screen, produced only privately between the viewer and the text, that escapes capture. I take the heteronormative insistences of these texts and the many readers who reject homoerotic readings thereof as evidence of the delicious things queers do in the shadows.

Using queer Arab critique on Golden Era film asserts the presence of nonnormative gender and desire in mainstream Arab texts, resists the erasure of queer subjects from Arab histories, and signals that queerness is neither absent from nor foreign to Arab culture. Despite their mainstream appeal, both films evidence a multifaceted dialogue about desire, gender, and sexuality in Golden Era Egyptian film. Because of their mainstream appeal and popularity in Arab culture, the films usefully operate as ambivalent objects in a transnational queer Arab archive.

The Golden Era offers space for queer identification with and queer spectatorship of an Arab canon. The Golden Era remains a central text to transnational

Arab audiences and has a robust queer contemporary life as noted in the chapter's introduction. This is significant insofar as it substantiates the production of and access to a queer history within dominant Arab cultural forms, and it resists the notion that those forms or cultures were forbidding to or absent of queer content. The use of "golden" to describe the cultural texts of the time period indicate some of its affective resonances. The Golden Era is itself steeped in nostalgia. As Svetlana Boym writes, nostalgia is itself a kind of desire—for something that has passed that is presumed to be preferable to what is currently offered. In Boym's assessment, there is something sad about nostalgia, a stuckness in desire for something that no longer exists, if it ever did. There is a certain anticolonial romanticism that we can locate in our longing, one that precedes naming and sexual identity practices that feel sticky and uncomfortable for queer Arab subjects—the same stickiness that drives us to use queer as nomenclature over lesbian or gay, the same stickiness that underlines Massad's romanticization of precolonial queer Arab formations. Boym reads such nostalgias as potentially troubling—undoing the subject's personal responsibility, an abdication of the present and future, where nothing compares to the past.[34] Like Boym, queer critics often read nostalgia as a negative affect: Berlant writes that nostalgia marks normative subjects' desire to erase queer presence and return to a more punishing and normative sexual past.[35] Muñoz champions a utopic future grounded in queer histories, but takes care to distinguish that from nostalgia.[36]

Queer Arab critique asks us to think differently about nostalgia and its affective efficacy for queer Arab archives and futures. For subjects whose histories are actively erased by Orientalist and heteronational violence, our nostalgia for the sexual playfulness of the Golden Era is nostalgia for the capacity to exist at all. As Elizabeth Windle writes, for queers of color subject to racist and heterosexist suppression of their pasts and contemporary violence, nostalgia disrupts time and brings the possibility of queer joy from the past to the viewers in the present.[37] Thus, to read queerness in the Golden Era both imagines a queer past and muddles homonormative constructions of a progressive, linear march to gay liberation.

At the same time, however, to read queerness through affective and ephemeral ruptures alone is not enough for queer subjects whose lives are material, for whom queerness is not a rupture but ongoing. I am concerned here with the tendency to reify a romantic precolonial queer subject at the expense of queer subjects who are living and organizing in the present. Many contemporary queer Arab subjects face daily discipline of their queerness, or yearn for their desires to take center stage rather than subplot. In those instances, attention to nostalgia, to queerness as ephemeral and gestural, and to queerness as only available via queer spectatorship underserves our queer Arab subjects in two ways: it can minimize the impact of heteronormative culture and its discipline on queer subjects. Their conditional and tentative visibility erases the violence perpetuated against them. It may also elide the very real way queers are themselves experiencing and reckoning with their own desires in more distinct and tangible terms. Queer women do analyze, name, and narrate their queer experiences around and against discourses that would relegate them to precolonial romantic figures or Western iterations of identity. In other words, queer Arab critique cannot only examine queerness when it travels under the heteronormative radar; it must also attend to moments when queer Arab subjects explicitly articulate queer identities and antinormative stances, even when their own articulations are ambivalent.

I have suggested that locating queer Arab archives amid the restrictive discourses articulated in the previous chapter necessitates developing a queer Arab critique that includes queer spectatorship, queer time and space, flipped homoerotic triangulation, and queer containment. Queer Arab critique begins by locating nonnormative gendered and sexual desires in mainstream texts and uses them to build a kind of queer archive often assumed unavailable to Arabs. In the following two chapters, I shift focus from texts where queer subjects are in the periphery to texts that center Arab women, banat, and femmes. I shift from texts where the onus of locating queerness is on the viewer to texts where the writers themselves name and narrate their experiences despite and against discursive restrictions. As in this chapter, the following chapters deal with longing in Arabic language texts. Unlike this chapter, chapters 3 and 4 name homoerotic and same-sex sexuality directly and centrally in their invocations of desire. Centering the voices of women, femmes, and banat is precisely what disrupts the impossibility of queer subjectivity eclipsed in Orientalist and heteronational discourses. Such voices produce a robust queer Arab critique and point us toward an expansive queer Arab archive.

longing in arabic 3

Ambivalent Identities in Arabic Novels

In the previous chapter, longing described moments of intimacy between women on-screen and, at the same time, longing from the spectator for that intimacy, for ephemeral moments whose significance to the viewer are belied by their brevity, their transience. The longing that animated chapter 2 crystalizes in chapter 3 via the work of Arabic novels that feature same-sex desires, practices, and identities explicitly and repeatedly. If the previous chapter poses the question of "if" and "when" we might read queerness in Arabic cultural texts, this chapter considers the "how" of queer Arab women's longing as it is imagined in Arabic literature. I argue here that study of queer Arab women, banat, and femmes produces a queer Arab subject with an interiority all its own, one that is not collapsible to Orientalist or heteronational scripts or to Western categories of LGBT identity. In the novels, queer Arab subjectivity is marked by ambivalence and fluidity with regard to sexual identities, practices, and desires. Queer Arab subjects are also marked by their social and political identifications, shaping their sexualities with and through their critiques of state and heteropatriarchal violence. Additionally, the novels suggest that intergenerational women's communities are a significant facet of queer Arab life. Finally, a secondary argument of this chapter is that Arabic novels are a potentially queer and feminist literary form.

While chapter 1 outlined discursive restrictions that limit queer representation and make queer subjects invisible and chapter 2 read against the grain to locate queerness within restrictive contexts, this chapter uses queer Arab critique to attend to the interiority and world-making of the self-identified queer protagonists in the texts under consideration. This chapter contributes to the queer Arab archive insofar as it features queer subjects who are ambivalent about their queerness, and their provocations teach us how to think and understand queerness in Arab cultures. Despite the discursive restriction Scheherazade animated in chapter 1, some literature and film has featured explicit homoerotic desire and/or sexual acts between Arab women. In the 2000s, several literary texts began to represent Arab women's sexuality more robustly. While this was often deeply heteronormative (as we saw in chapters 1 and 2), some texts explored torrid physical and emotional affairs between women and girls of various ages. Though the texts under discussion in this chapter are more explicit in their representation of queerness, the troubling discourses that shape Arab sexuality and Arab femininities withstand, and for that reason, it is still useful to approach the texts with queer Arab critique undergirding our readings.

It often comes as a surprise to Western and some Arab audiences that the majority of works about same-sex desires and practices between Arab women are not, as Orientalism would have us believe, originating in the West or in English.[1] They are works by Arab authors and artists, produced in Arabic, in Arab nations. Many are also translated into English and other languages. In this chapter and the next, I examine representations of queer desire between Arab women in the Arabic-language literatures available, with two small restrictions. First, I am only looking at work by Arab women and about banat Arab. Second, I am examining long works that center in plot or character homoeroticism between women. Utilizing these criteria, three novels emerge for consideration: Elham Mansour's أنا هي أنت (Ana Hiya Inti/I Am You), Seba al-Herz's الآخرون (Al Akharuun/The Others), and Samar Yazbek's رائحة القرفة (Ra'ihat il Kirfa/The Scent of Cinnamon). They originate and take place in Lebanon, Saudi Arabia, and Syria, respectively. The regional specificity in these works stands in contrast to the transnational Arab cultural experience of the Golden Era discussed in the previous chapter. At the same time, the texts' translation, circulation, and content extends their regional focus to a broader readership. The publication of the works by literary presses helps us understand the attention and circulation the novels might receive compared to the essay collections in the upcoming chapter. That circulation and reception come with expectations and criticisms regarding their alleged aesthetic value. At the same time, their publication by a known literary entity functions as an affirmation of the stories' social relevance, or at least, their presumed salability.

Under the criteria of long works that center homoeroticism between women and are by women, three collections of autobiographical creative nonfiction also emerged and will be discussed in chapter 4. I have divided the study by genre for a few reasons. First, the novels in this chapter offer a continuation of the subjectivity that animates chapters 1 and 2. Like film, the novel produces vis-à-vis its form an enactment of queer desire by characters on the page. In the following chapter, however, the texts are autobiographical with queer speakers. This shift in narrator warrants space and a slightly different theoretical approach than the works of fiction. Relatedly, the shift in narration accompanies a shift in narrative outcome. While both the novels and the autobiographical works consider the "how" of queer Arab experience, the attempt to resolve the question of queer Arab identity as such is done by critics (myself included) in the first instance and by the writers themselves in the second. While it's not my intent to offer here a genre study per se, how queerness is understood and mobilized in these divergent forms produces different kinds of queer subjects.

Second, how the novels circulate varies from how the essay collections circulate. Each of the three novels were published by Arab literary presses. Each has been translated into English and sometimes other languages. Each has received some amount of attention from Arab and Anglophone literary critics. Finally, all three, but especially Yazbek's, have "mainstream" cross-over appeal as a function of their publication house and translation, and in Yazbek's case, as part of the author's canon. Publication under a literary press produces a different kind of audience for the work than do other forms of publication, such as self-publication, which I will discuss in the following chapter. Texts produced for presses are also beholden to different expectations regarding their content; we can revisit from chapter 1 the question of quality or language mastery that concerns *Scheherazade's Legacy*. They also aim, seemingly, toward a different end: literary or aesthetic production over "political" representation. As texts subject to editors and their boards, the advice of agents, and so on, the texts must also be read as mediated by the multiple hands through which they pass. While texts that do not get published by presses certainly experience mediation as well, it is important to make transparent how and to what end that mediation functions in the case of the novels and, in the following chapter, the essay collections.

In this chapter I attend to the novel as a form and consider the publication and reception of the three "Arab lesbian novels" *Ana Hiya Inti*, *Al Akharuun*, and *Ra'ihat il Kirfa* in order to consider how Arab women writers navigate questions of gender and sexual nonnormativity in their work, how they represent and understand homoeroticism in Arabic and specific Arab cultural contexts, and how they imagine or undermine queer possibility for the novels' subjects. I argue that the texts engage in several significant rhetorical and political acts. First, they establish the existence of queer Arabs within Arab culture, despite discursive and material restrictions on queer life. They create and imagine queer Arab subjects that are not tokens of Orientalism, romanticized precolonial subjects, or "bad faith" Westernized Arabs. Instead, the texts evoke multilingual, transnational queer Arab subjects that are not reduced to the discourses that attempt to forestall them. Second, the texts offer interrogations of and interventions into the heteronormative, national, and state scripts that shape queer experiences. In their critique, I highlight the writers' agency and strategic normativity, wherein they manipulate common homosocial practices, heteronormative expectations, and the emphasis on reputation/respectability to secure secret intimate spaces for queer sex and love. The novels show that queer Arabs can look toward their own cultural producers and histories for salient critiques of heteropatriarchy, the state, and respectability.

To understand the significance of what these texts accomplish, it is useful to revisit briefly the debates regarding homosexuality and queer identity in the Arab world. Since this is discussed in my introduction and subsequently throughout the book, I will provide that discussion here through examining how the texts were received in literary and queer circles. With some minor exceptions, the novels in this chapter were met with complaints that can be deconstructed to reveal critics own longings, desires, and expectations for queer Arab literature. Here critics are a robust group that includes other queer Arabs, non-Arab queers, nonqueer Arabs, and literary scholars of all stripes. Obviously, the stakes in criticism for each group are varied. Queer Arabs may be looking for powerful representations that ring true to their lives, non-Arab queers may be seeking insight into Arab culture, and so on. Despite the intention behind the criticisms, the critiques themselves were surprisingly similar and fall into three categories.

First, critics asserted that the works capitulated to a Western canon of LGBT identity that cannot capture the nuances of sexuality in Arab societies. Massad suggests that the desire to "come out" and claim a distinct homosexual identity are homonormative benchmarks aligned with a Western delineation of LGBT identity, which, like the identity lesbian itself, cannot describe the facets of homoerotic desires and behaviors between Arab women.[2] While purveyors of this first criticism might recognize a precolonial queer subject in Arab cultures, their anxiety around Westernization and Orientalism forecloses possibilities for contemporary iterations of queer life for fear that they might be too easily coopted by Western imperial agendas, or what Puar calls homonationalism.[3] Amer suggests that this criticism can also alert us to questions of elitism and social class within Arab communities, where using foreign words (English and French primarily) "represents one of the legacies of colonialism and remains a distinctive hallmark of Western-educated Arabs, a mark of privilege, urban sophistication, and social class. This means that the use of Western terminology to speak about homosexuality leads to the exclusion of poor and working-class Arab gays and lesbians who may feel doubly alienated by foreign cultural semantics and categories."[4] Here, the recourse to non-Arabic language implies that queerness exists within certain social and economic classes of Arab society and is unavailable or alienating to poor and working-class groups. As a result of this rhetorical tendency, poor and working-class groups become invisible in conversations as queers or accused of elitism and/or Westernization should they articulate queer sexualities in their lives.

Second, works were criticized for "staying in the closet" and reifying queer sexualities as shameful by failing to make elaborate displays of "gay pride" and adopt LGBT identities. What use is a queer Arab novel, or a lesbian protagonist, if she is suffering and experiencing emotional trauma? This was particularly the case when writers struggled with historical queer Arab subject positions like سحق (sahq) or شذوذ (shuthooth) because of their negative social registers.[5] The ambivalence many writers displayed for categorical assertions of identity, in any language, made readers uncomfortable. Here were protagonists whose sexual desires, practices, and lives changed over time; here were characters who weren't ecstatic in their queer identities, but anxious and questioning. The writers' emotional ambivalence and struggles with their sexuality read to some as a lack of commitment to queer identity. In short, the writers were not queer enough.

Third, the works were critiqued for reifying the notion that queerness was not intrinsic in human behavior because in some narratives, banat allegedly turned to homoeroticism and same-sex partnerships in situations of violent, oppressive, or otherwise failed heterosexuality.[6] In other words, critics read queer subjects suffering under heteronormativity as evidence that homoeroticism is merely a phase, a response to patriarchy, or an adaptive strategy. In her work on Arab lesbian literatures, Iman Al-Ghafari asserts that the tendency to read queerness as failed heterosexuality results from an internalization of a heterosexual disciplining gaze that forms both the literature and its reception.[7] Despite this nuanced reading of how heteronormativity informs queer subject formation, this critique too discounts the work for its ultimate failure to present the right kind of homosexual, lesbian, or queer Arab subject. This critique is ultimately an anxiety around queer origins, wherein subjects are required to explain how and why they became involved in same-sex practices, and anything short of "born gay" narratives indicate a fake or performed queer identity. The stakes of this might be familiar: if queer behavior is anything but "nature" then it can be nurtured back out and does not require social transformation. If it is "nurtured" we are also free to disregard it, condemn its moral failure, and excise the perpetrators from our communities.

All three criticisms share a yearning or longing for a particular kind of "lesbian Arab" subject, and combined these criticisms reveal a double bind for women seeking to explore homoeroticism and same-sex desires. In this sexual double bind, queer subjects must adopt terminology and narrative arcs that are not apt to describe one's life or are dissonant with one's actual desires and experiences. This option would include both the Western LGBT nomenclature and the insistences on distinct gay identities and gay pride. Alternatively, subjects must invest in language or subject positions that, while one's "own," are already foreclosed within the surrounding social order and thus hardly desirable. This would include attempting to reclaim Arabic words like "sahq" or "shuthooth," and attempting to minimize their experience of heteropatriarchal oppression to guard against being read as failed heterosexuals. With this impossible double bind in place, "lesbian" Arab texts must fail.

I want to suggest we look at the double bind itself as the source of impossibility, rather than queerness, or the writers producing narratives. The desire to "resolve" lesbian Arab identity in the case of "not queer enough" is an attempt to assimilate Arab modes of sexuality into white Western categories. In the case of "not convincingly queer," the desire is to attempt to produce an "authentic" Arab history that does not include queers. These overdetermined discourses require a perfect Arab lesbian subject—a super heroic figure who must navigate the double bind flawlessly or face abjection as a proper queer subject or a proper Arab one. That perfect superhero is the impossibility.

Instead, by examining the three novels, I aim to articulate the facets and features of queer Arab subject formation as narrated in the texts—and not in accordance with my or others' longing for a particular kind of political subject. In the novels, characters relay their awareness and navigation of the double bind. They either explicitly or tacitly address critics and reception within their stories. The novels offer multiple experiences, perspectives, and responses to the criticisms and double bind that surrounds them. By examining three novels with varying national, historical, and social contexts, I aim to elaborate the many forms of queer Arab existence, how writers carve space for queer subjects, and the critiques they offer back to critics.

To do this, I frame discussions of *Ana Hiya Inti*, *Al Akharuun*, and *Ra'ihat il Kirfa* within feminist and queer criticisms of the Arab novel. I examine how the texts represent queer Arab subjects. I outline the three dominant features of queer Arab women's experience that emerge within the text: fluid, mutable, and nonlinear sexual desires, practices, and identities; intergenerational, intimate spaces for women; and critical consciousness regarding the state and heteropatriarchal violence. Ultimately, these three works offer us a literary history and present of queerness for banat and by banat. The texts are cognizant of the many tropes that surround queer subjects, reject singular or static renditions of their lives, and continue to exist in complex, multifaceted ways. *Ana Hiya Inti*, *Al Akharuun*, and *Ra'ihat il Kirfa* work to create space within Arabic literature to imagine queer Arab life. The novels are all written by Arab women and feature a central protagonist that engages in same-sex desires and practices. They take place in Lebanon, Saudi Arabia, and Syria, respectively. Each uses an intimate and interior-focused narration style done in stream-of-consciousness, often first-person narration. I offer here a brief summary of each novel as context for the remaining discussion.

Elham Mansour's *Ana Hiya Inti* follows Siham at the end of her high school years and into college. Much of the book is devoted to Siham's attempt to woo and win her college professor, Layal. Prior to Layal, Siham dated Nour (also a college professor) and Claire, a French student at her high school. While Siham begins her courtship of Layal to get over Nour, it soon becomes a torrid infatuation. The book also features Mimi, a married mother who is having an affair with a widow in her neighborhood, but who, like Siham, has her sights set on Layal. In this way, Layal becomes a foil for Siham's and Mimi's desires, even to the extent that they are only attracted to Layal when she is very feminine or very masculine, respectively. For her part, Layal revels in the attention of both women and finds Mimi particularly attractive. While desire is heady on the page, it seems Layal does not engage in any sexual acts with either woman. Eventually, Layal introduces Mimi to Siham, and the two develop a proxy relationship with one another, each still longing for Layal.

Seba al-Herz's *Al Akharuun* revolves around a nameless narrator and her lovers: Dai, Dareen, and Umar. The book is divided into three sections. It describes an abusive relationship with Dai, a rebound and friends with benefits relationship with Dareen, and eventually, the narrator's sex with and engagement to a man, Umar. The novel is saturated with Dai, who forms the first and most lasting impression on the narrator. Despite the narrator's florid descriptions of Umar compared to those she uses regarding Dai, her love of Umar is tangled with the death of her beloved brother Hassan, a grief she carries throughout the book. The book ends with the narrator pleading with Umar to never die.

Samar Yazbek's *Ra'ihat il Kirfa* alternates narration between its two central protagonists: Hanan Al Hashimi, an affluent Syrian woman in an unsatisfying marriage, and Aaliyah, a Black servant indentured to Hanan. The women are also lovers. The novel opens with a scene of discovery: Hanan catches Aaliyah giving Hanan's husband a hand job. Hanan throws Aaliyah out of the house. The novel flashes back and forth in time, covering both women's childhood and their time together. It ends with Hanan searching for Aaliyah while Aaliyah continues to travel away from her. It's written in third person and vacillates between Aaliyah's and Hanan's stream of consciousness.

These three novels overlap in their representations and offer us insight into queer Arab women's experiences with nonnormative gender and sexuality. The texts evidence how writers employ the genre of the novel and reject the dismissal of women's literature to explore and navigate queer Arab becomings. Specifically, they emphasize fluid and mutable sexualities; the primacy and intimacy of women's relationships with women through intergenerational communities; and queerness as critical consciousness regarding state and heteropatriarchal violence. In the next three sections, I will address how the works enable queer representation through manipulation of generic convention; how they establish women's homoerotic communities; and finally, how to read against a desire for queer origin stories and look instead toward the critiques the works offer.

The Arabic Novel: A Feminist and Queer Genre?

In this section, I discuss the parallels between the discursive constructions of the Arabic novel and Arab queers. I suggest that the Arabic novel, like dance in chapter 2 and graphic novels in an upcoming chapter, offer a space for queer and feminist subjects to emerge within and against discursive foreclosure. I suggest we read all three "lesbian Arab novels" against their critical dismissal and instead as rich interrogations and theorizations of gender and sexuality in Arab literature. The open-ended form of the novel is useful for queer Arab subjects because its narrative ambivalence reflects queer characters' ambivalence about their sexualities. Despite their reception, *Ana Hiya*

Inti, *Al Akharuun*, and *Ra'ihat il Kirfa* undercut or expand the Arabic novel's traditions by rending authorship of women's interiority from men and by challenging normative gendered and sexual structures through explorations of nonnormative subjects.

As I mentioned earlier, literary receptions of the novels were robustly negative in regard to their handling of queer sexuality. They were criticized for capitulation to Western notions around sexuality and for failing to clearly demarcate queer identity, through naming, displays of pride, muting of stigma and suffering, and/or articulating clear origins for their same-sex desires and behaviors. Additionally, all three novels were subject to critical scrutiny and broad readership because they were published by Arab literary presses, because of the genre itself, and because they accrued various forms of notoriety upon their publication. At the time of its publication, *Ana Hiya Inti* was dubbed "the first Arab lesbian novel" and thus bore a great deal of discursive and epistemological weight. Meanwhile, *Al Akharuun* sparked controversy in its native Saudi Arabia for its explicit and graphic portrayals of homoeroticism. The author of the work used a pseudonym and remained anonymous, along with the translator, when the work was later translated to English. This anonymity prevented al-Herz's social persecution and alienation, an outcome Mansour experienced after publishing *Ana Hiya Inti*. Finally, Yazbeck's *Ra'ihat il Kirfa* found broad readership through Yazbeck's ascending fame in Arab literature (particularly around her work on the Syrian civil war *A Woman in the Crossfire*). Wherever critics stood on the works' treatment of same-sex desire, they seemed to agree on one fact: the books lacked literary merit, or simply, the books weren't that good. While it's outside the scope of the chapter to delineate all Arab literary aesthetics, it's useful to contextualize that the three novels were received as examples of "women's literature" within an already contested genre for Arab writers, the novel. Let us discuss the genre (novel) and the designation (women's literature) in turn.

Many of the criticisms about queerness as a Western import to Arab cultures were also leveraged against the novel as an Arab art form. Namely, like queerness in the postcolonial Arab context, novels were seen as Western imports and inorganic elaborations of Arab cultural production.[8] The genre of novel opened up *Ana Hiya Inti*, *Al Akharuun*, and *Ra'ihat il Kirfa* to increased scrutiny as a form and in content. The production of the novel as "other" takes place against the backdrop of a literary history that esteems and prioritizes poetry as the ur-genre of the language and culture. Compared to poetry—the prestige form of Arabic literature with unquestionable cultural authenticity—the novel can already be read as an inauthentic or failed Arab cultural product by association with Western modernity and its relative recent emergence alongside other Arab responses to European colonialism. Like queerness, the outsider status of the novel was challenged through recourse to Arabic literary traditions that attempted to establish a longer history of Arabic prose narrative, specifically locating it in within the broader tradition of روايات عربية (riwayat Arabiya).[9] The novel, then, like queerness, holds an uneasy space in Arab cultures. It might be tainted with the stain of Western assimilation, and it might have roots in a precolonial Arab prose tradition. Rejecting queerness, like rejecting the novel, can be construed as part of an overall resistance to Western imperialism's effects on "authentic" Arab culture, or a desire for an unchanged "authentic" Arab subject located in the precolonial.

Like queerness, I suggest the novel is best understood as neither this nor that, but rather as a developing and mobile subject impacted by both one's literary and social history as well as their globalized present. Because of these parallels, it is delightful to consider how same-sex desire in Arabic literature has emerged strongly (but not exclusively) in the novel format. Queer novels double their dare: queer characters are attempting to articulate their rightful location within Arab culture through a similarly embattled form. We might say, with many grains of salt, that the novel is thus an ideal queer form regarding its position in normative Arab literatures.

I also suggest the novels are significant feminist interventions into the form. As works written by and about women, *Ana Hiya Inti*, *Al Akharuun*, and *Ra'ihat il Kirfa* challenge the heteropatriarchal and nationalistic trend evident in lauded work in the genre. Abd al Muhsin Taha Badr's schematization of the Arabic novel deeply influences receptions of the form.[10] In Badr's estimation, the Arabic novel took three forms: didactic, entertainment and recreation, and artistic. Badr disparaged the former two options and sought to privilege the last as the golden standard for the genre, particularly Egyptian novels of this type (Naguib Mahfouz's work, for example). According to Badr's schematizations of the novel, our novels were at best recreational or entertaining, and at worst (perhaps in the case of the somewhat mechanical *Ana Hiya Inti*) didactic. Simultaneously, *Ana Hiya Inti*, *Al Akharuun*, and *Ra'ihat il Kirfa* were considered examples of "women's literature," a genre subject to frequent dismissal in the Arab literary canon. Arab feminist critics have attempted to explain women's erasure from the canon in multiple ways: Bouthaina Shaaban notes that the content of women's novels were often considered threatening to patriarchy, and thus were stifled within the genre.[11] Similarly, Youmna al-Id suggests women's work was delegitimized via nationalist politics, while Hoda Elsadda argues this dismissal is a result of the combination of such forces: a liberal nationalist elite that instituted a gender hierarchy within the canon.[12] In each case, however, the fact remained that women novel writers were already at a disadvantage when it came to the reception of their works.

I suggest that the dismissal of the works relied on attacking form as cover for dismissal of content. While the formal elements of the works opened them to criticism, designating the novels "women's literature" reveals a slippage between "bad form" and "feminine" content. In both literary theory and critical responses, the novels fail to achieve praise as high art forms because of their "feminine" construction: first-person, stream-of-conscious narration, and "shocking" content. The novels were designated "women's literature" on the basis of the following points: (a) They were written by and about women. (b) The writing was overly personal. Because the characters often spoke in first person and spent a great deal of time detailing their emotional and physical states, the work was dismissed as sentimental and narcissistic, lacking broad application. (c) The writing was too political and thereby lacked artistic value. Because the works present without apology homoeroticism and question heteronormative sexual structures, they are read as diatribes, manifestos, or shock doctrines, and are thus outside the scope of artistry.

Conveniently, the designation "women's literature" makes invisible the discursive and political work the novels do perform, and undermines the credibility of the novels and the subjects they seek to represent, namely queers. As feminist critics note, the dismissive structure is frequently experienced by women writers, both in Arab literary circles and outside it, where writing is seen as inconsequential because it is produced by women, and where writing that is "feminine" (that is, emotional or experiential) is bad writing. The added emphasis on women's lives, especially their interior musings, consolidates the works' exclusion from high art. Writing on transnational women's literature, Lisa Suhair Majaj, Therese Saliba, and Fedwa Malti-Douglas all have pushed against the devaluation of women's voices and literatures in Arabic. They urge a more attentive ear to women's voices and experiences, as well as attempt to recuperate the many Arab women's novels erased from criticism and canon.[13]

The dismissal of writers and novels that depict queer Arab women provides an opportunity to highlight an intersectional concern: the erasure of the work results not only from the characters' or writers' presumed gender, but additionally from their sexuality. Writing about same-sex desire between men has rarely resulted in such lambasting or critical dismissal. As one critic muses: "Lesbian sex doesn't challenge social conventions like gay men do."[14] I have argued elsewhere that Orientalism and anti-Arab racism construct Arab men as the ultimate queer subjects, and that the fixation on the figure of the "gay Arab man" is a product of both Orientalist fascination and standard issue heteropatriarchy, which asserts and reasserts masculine subjects as the social center and most compelling narratorial voice.[15] Orientalism positions Arab men as hypermasculine and oversexed alongside quiet, oppressed women.[16] In his work on tourism, Joseph Boone argues that fantasies of male homo-eroticism underwrite Orientalism, producing Arab men as subjects of both fear and desire.[17] Anti-Arab sentiment after 9/11 also produced Arab subjects as hypersexual and seemingly queer, since their acts of aggression were read through a lens of sexual repression.[18] In other words, terrorism is rendered an outlet for repressed sexual feelings. Between these scripts, Arab men are nec-essarily hypermasculine and aggressive to make up for their (homo)sexuality. Both Orientalist and heteronational narrations around Arab men thus fixate on their sexuality as a facet of their otherness. By contrast, the dominant representation of Arab and Muslim women is first about silence and repres-sion by Arab and Muslim men; thus women's available narratives circle not around their own sexuality per se, but their rejection of their sexist Arab or Muslim cultures at large. Women unveil; men come out. At the same time, within and without Arab culture, men's voices and narratives continue to take primacy as universal subjects. Heteropatriarchy, coupled with Orientalist fixations on sexuality, position queer Arab men as the ultimate cultural radicals.

The notion that queer men are inherently more radical than queer women also reflects an internalization of binary gender and male supremacy. In his work on homosexuality in the Arab-Islamic workd, Khaled El-Rouayheb dis-cusses how men who bottomed (مأبون/ma'bun) rather than topped (لوطي / luti) during anal sex were seen as effeminate, failed men, while the luti re-mained a man, subject to less derogatory treatment and scrutiny. We can extrapolate from El-Rouayheb's example that "gay men" are perceived to per-form the ultimate taboo; they sacrifice their masculinity via having sex with men. As the privileged class, this "forfeit of power"/bottoming is seen as an inherently challenging act to structures of gender and sexual normativity.[19]

The notion that women's homoeroticism is somehow less revolutionary or radical fails to recognize, as many queer and femme writers have argued, that women's rejection of men and masculinity is also a threat to the heteronor-mative and patriarchal order, which places men's desire and pleasure above women's or imagines women without desires at all.[20] Badr's schematization and critics' dismissal of "women's literature" go hand in hand—they are both valorizations of masculine centered protagonists and a reflection of Orientalism and heteropatriarchy within the reception of the works. Criticism of the quality of the work cannot be abstracted from criticisms of its content. Both suffer from a devaluation of queer women's voices.

Rather than grounds for dismissal, I suggest we take the designation "women's literature" as one ripe with opportunity. Free from the demands of classic Arabic literature and "high art," the novels explore with more attention and nuance their protagonists' lives, and elaborate queer women's experiences. As I argue in the introduction, sentiment is one terrain in which queer Arab sexualities find purchase. Queer sexualities can unfold in the sentimental because it refuses tidy narrative progression or unambiguous closures. The process-oriented nature of the works and the narrators' uncertainty, cyclical fixations, and attention to body and emotion, all facilitate queer emergence in the discursive minefield outlined earlier and in chapter 1. In her analysis of *Al Akharuun*, Zeina G. Halabi resists that reading of Al-Herz's work as "feminine chatter with trivial perspectives."[21] She argues instead that Al-Herz offers a nuanced critique of Saudi politics and that she offers it via her rhetorical manipulation of the chick lit genre.[22] Halabi's recuperation of the novel from its gendered dismissal hinges on the work's approach to secularism vis-à-vis the Arab literary canon. Via *Al Akharuun*, Halabi valorizes the genre of chick lit as a politically salient genre for secular critique. Following Halabi's insight, I suggest the three novels' "feminine chatter with trivial perspectives" reveals women's emotional and social labor and offers us insight into queer Arab subjectivities. In her work on the feminist and avante-garde aesthetic in Levantine novels, Kifah Hanna argues that when women writers "[found] established novelistic forms such as the patriarchal family saga inappropriate for their subject matter, they employed original aesthetic forms."[23] All three novels employ an open-ended narrative form that eschews saga and the progressive narrative style lauded in Badr's characterization. Instead, they innovate the form to account for nonnormative subjects.

The most notable rhetorical feature across all three works is the cyclical narration style and lack of narrative closure. The open-ended form of the novel is useful to narrate the women's nonnormative, mutable, and fluid sexualities. The looped structure of the books and the stories' unfinished qualities are indicative of the characters' and writers' queer journeys, and significantly, their ambivalence regarding their sexuality. All three use flashback and resist a linear timeline for their narration. All three close ambiguously and leave the fates of their central characters up in the air. Thus, while each book features same-sex practices and desires and explores narrators' feelings regarding their experiences, the characters and readers never land on easy conclusions. The style of the novels—told from a first- or omniscient third-person perspective, in a cyclical stream of consciousness—is an effect of the characters' relationship to their sexuality. That relationship—unscripted, emotional, unresolved—emerges in the content and the style of the narration. Here, the interior-focused novel is an apt space for discursive discovery for the writers and their protagonists. In short, the novels hold space for characters to feel their way through their sexual lives. The novels lack narrative closure because the characters themselves do not "resolve" their sexuality in the books. Like the novels' narratives, the characters' sexualities need not resolve; it is in fact the failure of "closed" sexual identities like lesbian that create existential angst in the characters' lives.

Ana Hiya Inti ends without clarity for Siham regarding her love life and how she names herself. Siham's uncertainty is bolstered by the book's ending, where her often anxious tone is replaced with matter of factness and fantasy: she is in bed with Mimi but fantasizing about Layal. Siham has wrestled throughout the book with her desire for women; her ambivalence toward Mimi and inability to decide how to proceed with her love life characterize the book's closing. It is not a painful uncertainty per se; Siham's calm at the end of the novel relieves her tortured emotional state in the remainder of the work. By the book's conclusion, Siham has arrived at a moment where same-sex desire simply is part of her life. She no longer attempts to classify or code it or reject it. It's just there, like her exams or overbearing mother. Her relationship with Mimi is fulfilling in many ways and failed in others. Even her fantasy about Layal is rendered with a certain flatness: she assumes Mimi is fantasizing about Layal as well, and as such neither is overly emotionally invested in the other, and neither considers the other's fantasy a source of injury. This moment of reckoning, where queerness and her queer relationship is neither egregious nor triumphant, is a surprising respite from the rest of the book, where Siham's incessant processing leaves little room to breathe and exist. The book, like the character's queer self, ends with openness and the possibility of what's to come. Its open ending mirrors Siham's own status regarding her queerness.

I would argue despite its narrator's engagement to Umar, the novel *Al Akharuun* ends with similar ambivalence. Like *Ana Hiya Inti*, the closing scene of *Al Akharuun* features its narrator in bed. Here, the narrator is in bed with her fiancé, Umar, rather than either of her woman lovers from the book. The narrator is frenetically postcoital—she is urging Umar to assure her of his love and that he will never die nor leave her. This uneasy close, an unconvincing representation of the character's new heterosexual devotion, is not a queer happy ending—but it doesn't have to be. The novel has given us a slice of its narrator's reckoning with love and intimacy, within and against queer contexts. The novel produces ambivalence about its narrator's sexuality rather than the narrator claiming it (as in *Ana Hiya Inti*). The narrator in *Al Akharuun* speaks at length about her grief regarding her brother's death, her experience with Dai's controlling presence, and her tepid rebound relationship with Dareen. It is in fact the narrator's own insecurity and anxiety pushing toward the very last pages of the novel that allow us to understand her intimate story as one that continues to unfold, one that may or may not involve women in the future. By placing the narrator in the larger context of the novel and the relationship in the larger context of the writer's rumination on intimacy, I suggest that the story and the narrator's sexuality remain open rather than closed circuits. The narrator in *Al Akharuun* didn't experiment with women and conclude with a man. Rather, she sought and continues to seek an intimate relationship that will allow her to recover from and process the trauma of loss and abuse from her youth.

While *Al Akharuun* and *Ana Hiya Inti* conclude with ambivalent narrators, the two protagonists in *Ra'ihat il Kirfa* find themselves in much more dire circumstances. As in the two previous works, the novel ends with narrative uncertainty: we do not know what will happen to Hanan, and we are very worried about Aaliyah. The novel ends with Hanan driving through the streets of Syria looking for Aaliyah, who may have died during her travels. Again, the narrative need not be a happy queer ending, but it is unfinished. As I noted earlier, critical reception of this novel admonished it for failing to produce the right kind of lesbian subject—a happy one, a proud one. We do not know either character's fate, and this honesty regarding the dangers and fears that animate women's and queer lives brings into relief one of the stakes of women's same-sex eroticism—that it can fail, that it can bring danger into their lives, that it can be abusive, that it can, like any relationship subject to multiple power dynamics, be quite painful. I suggest that this novel offers us a different kind of ambivalence, one grounded in the dangers of women's lives rather than an attempt to "resolve" queerness as in the previous chapter, or falsely portray queer love as free from gendered, raced, and classed violence.

In each of the works, women fail to "resolve" their queer identities, and queerness is made ambivalent through the cyclical and open-ended narrative style. The writers' refusals of an easy resolution offers us an analogy to queer love and intimacy in Arab women's lives writ large: it is not easy, it can persist and end in many ways, it can be ordinary, it can be painful. Against the happy, heteronormative endings in Golden Era Egyptian film from the previous chapter, I value the open-ended narrative quality as commentary on the significance of ambivalence for queer Arab subjects. The novels also construct an archive of queerness that considers many kinds of intimacies—abusive, anxious, fantasmic—and witnesses the complexity of queer Arab loves and lives.

Ana Hiya Inti, *Al Akharuun*, and *Ra'ihat il Kirfa* are examples of women's literature that challenge the patriarchal and heteronormative genre of the Arabic novel by centering queer women's lives, emotions, and experiences. Rather than critique the works for failing to uphold heteropatriarchal conventions of the novel, their interior-focused narrations allow us to heed and imagine queer Arab women's lives. As evident in the books, women's sexual desires, practices, and identities do not all neatly align on a progressive homonormative and heteronormative continuum. Women experience a range of sexual desires and sexual partners and articulate a range of sexual preferences. They may name their identities or may eschew such categorization. They are no less worthy of queer subjectivity for these reasons. I would suggest that we interpret the novels as additional accounts of queer lives rather than attempt to authenticate them into a clear and distinct lesbian Arab subject. To question if any of these texts are "real lesbian novels" puts undo emphasis on authenticity as the defining characteristic of queer life. Who should define queer authenticity, and why should authenticity be the reigning categorical imperative? Instead here we might take the multiple experiences and articulations of women's sexuality as opportunities to expand and rewrite our heteronormative, patriarchal, and Orientalist accounts of women's homoeroticism without seeking to establish a concrete "lesbian" subject as such. In this sense, the lack of narrative resolution in the novels mirrors the structure of queerness between Arab women modeled in the book: sexuality is not a progressive narrative that ends at lesbian identity, but a mobile set of relations, feelings, and intimacies. The following section examines a second recurring theme across the novels, and a second significant facet of queer Arab women's lives: a social, intergenerational structure for homoeroticism between women that introduces them to their lovers as well as to broader queer communities.

Women's Homosocial and Homoerotic Spaces

This section uses the novel's "feminine chatter with trivial perspectives" to document a significant facet of queer culture between banat: the presence of an intergenerational, homosocial space that affords women and femmes opportunities for homoerotic exchanges. In other words, this section uses queer Arab critique to yield a new story for the archive. The presence of homoerotic, homosocial communities in all three novels is significant for several reasons: first, the referral to longtime queer communities substantiates queer Arab women's historical and contemporary presence. Second, it emphasizes how women use a seemingly heteronormative structure—gender-segregated spaces—to foster intimacy and eroticism against and within that heteronormative structure. Third, looking at these homoerotic spaces carved into heteronormative structures helps us see how the women understand their sexuality not as a fixed heterosexual/homosexual binary but as fluid and mobile constructions. In each work, characters make reference to women's communities where homoerotic relationships take place with, alongside, or in lieu of relationships with men. Their sexual desires and practices are not foreclosed by their relationships with men or with women; their sexualities are not fixed into heteronormative or homonormative identities. Finally, it offers us insight into how we must consider a different kind of story/telling to see queer Arab women, banat, and femmes. Arab homoeroticism is not collapsible onto other iterations of homoeroticism from other cultures and communities. The novels show that same-sex desire and homoeroticism between Arab women is neither an Orientalist, heteronormative fantasy for consumption nor an archaic facet of an old Arab past. It is also not a thoughtless duplicate of Western homosexual structures and communities. It is a contemporary shifting culture that is aware of, but not exclusively shaped by, these narratives. It is a queer interiority of its own.

All three novels make reference to women's homosocial spaces that afford them homoerotic possibility. Within the novels, homosociality is considered part of the dominant culture: many social spaces in Arab communities are gender-segregated, both within and outside religion. The characters in the novels take advantage of the homosocial space to facilitate homoerotic exchanges. In the novels, no indication is given that nonqueer members of the community realize how the women spend their time, which allows us to imagine (and I do) that homoeroticism is happening in all kinds of homosocial spaces.

Ana Hiya Inti's description of homosocial gatherings both reveals how queer subjects make space for themselves in heteronormative culture and challenges Orientalist, anti-Arab depictions of women's agency. In the novel, Mimi, a married woman who's been having an affair with a widow in her building, invites Layal to a women's gathering at her home. Even though Layal is a psychologist and has been positioned throughout the book as a liberal authority fluent in feminist thought on gender and sexuality, she is still surprised and uncertain about the gathering: the number of women, the multiple gendered styles, and the women's general joy and playfulness with one another.[24] Layal's discomfort can indicate more than her anxiety regarding her relationship with Mimi. We can read it as an indictment of feminist movements that erase queer women. Further, Layal's surprise acts as a corrective to the notion that queerness emerges from elite, Westernized circles. Layal symbolically occupies the elite, Westernized Arab subject position via her profession and education. Though Layal attempts to rationally explain and understand same-sex desire, she fails to account for the women's diversity and pleasure. I view Layal's reaction and the description of the gathering as evidence that queer women's lives, despite Orientalist or assimilationist oversignification, exceed discursive limits. At the same time, Mimi's party indicates the presence and regularity of same-sex intimacies in the book's Lebanese social setting. Mimi's own husband encourages her to spend time with the widow, not knowing they are lovers. Siham's mother trusts Mimi to watch over Siham. Normative homosociality between women ultimately enables their nonnormative sexual relationships and challenges Orientalist renditions of Arab women's sexuality.

Similarly, in *Al Akharuun*, homosocial spaces reveal how queer subjects maneuver heteronormativity and challenge the construction of queerness as only available to elite or Westernized Arabs. Dai introduces the narrator to a group of Saudi women who are described with wonder by the narrator. The women have multiple gender presentations, are openly affectionate with one another, and seem to be having a lot of fun. The narrator's surprise at the gender diversity of the group, like Layal's, challenges stereotypical depictions of queerness that imagine one kind of queer subject, usually a masculine woman. Apprehensive at first because she comes to the group through Dai, the narrator quickly becomes comfortable with the other women, though they share little of her social backstory.[25] Like Siham and Layal, the narrator of *Al Akharuun* accesses some social respectability via her university education, which helps offset the discrimination she faces as a Shi'i Muslim woman with epilepsy. As with Layal, access to elite or assimilationist discourses does not help alleviate the narrator's reckoning with her own desire, particularly her desire for Dai. Yet, her time with the women is marked by desire, camaraderie, ease, and excitement—particularly because she meets Dareen, her next lover. In this instance, the narrator's experience of queerness overrides the intellectual and discursive mechanisms that frame it. Like the women's party in *Ana Hiya Inti*, the "retreat" in *Al Akharuun* is described as a longstanding practice to which the narrator is newly introduced. In multiple contexts, then, women-only spaces serve (though not exclusively) as spaces from which women are able to create and foster homoerotic intimacies and offer constructions of Arab sexuality that defy its overwritten discourses.

Ra'ihat il Kirfa offers us two additional examples of homoerotic, homosocial spaces. Like previous novels, the depictions of these spaces challenge the oversignified discourses of Arab sexuality, but in this instance, they make room to consider harm and violence alongside joy and pleasure. As a child, Hanan is introduced to women's homoeroticism at a bathhouse by a bride the day before her wedding. Because Hanan is a child at this juncture, it is only useful to reference this insofar as it first reminds us of girls' and women's vulnerabilities, even within women's spaces, and second alerts us to the kinds of pleasure that might be available to women in such spaces. As a child, Hanan lacks power and agency to refuse the physical advances the bride makes on her in the bathhouse. At the same time, Hanan articulates that the bathhouse is a women's sexual space, something she intuits and finds pleasure in before her encounter with the bride.[26] Hanan describes the bathhouse as an erotic space, where women's nudity is on display for one another. She calls the bride a seductress and witnesses how the women are enamored of her and touch her. She too is hypnotized by the bride's body and beauty, commenting on her scent and skin. That erotic encounter becomes troubling when the bride uses Hanan as a kind of masturbatory object—Hanan is both pleasured and scared by her encounter with the bride, but ultimately it overwhelms her to the point of fainting. The bride's own young age, sixteen to Hanan's ten, makes the scene difficult to read. Unlike scenes in the previous two works, the stark difference in Hanan's age from those of the women around her forces readers to reckon with both the dangerous and pleasurable nature of the women's bathhouse and the potential for children's sexual awareness.[27]

The second insight into women's homoerotic spaces in *Ra'ihat il Kirfa* reveals both how homosociality is used to women's advantage and the limits of its power in a broader heteronormative context. The second instance of homosociality takes place after Hanan's marriage to Anwar. Anwar introduces her to a woman named Nazek and encourages her to "please" her because it will have a positive effect on their social standing and his work relationships.[28] Hanan describes the world of women she enters with the same erotic and magical qualities she experienced in the bath. She also notes how happy and alive the women feel in the space compared to when she sees them outside it.[29] She envies them their joy and wants it for herself. Through her attempt to acquire that lightness and joy, she begins a sexual relationship with Nazek. She describes the gatherings as known to the women's men, who are comfortable with them despite their intensity and peculiarity. In fact, Hanan remarks that the relationships were only severed if they became public and thus threatened the husband's reputation.[30] This suggests that the problem is not women's desires for women but how that desire might implicate and impact men. As such, this rendition of homosociality both produces space for Hanan to explore her homoerotic desires and reminds us that while homosociality has been optimized by queer subjects and their manipulation of it challenges the heteronormative order, heteronormativity still eclipses and binds women's freedoms.

Though there are consistent depictions of homosociality in each novel, how those spaces are described reveals and responds to different stereotypes, concerns, and discourses about Arab women's sexuality and agency. These depictions, while relevant to our imagination of a queer Arab history and archive, offer us important insights for queer Arab critique and queer Arab subjectivity. First, the suggestion that these spaces are a longtime feature of women's homosociality speaks to the historical presence of same-sex desire and practices between women. Second, despite their discursive oversignification and historical erasure, women find pleasure and exceed the discursive Orientalist or assimilationist arcs used to frame same-sex desire in Arab culture. Third, we can laud the means by which homosociality enables queer homoeroticism for women. Fourth, we must reckon with the fact the homosociality emerges from within heteropatriarchal segregation of women's private and men's public spaces. To that end, women's homoerotic spaces are always threatened by and threatening to men's social power and dominance within a heteronormative order. The turn from homosocial to homoerotic upends the normative order insofar as it rejects the seeming imperative of homosociality as a preventative to sexual desires and acts. It is important to hold homosociality as normative and homoeroticism as nonnormative at once, and to witness women's queer narrations and the significance therein. At the same time, we must attend to the critiques of society available through their narratives. The following section continues to closely read the depictions of queer subjects in the book to consider how they narrate their sexualities. Rather than seeking the "origin" of their nonnormative sexualities, I use the novels and their protagonists to show how queer Arab sexualities are formed in tension with and through critical interrogations of other kinds of normative structures, including ableism, heteropatriarchal and state violence, anti-Blackness, and classism.

Against Queer Origin, Toward Queer Critique

I mentioned earlier that the novels were often criticized for failing to offer a clear "reason" for the protagonists' nonnormative sexuality. I suggest in this section that the focus of queer Arab critique should not be an attempt to discern "where" queerness comes from, whether that search is discursive or individuated. It is not productive to attempt to frame queerness as either the precolonial Arab past or assimilated Western future, nor is it useful to look to individual characters and attempt to assess whether trauma or nature resulted in their nonnormativity.

Just as all three novels fail to offer closed narrative circles or clear-cut resolutions of the character's sexual identities, so too they fail to offer definitive reasons for their sexual desires. This is particularly true of Siham in *Ana Hiya Inti*, who is most concerned with finding out what makes her attracted to women. Siham reveals how constructions of women's homoeroticism are considered both banal and potentially dangerous to heteronormativity and heteronationalism. In *Ana Hiya Inti*, Siham narrates a childhood memory in which her father comes into her bedroom at night with an erection; she screams and he departs. She wonders if this might be the cause of her attraction to women, but later suggests she doesn't even remember if the event took place or if she is trying to justify her same-sex desires by fabricating the memory.[31] Siham's desire to locate a cause and origin for her sexual desires is not uncommon for queer subjects, particularly those who exist in a heteronormative social structure. Much of Siham's discomfort also emerges from her exclusive desire for women. Unlike Mimi or Layal, Siham is only interested in women sex partners, and this exclusive desire is what upsets her mother most and makes her life difficult. In this sense, Siham's and her mother's anxiety is rooted in the notion that same-sex desire between women could happen to the exclusion of heterosexual social relations and norms. It isn't that Siham has sex with a woman that causes a need for explanation—that is seemingly common and known.[32] Instead, it is that Siham rejects men entirely. In this sense, Siham's sexuality is ultimately threatening to patriarchy. The investment of Arab heteronormativity in patriarchy creates a red herring wherein queerness is read as inauthentically Arab. In other words, in these instances the cultural investment in patriarchy by way of heteronormativity abjects queer subjects to protect the patriarchy under the guise of protecting an "authentic" Arab culture. Siham's challenge to patriarchy is evident in the work's critical reception that, as discussed, attempted to route queer women's desires back through men and read homoeroticism as a failed encounter with masculinity and men.

Siham's record of her sexuality also foregrounds the significance of imperial and state violence on queer subjects. One aspect of Siham's experiences that often creates intimacies and urgencies between the women is the Lebanese civil war. Many gatherings are both interrupted and created by the recurring bombings, which force the women to head to the nearest shelter, huddled with one another in fear. On one such occasion, Mimi remarks she feels arousal when the bombings are over, especially when they've been severe. While neither Layal nor Siham seem to share this sentiment, Mimi's assertion of her body's sexual needs in the onslaught of the violence, amid the book's attempt to reckon with and understand homoerotic desire, reminds us that it is not useful to imagine gender and sexuality as postwar concerns. The trauma of the war and its impact on Mimi, Layal, and Siham is both ordinary and extraordinary—they retreat to and from the shelter with regularity at the same time that they wage a different kind of battle within Lebanese society. As Habib notes, the women are searching for liberation, love, and challenge to the norms despite, against, and within the tumult of violence.[33] I consider *Ana Hiya Inti* a feminist work invested in women's and feminine discourses. By foregrounding Siham's sexuality, it suggests that sexuality is a significant aspect in shaping women's experiences alongside economic, national, and other influences.

Finally, *Ana Hiya Inti* directly addresses the notion that homoeroticism is a classed phenomenon. It does so by juxtaposing Siham and Layal—two middle-class women with a Westernized history of education—and Mimi, a working-class wife and mother. Layal espouses a liberal Western feminist articulation of same-sex desire but appears to be uncomfortable with it in her own interactions with Siham and Mimi. Siham cycles through many of the names and identities ascribed to women who experience same-sex desire but never feels at home in one. Mimi does not ruminate on her identity as such, preferring to pursue and act on desires. Mimi is also the gateway for Siham and Layal to a community of women who have sex with other women and whose gender presentations vary. In this way, the book disrupts some common narratives around nonnormative sexuality that suggest it only occurs in elite circles. At the same time, it refuses to locate the "authentic" queer subject in either economic context. Siham and Mimi are both desiring subjects who disrupt heteronormativity through their sexual practices.

Al Akharuun offers us a similar nexus of criticisms regarding how to locate and understand queer desire in Arab culture. Most notably, *Al Akharuun* can be read for a critique of ableism in Arab nations. Its narrator understands herself as an outsider in many ways: she has epilepsy, she is Shi'i in a Sunni nation, and she's a woman experiencing homoerotic desires in a heteropatriarchal context. She rejects many popular markers of Arab culture, such as Egyptian film and cinema, perhaps because of its popularity. Her embodiment and desires make her feel other, despite her accounts of community belonging in college. In her account of the novel, Halabi suggests that the violence of the narrator's epileptic seizures is a reproduction of the violence of her personal, political, and communal losses in the Saudi state, which erases and forecloses histories of Shi'i loss in the Sunni nation. At the same time, Halabi argues that al-Herz offers a critique of secular Arab nationalism in favor of a grounded Saudi experience like the narrator's, one that urges us to consider sectarian ideologies and their impact.[34] Rather than read disability as metaphor in the work, I'd like to read Al Akharuun for a critique of Arab ableism. In ableist discourse, physical and mental illnesses are perceived as personal weaknesses and sources of familial shame. In Al Akharuun the narrator's illness reveals the ongoing generational effect of war and violence on the region, and her shame is a result of the social and political failure to create knowledge, access, and accommodation for disabilities.

Similarly, rather than read Al Akharuun's narrator's account of her sexual history as shock value or for a queer origin story, we might be better served by noting the many instances of sexual violence the narrator experiences, and how those impact her understanding and enactment of sexuality and intimacy.[35] Throughout the work, the protagonist attempts to understand her physical desires but finds the literature in both same-sex and heteronormative circles overwhelming to the point that she withdraws from chatrooms and ceases attempting to read about homosexuality in internet searches.[36] When those measures fail, she attempts to secure understanding through her body itself, specifically through sex with Dai. But Dai is an abusive and controlling partner, and the narrator leaves that relationship without any additional clarity. Like the narrator, readers are unable to locate an originary point to homoerotic desire. Instead, it is more useful to take seriously how misogynist violence, both physical and epistemic, shape her unhappiness. Al Akharuun's narrator's sexual history offers an indictment of sexual abuse and its impact on her capacity for security and intimacy. In a letter to Dai, the protagonist details a sexually abusive relationship between her and a tutor ten years her senior who begins physically and sexually assaulting her even before she experiences puberty. The protagonist becomes "obsessed" with the tutor, Balqis, and understands her relationship to violence during sex as formed by

Balqis's own sadistic sexual preferences.[37] It is important here to delineate the narrator's nonconsensual sexual assault by Balqis from the consensual sex she originally has with Dai and that which becomes abusive later in their relationship. Outside of her consensual explorations, the narrator is mugged and sexually assaulted on her way home from a college function. The narrator's attempt to understand her sexual assault and abuse by three different sources (Balqis, Dai, and the anonymous muggers) influences the shape her relationships take in the course of the book. In this sense, the book offers nothing pertinent regarding "a queer origin" and instead articulates the impact of childhood sexual abuse. Attending to the narrator's exposition of her sexual history centers the work's critiques of heteropatriarchal and heteronormative structures that foster sexual assault and abuse.

As in *Al Akharuun*, *Ra'ihat il Kirfa*'s search for "queer origins" can and should be replaced by a critical assessment of how young women and girls are vulnerable to multiple kinds of sexual violence across and within their varied social statuses. At the same time, it alerts us to anti-Blackness within Arab communities. *Ra'ihat il Kirfa* differs from other works in this section in that its characters are not vocal in discussing their queer origins. Instead, the sexual histories presented, particularly Aaliyah's sexual assault and abuse both before Hanan and by her, are elaborated without the narrator's rumination on their impact. Yazbeck's slow reveal of how Aaliyah came to be Hanan's sexual partner alerts readers to how Aaliyah's life, informed primarily by her status as a refugee Black girl with no privacy or resources of her own, is exceptionally vulnerable to sexual assault by boys, men, and women.

In *Ra'ihat il Kirfa* the physical descriptions of Aaliyah and the eroticization of her figure reveals anti-Black racism in Arab cultures, which shares the hypersexualization of Black women's and girls' bodies that animates misogynoir in other contexts.[38] The book achieves this by describing and dramatizing Hanan's and Aaliyah's differences. For example, Hanan is often referred to by her full name, emphasizing her rootedness and class standing, whereas Aaliyah is never given a last name. Hanan is described as fair and pale next to Aaliyah's darkness. Hanan is tall and flat in figure. Aaliyah is petite and curvaceous. Additionally, Hanan is well established in her marriage and at least in her late teens when she takes in and begins sexually abusing Aaliyah at the age of ten.

The racialization of Aaliyah is inextricably linked to her class standing. In contrast to *Ana Hiya Inti*, *Ra'ihat il Kirfa* locates women's experiences with homoeroticism in elite circles. I read this in two ways: first, it gives insight into how women within "elite" economic circles can experience heteropatriarchy and its attendant normativities to the detriment of their bodies, minds, and lives. At the same time, it offers us insight into how class differences (aligned with racial ones as we shall see) enable women to harm other women. Though Hanan is herself bound by heteropatriarchal norms, Hanan's moneyed economic status enables her to enslave and abuse Aaliyah.

Aaliyah's history reveals how classism and anti-Blackness intertwine with heteropatriarchal state and imperial violence. Some critics describe Aaliyah's relationship to Hanan as socioeconomic respite.[39] I suggest instead that it is precisely Aaliyah's precarity as a young Black girl that enables all the violence visited upon her before and after her time with the Hashimis. Aaliyah's family's poverty and refugee status amplify her vulnerability to violence. Her family's home, a shack in al Raml, a Palestinian refugee camp in Syria, offers no privacy or protection from the boys that prey on Aaliyah and her sister. Aaliyah's first experience with sexual assault happens at the hand of a neighborhood boy she meets after dropping out of school to earn money. Her sale to the Hashimis reflects Aaliyah's family's precarity as refugees in Syria. In Aaliyah's narrative, her family's refugee status and poverty are a result of state violence; her abusive father and the boys who assault her are agents of heteropatraiachal violence, enabled by a masculinist and misogynist society. But this is only part of Aaliyah's story. Hanan also enacts violence, by purchasing Aaliyah and sexually abusing her. Hanan's actions are enabled through the intersecting oppressions of anti-Blackness and classism that offer Hanan respectability or power at the cost of Aaliyah's oppression. Rather than position Hanan as Aaliyah's light-skinned and rich savior, we should center Aaliyah's narrative and use it to critique the anti-Blackness and classism that underwrite Arab heteropatriarchy.

At the same time, it is important to not read Aaliyah only as a reactionary subject or simple victim. Similarly, Hanan is not only villain or victim. I suggest that depictions of both reveal how women explore sexuality as a means of disrupting dominant power structures. Hanan's sexual history, while not without trauma, is significantly more pleasurable than Aaliyah's. Hanan discovers masturbation at a young age and practices it regularly.[40] Aaliyah is not Hanan's first sexual experience with a woman. She meets and has an affair with a prominent society woman named Nazek. Hanan describes her sexual encounters with women as pleasurable and highly preferable to those with her husband, whom she repeatedly describes as a crocodile who smells and feels like death. In her love affair with Nazek, she learns "there is something beautiful, something more sensitive about women, something that makes you shine . . . with women, love is different. When passion takes hold of you and you're completely absorbed in your lover's kiss, she's all of those men in one: a lover, a friend, and an everlasting object of desire . . . In your arms, a woman is like silk; she gives away her heart before giving away her body. A man would never do that."[41] Nazek also introduces Hanan to other women like them: women who have married young and have same-sex lovers. Hanan describes the double face of these women, who seem boring and sad in the company of men but joyful and light around women.[42] She stops trying to have a relationship with her husband at all and seeks all sexual gratification with other women, and eventually Aaliyah. Critics have interpreted Hanan's relationship and preference for women and girls as a commentary on hetero-patriarchy: that rather than index a "true" homoeroticism, it is the result of repressive gendered and sexual paradigms in Arab nations. While it is true that Hanan's sexual history is marked with abuse and heteronormative violence, this narrative does not account for Hanan's experiences of pleasure or agency. Rather, it positions Hanan and other women as strictly reactionary subjects. Instead, I revisit Hanan's story to discuss how her homoerotic and same-sex relationships offer her pleasure and power and allow her to explore her own subjectivity.

Aaliyah's narrative voice is strong and agential in the novel, and she finds ways to access pleasure and power despite the intersecting structures of violence that surround her. As I noted earlier, Hanan is deeply predatory to Aaliyah. In her sequences of narration, Aaliyah confesses to fearing Hanan at the beginning of her time in the Hashimi home and to dissociating when she is forced to bathe and massage Hanan. When Hanan and her husband buy Aaliyah, Hanan brings her to the bath, strips her, and explores her body. She talks to Aaliyah about the pleasures of women, fingers, and orgasms.[43] Hanan promises she will teach Aaliyah the pleasures of her own body and the pleasure of others. As descriptions of the scene unfold in both narrators' sections, it becomes clear that Aaliyah has been touched and forced to touch Hanan at the age of ten, from the very beginning of her time at the Hashimi house. Eventually, Aaliyah describes her decreased fear during their interactions, and some enjoyment of them. She discovers pleasure in touching and being touched, and especially pleasure in giving or withholding sex from Hanan.[44] Aaliyah quickly realizes that though Hanan claims to love and desire her, she still does not see her as an equal or worthy of respect. Though Hanan wants Aaliyah at night, she also wants her to leave the bedroom and resume her station before morning. One night, Aaliyah stays through the night and Hanan becomes enraged. At this point, Aaliyah becomes dominant with Hanan sexually and begins sleeping with Anwar, Hanan's husband. Aaliyah describes her newfound power in the bedroom as the power of the night, over which she reigns as queen and mistress of the household.

Though I am reluctant to overemphasize the power of sexuality in this instance, I am more reluctant to position either Aaliyah or Hanan as merely reactors. The novel offers opportunities through the narration of the characters' interiority, opportunities to Hanan and Aaliyah as occasionally agential subjects rather than strictly reactionary. Hanan enacts her power over Aaliyah, while Aaliyah strategizes what little power she holds over Hanan to make her experience in the Hashimi house survivable. Both offer us a way to think through when and how violence is perpetuated between nonnormative subjects, and how sexuality intertwines with other facets of identity.

In all three novels, characters' queer experiences and embodiments can offer us critical readings of heteropatriarchy, classism, anti-Blackness, and ableism. Thus, the works engage not only in queer world-making for the protagonists but do so within the specific contextual spaces the novels create. The differing national contexts of the works (Lebanon, Saudia Arabia, Syria) asks us to consider how local histories and cultural facets impact the characters' queer becomings (e.g., the Lebanese civil war in *Ana Hiya Inti*, the Sunni majority of Saudi Arabia in *Al Akharuun*). Though not generalizable in the least, Arab queer histories and presents are impacted by colonial and national discourses in each case. Within the transnational Arab frame, we can consider the specificity of these experiences while at the same time articulating the shared experience of state violence for queers. To make queer worlds, the novels offer critique and interrogations of the heteronormative, patriarchal, and other oppressive structures that surround them. It feels particularly important in these works to attend to banat's vulnerability in each work, to attend to the sexual and physical violence they experience. The characters' embodiments and social, racial, and economic standings impact their agency and exposure to violence. Rather than look toward a queer genesis point, I suggest we pivot our analysis to the ways that queer narration offers us insight into multiple and intersecting heteropatriarchal, economic, and state violence. Through an intersectional reading of their stories, the novels both explicate and animate a sense of queer interiorities for Arab women: the sexual fluidity and rejection of categorical lesbian identities; the prominence, problem, and promise of homosocial, homoerotic spaces; and the repressive and discriminatory social structures that concern their daily lives.

☾

In this chapter, I have examined three novels that attempt to narrate and navigate Arab women's queer lives. Through *Ana Hiya Inti*, *Al Akharuun*, and *Ra'ihat il Kirfa*, I illustrate how queer Arab experiences both undercut and exceed heteropatriarchal and authenticating discourses that would otherwise erase them. The texts use the Arabic novel to better represent a queer subjectivity that is not collapsible to Orientalist or heteronational discourses; through their ruminations, I argue against a desire to "resolve" an Arab lesbian subject and instead foreground how characters experience their homoerotic desires and practices in nonlinear ways, and in ways that suggest queer sexuality is better articulated through an open circuit rather than a resolved identity. Moreover, the novels attest to the historic and ongoing presence of homoerotic women's communities. Significantly, they teach us that an absence of queer origin stories is not an absence of queer histories. They center women's lives and voices, particularly their experiences with violence, abuse, and assault, which offers insight into aspects of Arab culture that are often unattended, like anti-Blackness and ableism. At the same time, the novels offer critiques of heteropatriarchy, heteronormativity, and national and colonial violence. As such, the works demonstrate how some Arab writers are navigating the multiple discourses that surround sexuality and sexual identity. These writers offer meaningful critiques of heteropatriachal and normative Arab cultures that emerge from deeply contextual locations within the novels, and thus reject the insinuation that criticisms of Arab patriarchy only emerge from transnational or global encounters with Western or white modes of gendered and sexual liberation. Instead, the works foreground Arab feminist and queer critiques of Arab state violence, Arab normativity, and ongoing imperialism in their respective locations. The ways the novels echo these three concerns over three disparate locations with specific regional and state histories points us toward some of the shared histories that animate transnational Arab subjects. Finally, the circulation, translation, and critical reception of the novels move us outward as we imagine and construct a queer Arab archive.

While the first two chapters focused on texts that foreclosed queerness or read queerness against the heteronormative arc, these novels assert a nonnormative sexual presence in the works and assert that subject's rightful belonging to Arab communities. Unlike in chapter 2, these texts are available as "queer" with or without queer readership. The novels attempt to represent and consider queerness through their imagined characters. In contrast, the following chapter takes up autobiographical narrations of sexuality from queer people living in Palestine and Lebanon. The stakes of the two sets of texts are very similar: how to navigate repressive discourse, how to substantiate queer Arab sexualities, how to represent queer experiences. But the arguments the texts make differ in tone and tenor as a result of the multiplicity of speakers and those speakers' positions. In the following chapter I consider how the writers in nonfiction collections articulate their sexuality. While writers in this chapter make use of the Arabic novel, I suggest that writers and editors in the collections manipulate the Arabic language itself. Their testimonies and representations of self imagine and produce a new set of questions and considerations in the making and unmaking of queer Arab archives.

love letters   4

Queer Intimacies and the Arabic Language

During a visit to Palestine in 2011 I met with a friend and member of Aswat, a feminist and queer organization that advocates for LGBTQI communities. The Palestinian organization began as a queer women's collective in 2003 and is one of the longest-standing queer organizations in the Arab world at large. Over coffee my friend handed me one of Aswat's recent publications, an essay collection called *Waqfet Banat* that gathered the voices of queer Arab women and gender-nonconforming people. In fact, she gave me two copies—one for myself and one to give to a friend or a library. I met my friend through a private network and had become aware of the book and others like it through the same network. I begin with this moment because it highlights a different kind of queer exchange and representation than what has animated the previous chapters. In the texts of previous chapters, queers are subjects of representation I disentangle to imagine queer Arab selves and others. Here queer subjects engage in that process directly, grappling with discourses around naming and identity via lived experiences. These texts move us from the hypothetical question of how might queer Arab life be represented toward the question of how queers represent themselves. Of course, "autobiographical" texts are always mediated, and my analysis of them is another mediation. As such, in this chapter I attend to processes of mediation and translation that inherently shape the texts and the queer subjects within. This chapter uses three essay collections to argue that queer Arab subjects are unassimilable to

Western narratives of LGBT identity, to Orientalist visions of Arab sexuality, and to heteronational responses to both. The texts studied record the queer Arab present and demonstrate that queerness for Arabs is a relational, transnational construction. I make this argument through a study of the texts' composition and circulation, as well as through a study of the language employed. I argue that the writers manipulate the Arabic language to make space for queer subjects within Arab cultures. At the same time, their play with language underlines some of their ambivalence regarding their sexual identities. Finally, I foreground how queer subjects are at the center of social justice and liberation movements via their strident critiques of heteropatriarchal colonial and settler colonial violence.

As in the previous chapter, my focus here is Arabic texts written by banat and femmes about Arab women's queer and homoerotic lives and experiences. Unlike the previous chapter, the three texts here are edited collections produced and self-published by queer activist organizations. They include بريد مستعجل (Bareed Mista3ji/Priority Mail) by ميم (Meem); حقي: أن أعيش، أن أختار، أن أكون (Haqi: An A'ish, An Akhtar, An Akoon/My Right: To Live, To Choose, To Be) by أصوات (Aswat); and وقفت بنات (Waqfet Banat/ Women's Stand) also by Aswat. Meem is in Lebanon and Aswat in Palestine. The regional and personal modes of production, publication, and circulation in these texts are very much at odds with the texts in the previous works, but foreshadow the following chapter. These collections center queer voices and are published independently and thus offer an interesting counterpoint to the process of anthologization and minority literature formation discussed in chapter 1. I titled this chapter "Love Letters" to capture precisely the intimacy of the works' movement and to attest to the labor of love the works perform, in staking their histories and in creating and imagining community. One of the collections, Bareed Mista3jil, also underscores this point in its title, which literally translates to "Mail in a Hurry." Finally, "Letters" also operates in reference to the alphabet, hinting at how writers in the collections manipulate the Arabic language.

The production of Bareed, Haqi, and Waqfet Banat by queer Arab activist organizations and for queer Arab communities allows the collections to do different kinds of cultural and social labor than the texts of previous chapters. The three collections are produced by and for queer writers, written toward the community from which the writers both seek and emerge. This is unlike either Golden Era film with its massive circulation and production oversight, or literary presses with specific audiences and editorial styles. As such, the three collections studied here do not face the censorship or regulations placed on film, and they do not garner the attention of literary critics that the novels experienced. Instead, the works travel and are received in private, by word of mouth, and in largely noninstitutional ways. They do their work in intimate ways that refuse a mainstream public while at the same time creating a community within their readership.

I consider the shift in production and circulation meaningful insofar as it signals a different kind of rhetorical labor for the texts produced. The collections are often explicit about their aims in ways that inform and temper our reading of the content. Moreover, as texts emerging from activist organizations, the collections are interpreted as performing political and social labor within their broader communities, whether or not they do so explicitly. In contrast to the novels from the previous chapter, whose framing and reception were contested in critical response, the texts under consideration here are not necessarily received as works of creative culture, but offer a kind of evidence of experience, a record of difference articulated by those differently positioned in their communities.

On the one hand, as we saw in chapter 1, collections are an open and explicit attempt at archival practice, performed here by social organizations seeking community and structural changes to their cultures. On the other hand, these specific collections and the archive they attempt are often undermined or refuted by the very subjects within them, who express a great deal of ambivalence and anxiety in their narration of their experiences, identities, and communities. Through study of the collections' rhetorical and cultural labor, this chapter crystalizes the difficulty in locating a queer Arab archive and, more specifically, outlines reasons why that archive is challenging that are not merely about the discourses framing it (Orientalism, heteronormativity, heteronationalism). Instead, writers use their mediated experiences to explore queer Arab understandings and enactments of sexuality that are not neatly narrated; they do not result in a clearly named and recognized queer subject. This is to say, the discourses that forbid queer Arab sexuality (chapter 1), the ephemeral and gestural traces of women's desires (chapter 2), and the challenged and challenging longings for queer subjects (chapter 3) become intertwined in this chapter (4) with queer subjects' own multifaceted desires. These collections reflect the anxiety and ambivalence of queer Arabs toward their sexualities. At the same time, they insist on their place and presence in Arab societies and challenge Arab linguistic, social, and political structures that would exclude them. Insistence and ambivalence: they demand to be seen with a simultaneous refusal to be known. I consider insistence and ambivalence a tactical position that both protects their safety and existence within Arab culture and refutes discourses of Orientalism, heteronormativity, and heteronationalism that foreclose their flourishing.

Here I argue that the texts engage in a number of significant rhetorical and political acts. First, as in the previous chapter, they evidence queer Arab women's lives. They invoke multilingual, transnational queer Arab subjects. Second, the texts utilize the Arabic language to make space for queer subjects. Rather than framing Arabic as a restrictive language, the texts illustrate the fluidity and sexual possibility within it. While the previous chapter mobilized the "othered" status of the novel, this chapter uses colloquial Arabic, Arabish, and transliteration to make linguistic space for queer Arab women. Third, the texts explicitly critique heteropatriachal and heteronormative Arab cultures as well as the imperial violence that impacts Arab subjects. They refuse to locate homophobia or heteronormativity strictly in Arab culture and look instead to how ongoing colonial and settler violence impede queer life.

In the first of three sections, I frame the three collections as acts of testimony that insist on the existence of queer Arabs. In the second, I examine how the writers deploy Arabic, translation, and transliteration to create space for queer Arabs that is transnational in scope. In the third, I outline the critiques of heteropatriarchy and the state that the collections provide.

Ontological Insistence in Autobiographical Formats

While the previous chapters examined novels and film as sites of queer emergence, this chapter examines the use of autobiography and testimony. We might consider these texts examples of testimony that insist on the presence of queer Arab life. As in the previous chapter, I encourage us to consider the sometimes negative and painful content relayed as the means by which to refuse essentializing queer subjects, rather than dismissing their queerness or Arabness as failed or inauthentic. In 2007 and 2010, Aswat released two collections of personal narratives: *Haqi* and *Waqfet Banat*. In 2009, Meem, an LGBTQ organization in Lebanon, released a similar project, *Bareed Mista3jil*.[1] All three texts favor a light editorial hand and forward first-person narrations of queer life in their respective countries. All feature cis and trans queer voices. All are published anonymously, though *Haqi* includes first names that may or may not have been edited for privacy. *Waqfet* and *Bareed* are organized thematically and offer no indication of the authors. *Bareed* organizes its stories around themes including discrimination, self-esteem, gender identity, activism, coming out, family, relationships, sexual diversity, religion, community, self-discovery, and emigration. *Bareed* states that the editors conducted interviews with over 150 queer people in Lebanon in order to produce the collection, selecting stories that were most representative of the interviews conducted. *Waqfet* does not offer the same framing device, but stories are grouped thematically, concerning (in order) gender nonconformity, religious restrictions, trans experiences, family (the longest section), and queer liberation.

First, I suggest that these works are not stifled by the sometimes negative representations of queerness relayed, or by the seemingly unrealized LGBT identities within the covers. Instead, we should think of the works and the complicated lives represented as artifacts of queer life and narrations of queer Arab becomings. The texts present queer Arab life as incredibly fraught, relaying stories of longing, shame, and violence. They catalogue the many axes of power that inform queer experiences, as well as the interpersonal and community interactions that shape queer life. The emotions generated in the entanglement of power, personhood, and community—emotions like shame, lust, grief, and even joy—are vital aspects of the stories.

Second, I suggest we think of the three collections as testimonial literature. I draw my definition of testimony from the field of trauma theory, where testimony marks work that is not "a completed statement, a totalizable account" but a "discursive practice."[2] Thinking with Linda Tuhiwai Smith in *Decolonizing Methodologies*, I also consider testimony a form of epistemic justice utilized by Black, Indigenous, and people of color to combat their erasure from arts and history, as well as their frequent casting as unreliable subjects.[3] Finally, I chose testimony precisely because it honors those who are inclined to speak but recognizes how speech is mediated by questions of editing, translation, and reception. To be clear: by marking these texts as testimonies, I am not suggesting that they offer an unmediated Truth. I am not unveiling, in a classic Orientalist fashion, the Secret Lives of Arab Lesbians. Rather, collectively, *Haqi*, *Waqfet*, and *Bareed* create queer Arab subjects and histories through the act of narration itself. As Jackie Stacey and Sara Ahmed note, marginalized subjects develop through testimony "the conditions for their own existence and reception, by constituting different configurations of self, space, and community."[4] These collections produce multiple configurations of self, space, and community via their representation of diverse individual writers, their attention to their national context, and their commitment to cataloguing queer life in order to create a history and present for other queers.

Despite differences in organization, structure, and writers, each collection can be considered an example of testimony, an insistence on queer Arab history and presence. *Haqi* is organized by author, rather than thematically as are *Waqfet* and *Bareed*. Rather than offer a broad experience of queer subjects in Palestine or Lebanon, *Haqi* narrates relatable but individual lives that do not aim to stand in for or represent a broad swath of experiences, which is part of the explicit goal of *Bareed*.[5] At the same time, the introduction and dedication mark the text as an act of testimony: the editors suggest that the book offers information on same-sex desire while raising consciousness around it as a social issue. They write that *Haqi* is a book for people who need it to know they are not alone, so that they may find themselves and each other, and through this process create new work for the community the book creates.[6] The function of the book becomes explicit as a community forum and creator of community. As one contributor remarks, she decided to write her story because she had difficulty finding queer stories in Arabic. She wanted to leave a record for others who might go looking.[7]

Like *Haqi*, *Waqfet* has ambitious goals for its collection: to document "the struggles marginalized groups face in a heteropatriarchal society," to foster awareness and understanding about the LGBTQI Arab community, to be a resource to other folks questioning their sexuality, and to stand firm in their belief that they are of and belong to their communities.[8] In both cases, the collections create what their writers seek: the trauma of queer erasure is acknowledged and made possible via the presence of queerness in the testimonies.[9] Queer Arabs are made tangible in the object of the collection, which is at once the evidence of their own existence to the writers and the affirmation of queer life to its readers.

Bareed enacts a similar insistence. The editors remark in the introduction that the book is didactic in nature: to introduce Lebanese society to "the real stories of real people whose voices have gone unheard for hundreds of years . . . so that we can come together as Lebanese from all religions, beliefs, and backgrounds to respect and embrace all differences, especially those of gender and sexual orientation."[10] At the same time, the book's second function is not instructional, but rather to create a work by and for the community it represents, which is supported by the book's dedication "for all of you with stories that are yet to be told." Here we see the writers use the foundation of *Bareed* as a stage for future becoming.

All three collections insist on their existence and their right to exist. This act of narration—because of its potentially dangerous fallout for queer Arabs, because of its challenge to the heteropatriarchal order of things, and because of its capacity to build queer community—is itself a radical act. It is a crucial step toward creating queer Arab life in the present. Writers reinvent their sexualities on every page. Writers narrate ordinary and extraordinary circumstances, varied and diverse lives. At the same time, shared themes do emerge within the texts. By studying the texts and looking at shared features and experiences, we can begin to delineate the facets of queer women's lives in Arab contexts. At first, *Haqi, Bareed*, and *Waqfet* struggle with naming and translation, but they ultimately reform and refigure Arabic and English in order to make space for queer Arab existences. Second, the texts present queer Arabs as transnational and critical subjects whose identities are forged across national and linguistic boundaries, within and against colonialism, occupation, apartheid, and state violence. Their critiques of this violence are interwoven with their consciousness around and critiques of patriarchy, heteronormativity, and respectability within their communities. Both facets contribute to the construction of a transnational and relational queerness as well as Arabness. I will address the questions of language and naming next, and the critical provocations the texts provide later.

Translation, Transliteration, and Naming

This section offers three related claims: first, through the manipulation of the Arabic language, transliteration, and neologism, writers make room within Arab culture for queerness and nonnormative subjects. Second, translating Arabic words like مثليّة (mithliya) or سحاقيّة (sahaqiya) into "lesbian" disappear the specificity of Arab queer experiences. Third, transliterations and neologisms provide opportunities to disrupt the field of signification and alert us to the specificity of Arab queer experiences that are not collapsible or assimilable to the referent "lesbian."

Two related concerns around translation weave through all three collections. The first concern is the translation of their experiences into language itself and the choice around which language(s) best serve the collections' missions. *Haqi* was originally published in Arabic and has never been translated. *Waqfet Banat* was simultaneously released in English and in Arabic. *Bareed* was first released in English and then translated into Arabic. What are the ramifications of these choices? How does publication in Arabic and/or English impact the readership, reach, and goals of the collection? How and why these language choices were made is integral to the second concern: how to name or identify queer Arab experiences. Would writers use Arabic neologisms, transliterated Arabic or English, or Arabic or English phrases? Each collection grapples with the processes of translation, transliteration, and naming. I will discuss *Haqi, Waqfet,* and *Bareed* in turn.

While *Haqi*'s Arabic language choice prioritizes its immediate local audience, it does pose a challenge for nonreaders of the language. At the same time, using Arabic signals Aswat's commitment to reading and writing queerness as part of Arab culture. As the first collection, and the only published in Arabic alone, *Haqi*'s first audience is Arabic readers (primarily in Palestine). While the collection uses a mix of colloquial and formal Arabic, it still relies on literacy as the means for access, which limits its reach for illiterate Arabs. As an example, in 2013 in Palestine, the illiteracy rate among individuals aged fifteen and over was 3.7 percent, with decreased percentages for younger groups.[11] For these individuals, reading itself provides an access barrier. The use of Arabic alone also limits the collection's reach to Arabs who cannot read Arabic. Given the number of Arab refugees and immigrant populations outside the Arab nations, that group could be quite large.

I suggest that *Haqi* makes deliberate space for multiple gender and sexual identities by using neologisms and reformatting formal Arabic. In its foreword and introduction, *Haqi*'s editors refer to homoerotic relationships between women and same-sex desires with the phrase مثليّة الجنسيّة (mithliya al jinsiya), a neologism based on the English phrase "same-sex" (مثليّة mithliya = same; الجنسيّة al jinsiya = sexuality). However, that is not a neat translation process. Al jinsiya derives from الجنس (al jins); the former can refer to sexuality or nationality, while the latter can refer to sex, gender, or genus. Mithliya derives from the root مثل (mithl), which, depending on diacritics, can be "like, as, or such as" or a noun meaning example or proverb. The writers call women مثليّات (mithliyat, the plural of mithliya). *Haqi*'s editors and some writers also adapt the gendered nature of Arabic by including both feminine and masculine prefixes and suffixes on words, separated by a backslash. They also use "she and/or he" for singular formations and offer both masculine and feminine plurals. We can look to the use of "الكثيرين والكثيرات مثلك" and "الإنسان/ة التي/الذي" in the introduction as examples.[12] This is notable because formal Arabic uses masculine endings for heterogeneous audiences. It might be tempting to read *Haqi*'s insistence on feminine and masculine language as a reification of the gender binary. Instead, I argue that by insisting on the feminine prefixes and suffixes, *Haqi* argues that women's experiences cannot and should not default into a monolithic masculine queer subject, or even into a heterogeneous "us." In recognizing a feminine plural, *Haqi* refuses to allow a queer masculine subject to stand in for all others, which often occurs in queer and queer of color representation. Instead, the work explicitly hails women and femme of center subjects without erasing or ignoring men or masculine of center audiences. Both are welcome and represented.

Individual essays within *Haqi* reflect how language can be a site for negotiating cultural belonging for queer subject. Here we can also see writers attempt to navigate their complex social locations through questions around naming. Their language choices and experiences reflect an ongoing engagement with the scripts that inform their lives. In this excerpt from her essay, writer Zizi asks:

هل أنا سحاقيّة أو مثليّة أو متنوّعة الجنس، هل أنا فرد أو مؤسّسة أو ثوريّة أو تجريبيّة أو مموّضة؟ لستُ أعرف أن كنت أيًّا من هؤلاء أو بعضًا منها/منهنّ أو أنّي لست أيًّا منها/منهنّ أبدًا.

Am I sahaqiya, or mithliya, or mutinowiat il jins, am I an individual or founder or revolutionary or experimental or trendy? I don't know if I am any of these words or some of them, or if I am none of them.[13]

Zizi's exploratory questions characterize the work of the collection. Like other protagonists, she tries on multiple names for herself, including mithliya and متنوّعة (mutinowia). I mentioned mithliya earlier, but it's worth noting that mithliya and mutinowia emerged at the same time. The latter is a rough adaptation of heterosexual or varied/diverse sex. She also brings up the historical term for same-sex behavior between women—سحق (sahq). Other writers question their identities as سحقيّات (sahaqiyat), or women who practice sahq, as well as consider the ramifications of the term شذوذ (shuthooth), which can be translated as abnormal, weird, and/or queer. I will return to sahq in the following chapter as a significant axis of queer thinking, but Zizi and other writers often find the term difficult to incorporate into their sense of selves. Zizi is also keenly aware of ways queer behavior has been interpreted: she internalizes and considers the notion that she might be experimenting or in a trendy phase. She wonders if her sexuality positions her as a revolutionary or a leader in her community. Even her question "هل أنا فرد؟" can be interpreted as "am I unique?" or contextually as "am I an individual/alone?" rather than someone within a larger community. Here Zizi is considering how her sexuality aligns or misaligns her with community norms. Though Zizi does not reference lesbian, gay, or queer in this essay, other writers in the collection and elsewhere transliterate them into Arabic and consider them as options. Zizi's interrogation of naming practices and of her own experiences with desire and erotic activities with men and women offers an example of how subjects are grappling with their identities at the intersection of transnational Arab culture and demonstrating their familiarity and tension with the politics associated with claiming and naming an identity like lesbian (Western assimilation) or sahaqiya (allegedly precolonial Arabic literatures) or mithliya (contemporary Arab culture, which is marked by postcolonial negotiations, the ongoing occupation of Palestine, and globalization). Zizi and other writers identify with and reject multiple names and facets of the identities offered to them. They also develop and adopt new language to describe their experiences. The negotiation of language reflects that Arab queers are dynamic subjects making and remaking their language, and through it, their identities and communities.

Waqfet frames its mission in similar terms to *Haqi* and *Bareed*. The choice to release *Waqfet* in multiple languages accomplishes three feats: *Waqfet* invites and attends a transnational audience, rejects the notion that queerness is an inauthentic Western import, and produces localized knowledge about queer Arabs. *Waqfet* is simultaneously published in English and Arabic in order to "broaden its reach to the Arab LGBTQI community in Palestine and around the world."[14] Here, Aswat, as the organization that published both *Haqi* and *Waqfet*, redresses part of the limit of *Haqi*'s readership by drawing in readers of English. At the same, it recognizes an Arab LGBTQI community in Palestine and around the world, which constitutes queer Arabs as a transnational and multilingual group. In choosing to release in multiple languages, Aswat positions a queer Arab community across real and imagined divides and complicates the simplistic double bind of East and West that underwrites the criticisms I outlined in the previous chapter, as well as the naming practices in the previous paragraph.

Differences in the Arabic and English versions of *Waqfet* speak to how Aswat imagines and frames its transnational community. While the Arabic and English versions are almost identical, one major feature distinguishes them from one another. In the Arabic version *Waqfet* opens with a glossary titled بعض من المصطلحات الأساسيّة في الهويّة الجنسيّة (Some key terms for sexual identity), which includes entries for the following:

sexual identity الهويّة الجنسيّة
biological sex الجنس البيولوجي
social gender/gender identity النوع الاجتماعي/الهويّة الجندرية
masculinity and femininity الأنوثة والذكورة
coming out of "the closet" or declaring mithliya
الخروج من "الخزانة" او الإشهار بالمثلية
mithliya al jinsiya مثليّة الجنسيّة
mithli al jins مثلي الجنس

possible neologism for bisexuality ازدواجي الميول الجنسية

fear or terror of/for mithliya, possible neologism for homophobia
رهاب المثليّة

variations/changes in social gender identity, possible neologism for
transgender مغيّرو/ات النوع الاجتماعي

variations/changes in biological gender/sex, possible neologism for
transsexual[15] مغيّرو/ات الجنس البيولوجي

The presence of this glossary in Arabic underlines one of *Waqfet*'s goals, which is education of Palestinian and Arab society about gender and sexual variation.

The fact that the glossary appears in the Arabic but not in the English translation has competing consequences. On the one hand, it imagines that a keyword section is not necessary for English readers—that alongside English fluency is an assumed familiarity with language around gender and sexuality. It also assumes that queer Arab identities can slot into a preexisting English vocabulary. It may be the case that English language speakers or societies for whom English is a first or primary language are readily familiar with generic understandings of gender nonconformity or homosexuality. Yet, the use of similar glossaries in introductory texts on sex and gender and on websites like the Human Rights Campaign, Planned Parenthood, and the Trevor Project suggests that the distinctions around biological versus social gender, the difference between gender and sexual identities, or the biological variety in sex are also unknown to a great deal of the English-speaking population.

On the other hand, the presence of a glossary in the Arabic version of *Waqfet* attests to how Arabic can be reimagined and repurposed to reveal and accommodate queer Arab sexualities. The stories themselves attest to the unease queer subjects feel in the process of translation, as noted in Zizi's story. As in *Haqi* and *Bareed*, writers in *Waqfet* demonstrate varying levels of comfort and discomfort with Western terminology for queer identities and often refuse to use any distinctive label to describe their identities, focusing instead on how they feel and if they are happy in their lives.[16] Across all texts, many use the original nomenclature of mithliya rather than transliterating lesbian or queer (which sometimes occurs in Aswat's and other organizations' Arabic literature). This indicates a discomfort with both categorical options but a preference for the Arabic neologism overall. Despite this, reading the two versions of *Waqfet* side by side reveals a surprising editorial choice—the tendency to translate mithliya back into English as homosexual or lesbian *rather* than transliterate it into English characters. Similarly, sahq and sahaqiya are translated into lesbianism/lesbian. This is surprising precisely because what all three collections indicate, over and over, is how much discomfort writers feel with those English categories.

I suggest that this translational practice is part of the difficulty in seeing, establishing, and distinguishing Arab queer subjects. It also makes it difficult to see queer Arab subject formation as a distinct historical and contextual process. The tendency to translate rather than transliterate Arabic contributes to the anxiety Arab queers feel around understanding their sexuality through a Western lens. At the same time, the translations help make queer Arabs more legible to broader audiences, Arab and non-Arab. However, adopting known categories with distinct definitions, histories, and subtexts risks erasing the specificity of queer Arab experiences.

I propose that transliterations of mithliya and sahaqiya accomplish what the translations fail—to capture Arab women's experiences with queerness in their own voice. This is not to say that Arabs cannot or should never refer to themselves as homosexual, lesbians, and so on. Rather, there is capacious possibility in defining and redefining mithliya and sahaqiya by and for queer Arab subjects.[17] To refuse to translate those terms into the equally specific categories of lesbian and homosexual allows both communities to maintain their historical context and nuance. In this chapter and elsewhere, I reject the translations of mithliya or sahaqiya into English as homosexual or lesbian. I stay with the Arabic versions as the nomenclature queer Arab subjects create and utilize. In choosing to transliterate them, I put the onus on readers to understand and make room for queer Arab subjects as in conversation with, but nonassimilable to, Western queers. As I have argued throughout, queer Arab subjectivity may be comparable but not assimilable to other constructions of sexuality and sexual identities.

Despite its initial publication in English and many of the writers' unease with the Arabic language, Bareed can and does manipulate the Arabic language to make space for queer Arab subjectivity and to challenge heteronormative Arab cultures. Unlike Aswat with Haqi and Waqfet, Meem has not made Bareed Mistaᴣjil available online. Of the three, Bareed is the only collection published originally in English, followed by an Arabic version. The editors offer the following comments regarding language:

> The authors were personally more comfortable writing in English. But when we began the process of translation into Arabic, we were faced with a powerful blockade against talking about sexuality. The words didn't exist to express exactly what we wanted them to, and we were constantly straddling between the Lebanese Arabic dialect that we speak in our everyday lives and classical Arabic.[18]

The writers' take on language makes clear that classical Arabic rather than colloquial is often more exacting and less in tune with real-life experiences. They note that Arabic has not adapted itself to create new words or forms of expression and that rigid gendering of the language makes it difficult to relay stories regarding gender nonconformity. Finally, they noted that writers often turned to English and French, common languages in Lebanon, where discourses on sexuality were more common. While respecting the medium and explanation the editors here provide, the writers do use colloquial forms, which incorporate other languages and resignify gendered terms to make space for queer invocations. At the same time, the writers' suggestion that Arabic does not lend itself to movement is undermined by the multiplicity of the dialects represented in the collection itself. Even in the English-language version, many exchanges and words are written in Arabish, a transliterative writing of the Arabic language with English letters that incorporates Arabic numerals in order to signify Arabic letters with no match in English (e.g., ح = 7).[19] Within this invocation, writers reveal their attachment to Arabic and to what is untranslatable to English. This use of Arabish further evidences the malleability of Arabic despite the editors' contestations. I would make a case here against rejection of Arabic as the stodgy and unmoving language of the classics and for an embrace of Arabic as the mobile, vernacular language that exists in people's experiences.

Despite the restrictions the community and the translation process creates, *Bareed* manipulates language and uses neologisms to create the identity it seeks to explicate. Take for example the original nomenclature one writer uses to describe the online queer community in Lebanon, dubbing it Lesbanon. The choice is both a reading of lesbian with an Arab twist and a way to create space for women in queer cultures that were at the time dominated by men.[20] While the Lesbanon chatroom dissipated after some time, the function of Meem— the organization from which *Bareed* emerged—became for many writers the real-world Lesbanon. Of her quest to find lesbians online, one writer remarks, "I often wonder if the new generation of lesbians appreciates their much easier (and much cheaper) access to the internet and the availability of a welcoming support group like Meem."[21] Meem—the letter *M*—is its own creative neologism. It symbolizes the first letter of every word in the name of the organization (مجموع مؤازرة لمرأة المثليّة / majmua mua'zara lil mar'a al mithliya). Thus, the Lesbanon that Meem creates is a forward gesture in the creation of queer utopic space and a validation of its historical presence.

Part of the collections' capacity for multiplicity, freedom with the Arabic language, and nuanced political vision is underwritten by the fact that the collections were created and published by queer organizations rather through a publishing house. As agents of social change in Palestine and Lebanon, respectively, Aswat and Meem challenge their community's silence by seizing the means of knowledge production. They hold themselves accountable for representing local communities and attending to intersectional social positions. At the same time, they are aware of the larger geopolitical and global roles they hold and use their publications to speak to both contexts.[22] They also directly distributed their books to members, libraries, and other organizations, as I narrated in my chapter introduction. They announced their publications in groups for queer Arab women that include Arabs across the globe and offered to ship readers copies discreetly if needed.[23] Arabs traveling in and out of Palestine and Lebanon carried copies for one another to ship in the United States, United Kingdom, and elsewhere. By relying on community dispersal they instantiated challenges to queer restrictions in their locations, and the global erasure of queer Arab subjects, in a grassroots fashion. Independent publication also allows them to describe the facets of their lives and make substantial critiques of the Arab communities in which they live, without fear of censor. As such, the three collections underline the transnational and relational formation of queer Arab subjectivity that is at the core of queer Arab critique.

Queer Arab Critique and Transnational Arab Communities

In the first section, I articulated how the collections served as testimonies to insist on queer Arab existence. In the second section, I discussed how they used Arabic to create space and language to describe queer Arab existences. I turn now to the content of the collections, which illustrates some of the defining aspects of queer Arab identities. I propose that we use *Haqi, Waqfet,* and *Bareed* to establish a nuanced understanding of queer Arab subjectivity that is unique but in conversation with the multiple discourses around queer Arabs and queerness at large. As in the previous chapter, I argue that we should not dismiss the narratives that invoke negative affects, such as shame. Rather, we should use shame to critique heteronormative Arab cultures. Finally, the collections all discuss how queerness is eclipsed, often violently, by colonial and settler colonial forces. Rather than locate heterosexism strictly within Arab culture, these collections index how colonial and settler violence harms queer subjects. Each of these arguments underlies some central claims of the book, namely that Arab queerness is not reducible to the discourses that circulate about it and that critiques of heteronormativity and imperialism are readily available from queer Arab spaces, if one attends to them.

The collections articulate experiences that are shared with other queer communities but not collapsible to them. Some themes within the collections are gender binary/rigidity; shame and respectability; critiques of heteropatriarchy, the state, and imperial violence; and concerns around transnational identity and authenticity. These themes are shared across the stories, with writers in each book commenting on some facet of how their queer lives are formed and informed by the topics. For example, all three books feature multiple stories wherein writers come to understand their homoerotic desires through defying normative gender expectations. This script is familiar for many queer subjects, as evidenced by numerous cultural and local iterations of tomboy girls and effeminate boys. Similarly, like other queers, Arabs too struggle with religious, familial, and social acceptance of their nonnormative sexual and gendered identities. Writers discuss being estranged, welcomed, or ignored in their families, religious institutions, and social circles.

Another common narrative arc within the stories is writers reckoning with their reputations and their relationship to shame. In the collections, interrogations of shame become a way to challenge respectability politics for queers. As Georgis suggests in "Thinking Past Pride: Queer Arab Shame in *Bareed Mista3jil*," Arab queers articulate and engage with shame differently than expected in heteronormative Arab or Western queer communities. Georgis argues writers use shame as a catalyst for creation and critique.[24] Following her logic, in *Haqi*, Samirah writes about being "weird" or "strange" in her experience of queerness insofar as she questions whether her feelings or thoughts are real or normal given their unusual subject—her love and lust for a woman.[25] Despite describing her "ordinary" childhood, Samirah feels an unrelenting sadness, an emptiness that doesn't abate until she meets and falls in love with a woman. In this moment, she wants to share her joy and her love with her family but quickly realizes that though her family wants her happiness, they only want it if it aligns with their notion of normalcy. Samirah chooses to cleave her "true life" from her family life not because she experiences shame or doesn't believe in her truth, but because she places maintaining a relationship with family, even a shallow one, over the fracture an open and ongoing discussion of her sexuality would create. She closes the essay by claiming that the strangeness she now lives is not her romantic or sexual life, but a life in which the people she loves are far from her. Her home is strange in the absence of her family.[26]

This rhetorical turn in the essay, where weirdness goes from an internal metric to an external state of being, offers an alternate reading of shame and respectability where shame can diagnose heteronormative and patriarchal failure of Arab cultures rather than individually failed subjects. Samirah's story expands the onus of shame and respectability from her individual responsibility to a family and communal failure. Because her individual weirdness could cause a loss of respectability, she creates a new reality where she can be "strange" and "respectable." Through the essay strange becomes estrangement, and so Samirah neither claims nor rejects how shame is operating in her life—it is both hers and her families', theirs for their failure to love her and seek her happiness, hers for its capacity to create estrangement. Here then shame shapes Samirah's queer life in unexpected ways. It moves from an internal source of pain to an external organizing feature of queer Arab life. A writer in *Waqfet* makes this reorientation of shame explicit: "It's a shame that I can't find a safe and reliable shelter within my family and my home."[27] Rather than stifle her queer identity or police her actions, shame is turned back on the broader community that has ultimately failed banat.

Writers also locate the oppression of heteropatriarchy and heteronormativity in their nations as one invoked and sustained through colonization and settler occupation. For example, in *Bareed*, the essay "We Are Not Safe" relays the story of the protagonist's rape by a group of men who accost her on her way home from a party. The writer claims she is often held up as an example of "Lebanon's booming gay life," but in that moment the violence and discrimination she experiences witnesses how sexism, misogyny, and patriarchy make women—queer or otherwise—distinctly unsafe.[28] Her rape is not framed as LGBT discrimination but as patriarchal violence that any woman can experience. In this way, the story both refutes a particularly homophobic or homophonic version of Arab culture and Lebanon in particular. Instead, she focuses her criticism and the source of her oppression on Arab heteropatriarchy.

Aswat frames the discrimination and oppression for Palestinian queers as the combined result of heteropatriarchy and the Israeli occupation. They reject the notion that Arab queers suffer unduly at the hands of religion by featuring work from Muslim, Jewish, and Christian writers who experience varying degrees of acceptance and rejection. One example is in "A Voice from Aswat," where Saraya narrates her queer coming of age via Aswat and refuses to disentangle the Israeli project of Palestinian erasure from queer liberation. She writes that the founding of Aswat as a society for Palestinian women brought about a great deal of internalized racism from Palestinians who had learned to fear and hide their Palestinian heritage as subjects under occupa-

tion.[29] For Saraya, the primary mission of Aswat is queer Palestinian liberation, which cannot be achieved without the liberation of Palestine and the
rejection of Palestinian heteropatriarchy.[30] Thus Saraya, with and through
Aswat, firmly dispels pinkwashed misconceptions about Israel as a haven for
Palestinian queers and locates it as a source of dispossession and a barrier to
queer liberation.[31] When writers do reference freedom in Israel they do so
with loss—dispossession of their ancestral homes and estrangement from
their families who live in the West Bank and/or Gaza.[32]

Thus, in both collections, Aswat highlights apartheid violence as a facet
of queer Arab life alongside more commonly discussed concerns like gender,
familial acceptance, and religious struggle. In a *Waqfet* story, Haya Suleiman
narrates falling in love with a woman in the midst of her job documenting
humanitarian crises in her homeland. Her love for the woman is entangled
with the woman's capacity to empathize and understand Suleiman's secondary trauma and the woman's softness in the face of the horrors Suleiman
documents.[33] In this way, Suleiman's story, like those of Saraya and others,
marks queer Arab identity formation and articulation as inextricable from
the violence of the occupation. To understand queer Arab identities and
social formations requires not only an articulation of how heteropatriarchal
gendered and sexual tropes are enacted in Arab societies, but additionally,
how those tropes are informed by ongoing violence and political maneuvers
around, through, and with Arab nation-states and those states that intervene
in them: Israel, the United States, or other Arab nations.[34]

All three collections also respond to the discursive and material restrictions presented in chapter 1 that attempt to foreclose the emergence or
existence of queer Arab subjects. To this end, writers reaffirmed the editors'
construction of queer Arabs as transnational subjects via their discussion of
movement, diaspora, and authenticity. While all three collections highlight
specific nations (Palestine and Lebanon), the writers within come from all
over those nations, and in the case of *Haqi*, feature Palestinian refugees in
Jordan, Egypt, and Lebanon. For many writers, understanding their queer
identity is inextricable from understanding their social location within and
without the Arab world. In *Haqi*, Rauda discusses her relationship to movement and travel as she seeks to understand her identity and social location
as a queer Palestinian woman impacted by the occupation.[35] Another writer,
Rima, details her heartbreak over loving a woman who lives in a city she
cannot visit because of Palestinians' limited mobility within occupied Palestine.[36] In "The Closet and the 'Truth,'" Aden explores the metaphor of the
closet and the idea of coming out as it relates—if it relates at all—to her life in

Palestine.[37] In other words, these stories reflect a complex and varied sexual history for queer Arab women that is impacted by their relationship to the apartheid state and to transnational queer culture.

The collections also reject the notion that queerness is antithetical to Arabness, and the movements of Arab queers attest to understanding both Arabness and queerness as mobile, transnational categories. In *Bareed*, one of the highlighted themes is emigration and the role it plays in the writers' lives. The editors remark that writers in the collection experience higher rates of emigration than others, which is in part because Lebanon has high rates due to the war and the economy. Queers in particular might imagine a "better" life outside their Arab nations. The notion that their queerness is incompatible with the Arab world imagines an Arab world to which queerness is inorganic or impossible. Yet, all the collections demonstrate how queers make lives in Arab spaces and how their queerness does not erase or abject their Arab identity. At the same time, queers who do immigrate remark on the sense of loss they experience during immigration and how they do not experience the liberation they hope to in their travels. In some ways, these people become "more Arab" in their contact with systems of discrimination in their new locations. In "This Land Is Not My Land," the narrator living in the United States has become "an Arab Ambassador" in the face of the anti-Arab and Islamophobic communities she encounters.[38] The act of physical movement many Arab queers experience underlines the literal and figurative transnational nature of Arab queer identity. For many, queerness takes place online and across virtual and national borders. And for many, questions around authenticity are not organized around whether or not they are good or real Arabs, but whether or not they are good people, lovers, or activists. In the collections, queerness is not outside of Arabness, and Arabness is not an inside one can inhabit. Both happen in relation to, and in between, multiple transnational discourses, spaces, and languages.

❦

Ultimately, the collections *Haqi*, *Waqfet*, and *Bareed* accomplish a number of significant discursive and material maneuvers in order to establish and make space for queer Arabs. They function as testimonial literatures that witness queer Arab experiences and create queer Arab communities. They use the Arabic language, translation, and transliteration to create discursive spaces for queer Arabs to exist and to mark queer Arabs as a transnational community. Their expositions regarding gender and sexuality both provide a map of queer Arab experiences and offer critiques of authenticity, binary gender, respectability, heteropatriarchy, state and imperial violence, and the Israeli occupation of Palestine.

Through analysis of *Haqi*, *Waqfet Banat*, and *Bareed Mista3jil*, I have shown that queers testify to and insist on their past, present, and future existence within Arab society. They manipulate and remake the Arabic language in order to find new ways to represent and capture their experiences. They imagine queer Arab communities as multilingual and transnational, eschew fixed or definitive iterations of their sexualities, and offer interrogations and interventions into the binding discourses that frame queer Arabs: assumed assimilation to Western norms, the failure to be proper gay subjects, the failure to be proper Arab subjects.

Across my discussion of the texts' archival creation and obfuscation, I discussed how the texts mediated and were mediated by multiple kinds of discourses. I argued for the saliency of Arab neologisms and transliterations in expressing queer experiences. I attended to the content of the collections to give some of the texture of queer Arab women's lives. Per the literature, that topography is often difficult and dangerous, anxious and ambivalent. The content of the collections left me wondering: How and where do we locate pleasure, resistance, and freedom in queer Arab women's lives? In the following chapter, I examine graphic novels, prints, and film to locate ways women find pleasure and intimacy with one another and make possible queer futures.

sahq

5

Queer Femme Futures

As I noted in the introduction, the affective question that has undergirded this project is: What would it mean to be queer, Arab, and OK? I have eschewed an approach to thinking about queer Arab life that would amplify erasure and death. I consolidated impossibility to chapter 1, where I outlined the discourses that limited the capacity and availability for queer Arab subjects and representations, particularly for women. In chapters 2 through 4, I demonstrated instead how queer readings and queer subjects sidestep their erasure, insist on their presence, and create intimate, complicated lives. In chapter 2, I developed queer Arab critique to locate queer stories and histories within mainstream and heteronormative texts, circumventing the discourses outlined in chapter 1 that made queer stories and histories seem impossible. In chapters 3 and 4, I used queer Arab critique to examine what queer life looks like in contemporary representations and when writers made explicit claims to same-sex identities like queer, lesbian, mithliya, and others. I highlighted the ambivalence that underwrites many queer Arab women, femmes, and banat. At the same time, I foregrounded their manipulations of Arabic and Arab literary traditions and their powerful critiques of heteropatriarchy, multiple normativities, and colonial and settler violence in their communities. Via queer Arab critique, the central three chapters offered a tentative queer Arab archive that records our past and manifests our present. In this concluding chapter, I imagine what our queer Arab future might hold with banat at its center. This chapter continues to reorient our understanding of queer Arab culture as one that is both legible in homoeroticism and recognizes queerness as resistance to Arab heteronormativity and patriarchy. Specifically, in this chapter I am interested in how artists and writers disrupt gendered and sexual norms through their transnational cultural organizing and production.

This chapter discusses multidisciplinary work by multidisciplinary Arab artists. My texts here include the narrative film بر بحر (Bar Bahar/In Between, directed by Maysaloun Hamoud); workshops and apparel from نول (Nöl Collective, formerly Babyfist); and prints and books from Maamoul Press. In contrast to previous chapters where texts were collected and discussed via a more transparent organizing impetus (e.g., Arab American texts that evoke Scheherazade in chapter 1 or homoerotic Arabic-language novels by women in chapter 3), this chapter uses feeling as the binding apparatus of the archive. The texts selected are bound by the feelings of possibility they produce, their capacity to illustrate and imagine a pleasurable, joyful world between banat. In *An Archive of Feelings*, Cvetkovich discusses how affective experience can provide the basis for new cultures; she suggests that cultural artifacts become the archive of something more ephemeral, of culture as a "way of life."[1] This chapter considers the emotions embedded in the texts as well as those evoked in the process of the texts' production and reception. I ask these texts: What is it to feel Arab, queer, OK? What might it feel like to be OK as a queer Arab? The texts respond to both kinds of questions, but more than anything, they feel possible. My analysis of these texts emphasizes the shared strategies they employ to create intimacy and capacity in an unrelenting and violent world.

The selected works think critically and provide provocations against the gendered and sexual norms of transnational Arab culture that we untangled in chapter 1. The principles of queer reading established in chapter 2 are also at work here: we are an attendant and receptive audience to queer ephemera; we highlight queer time and space; we delight in intimacy between women; we anticipate and read against the grain of queer containment. At the same time, the principles that emerged from chapter 3 and 4's readings of queer Arab subjectivity are at work: an insistence on a transnational formation of Arabness, a commitment to nonnormative expressions of gender and sexuality, and a critical reception of Arab heteronational and authenticating projects. In this concluding chapter, these three investments take a sharper, more directive form.

In my analysis, I suggest that contemporary Arab artists are remaking sexual and social norms in their cultures through their creative labors. They disrupt heteropatriarchal institutions and create alternative pathways for existence and resistance in three ways: through rejecting respectability politics, through rejecting the cultural politics of re/authenticity, and through transnational collective organizing. To imagine a queer Arab future that includes being OK—and if we dare, a future that includes joy, pleasure, and hope—we must insist on these three tenets. We must establish and engage in transnational collectivity; we must reject gender and sexual respectability; and we must reject authenticity politics, both precolonial and heteronational, as the defining metrics of Arab identity. I use سحق (sahq) to encompass these three acts of queer Arab existence and resistance.

I use sahq *both* as an option to describe same-sex practices, intimacies, and identities between banat Arab *and* as the direction and shape of a queer Arab social and political praxis that circumnavigates the discursive and material limits outlined in chapter 1. Sahq is a medieval Arabic term that refers to same-sex acts between women.[2] In her work on medieval Arab lesbians, Amer argues that sahq offers queer Arab women Arabic language with which to reject Western articulations of sexuality. Building on Amer's work, I argue that sahq is a useful description of queer Arab subjects as well as a direction for queer Arab praxis. Sahq is both fleshy and fricative, supple and mobile. It is in its versatility, in the movement sahq necessitates, that queer Arabs might find the most useful form of the word. Sahq can describe a sexual act, a sexual subject, a social and political praxis, and/or an orientation toward action that is grounded in women's bodies, in transnational movement, in queer resistance. In the first section of this chapter, I outline how sahq is a useful description for queer Arab life while at the same time offering sahq as a direction for praxis that enables a queer Arab future. In the second half, I analyze the film *Bar Bahar* and texts from Nöl Collective and Maamoul Press to see examples of sahq in action.

Sahq as Description and Direction

I argue that sahq can operate not only as a description for queer Arab subjects and lives, but as directions for enabling queer futures. As Amer suggests, sahq can be a useful description for queer Arab practices and subjects. Amer argues that using sahq resists coopting gender and sexually diverse Arab communities into ill-fitting identities like lesbian or gay. She suggests we use sahaqiya (the subject version of sahq) to name women with same-sex desires, practices, and identities. In *Female Homosexuality in the Middle East*, Habib, like Amer, locates sahq and sahaqiyat (plural of sahaqiya) firmly in Arabic and Arab histories and traditions.[3] I follow Amer's and Habib's lead in using sahq to describe queer Arab life and also suggest that it has more expansive utility and function.

One such function of sahq is that it offers a sensorial disruption of the contemporary queer naming landscape for Arabs. In both Arabic and transliterated Arabic, sahq requires us to think critically about the community and acts that it describes. It provides opportunities for disruption and multiplicity. The literal definition of the term refers to the friction between a mortar and pestle, or the act of grinding spices, an allusion to the act of women rubbing their bodies against one another, an aromatic scissoring. As such, it names the work of resistance itself—the grind against heteronormativity and patriarchy that queer Arabs must engage in order to exist in any form. Even as a noun, then, sahq describes action and evokes sensorial data—smell and touch at the very least. Sahaqiya, the subject form of the noun, maintains this emphasis on action—a sahaqiya is one who performs sahq, sahaqiyat are a group of sahaqiyas. Arabic to English translations of sahq include the following verbs: crush, smash, bash, squash, quash, overwhelm, and grind, to use a few. These translations can be playfully invoked: banat smashing the patriarchy, or queer Arab femmes, the original Grindrs. Sahq yokes and evokes sensation and action.

Sahq places banat and sahaqiyat at the center of our queer futures. Sahq as a denotation of intimate acts between women underlies the ethos of this book. Rather than assume a masculine collective default (e.g., gay) or rely only on translated or transliterated Western languages (e.g., queer), sahq forces us to think queerness through women and femininity first. This is not a "talking back" to imperialism or patriarchy per se, but an attempt to start a new conversation in which banat are at the center.

Sahq also invokes multiplicity. In English, sahq is transliterated on the page as its own entity, where it becomes a shifting signifier. Amer notes the interchangeability of sahq, sihaq, and sihaqa in her work. I use sahq over the others because the pronunciation and therefore transliteration is, like all spoken Arabic, regionally inflected. Sahq reads for me as the closest transliteration for my transnational Palestinian tongue. The same applies to the subject form, which Amer transliterates as "sahiqa" or "musahiqa." I use sahaqiya, a choice undoubtedly influenced by my first encounter with the term in the collections discussed in the previous chapter. Though I stick with sahq and sahaqiya for consistency in the chapter, I value the multiple spellings and pronunciations as further evidence of the heterogeneity of the concept and category.

Queerness is ever shifting, ever moving, and sahq's many definitions and transliterations underline this multiplicity.

Sahq emphasizes the distinctness of queer Arab formations. Throughout the book, I have suggested that queerness in Arab communities is not consolidated to a single narrative arc or easily assimilated to lesbian or gay identity, nor is it simply a romantic Arab tradition resurrected, nor still a Western construction coopted. Sahq's unique Arab etymology offers a means by which to discuss the specificity of queer Arab subjectivity. At the same time, sahq's multiple meanings and multiple translations and transliterations help describe those Arab experiences without totalizing them into a monolith.

As a direction, sahq urges us to reject authenticity as the defining metric of Arab identity. Sahq grounds queer activisms and politics in Arabic and Arab traditions, a move that rejects the notion that queerness is inauthentic to Arab culture. At the same time, "authenticity" cannot be the metric by which we regulate or imagine queer Arab life. As I discussed in the introduction and chapter 1, authenticity is a damaging and double-bound framework for understanding minority subjects because it essentializes those cultures, reducing them to a handful of typical traits. It also erases cultural differences within the group, suggesting that all members of a minority group have the same experiences, values, and traditions. Using the narrow and essentialized version of the culture, authenticity is the means by which a group can be policed both from within and without the group's boundaries. To that point, authenticity can often function as the gatekeeping metric for group and group identities. We can look again to Naber, who defines the politics of cultural authenticity as the doubling down of minority cultures on certain gendered and sexual norms in their communities in order to distinguish their identities from dominant and white Eurocentric communities (e.g., loose Americans, respectable Arabs).[4] Cultural authenticity is at the core of heteronationalism, where insisting on "authentic" Arab values, identities, and practices operates as a strategy to resist assimilation and colonial erasure. Heteronationalism calls on cultural authenticity to restore a postcolonial Arab subject to its "pure" precolonial Arab status via policing gender and sexuality. Authenticity is thus a laden and nuanced subject for ethnic minorities.

I suggest we reject authenticity as the defining metric of Arab identity and look to sahq for new ways to imagine Arab subjectivities. As we have seen, for queer Arabs in/authenticity is often wielded to label some sexual practices as foreign to the culture: usually same-sex desires and practices, alongside their attendant "Western" identities (e.g., gay, lesbian). The idea that sexuality can render subjects in/authentic operates in the diaspora and in the homeland—where queerness marks an overly assimilated Arab subject in the former and a traitor or failed cultural subject in the latter. In claiming nonnormative gendered and sexual desires and practices, queer subjects are then faced with the threat of not being Arab enough or with being too queer to be Arab (and often too Arab to be queer for other queers). In other words, according to the politics of cultural authenticity, queer subjects aren't "real" Arabs. The threat/enactment of cultural erasure can have intense negative psychological and physical impacts on queer Arabs in both ancestral and diasporic contexts. Of course, threats of violence and erasure are not limited to categorically queer subjects per se and can be invoked anytime Arabs walk outside the lines of what is deemed "authentic" Arab culture.

As a relation produced through friction, sahq articulates an Arab identity that does not necessitate erasure or opposition to other minorities both within and without that identity. Instead, sahq is only achieved through the cumulative, through the contact between groups that might otherwise be erased in order to arrive at an authentic "Arab" subject. Rejecting authenticity as a metric of Arab identity is daunting because it risks subjects becoming abjected from their cultural, social, and familial homes. Rejecting authenticity is also difficult because it asks subjects to think critically about how they define their Arab identity and how that script might be rewritten without recourse to gendered and sexual norms. Because sahq is a formation in tandem—an act performed between subjects—it emphasizes the relations between subjects rather than the singular identity of the sahaqiya. As an attention to the in between, sahq allows for cultural shifts as peoples, texts, and institutions travel transnationally. I am thinking here of course about queers but also about diasporic Arabs, Black or Afro Arabs, and Arab-adjacent groups who often experience the impact of anti-Arab racism and/or Islamophobia though they might not identify with said groups.

Sahq rejects authenticity, a bounded project, and directs us to relationality, an evocative one. In rejecting cultural authenticity as the primary metric of Arab and/or queer identity it is not my intention or desire to offer a definition of Arab that could resolve the heady debates I outlined in my introduction. Instead of insisting on a set definition, I suggest that Arab becomes as multifaceted and diverse as the bodies that claim it. The texts of this chapter, and the book overall, reveal how Arabness and queerness are mutually constituted. They show how queerness is intersected, in tandem, and essential to articulations of Arab identity. Sahq resists upholding a narrow heteronormative authenticity by recognizing already extant queer strains within the culture, as evinced in its medieval etymology.

Sahq's sensorial and physical description underlines its directive toward transnational collectivity. Sahq is a tactile, intimate act that is only possible between two bodies. It is a generative, fricative relation between subjects that is driven by sensation. Each chapter before this has emphasized queerness as a relation to heteronormativity and power and highlighted the transnational organization of Arab queers. As it exists within the framework of sahq, the transnational collective is thus both descriptive and directive. To flesh out sahq, I draw on the work of Amber Jamilla Musser and Keguro Macharia. In her works on sensual excess and flesh, Musser notes that attending to fleshiness allows us to see the materiality and movement of the body without recreating it as essential.[5] In concentrating on fleshiness, we can access the specificity of the raced and gendered body without defining it categorically. This is especially useful for us in thinking about queer Arab subjects who, as I have noted previously, may or may not articulate their sexual practices and intimacies into a coherent and categorical identity. The fleshiness of sahq encourages us to consider the multiplicity of bodies and that which is generated between them—as Musser states, a self that coalesces into openness rather than fixity.[6] In this instance, transnational collective organizing refers to how queer Arab communities are constituted across, around, and through national boundaries: that which is generated between, a collective that coalesces into openness rather than fixity. We saw the expansive movement of Arab culture and texts, affective and conceptual kinds of bodies, in chapters 1 and 2, in the circulation of Scheherazade and Golden Era films. Sahq as transnational collectivity shows us how queerness emerges in the movement of Arab culture between people as well as the movements of people themselves.

Sahq, with its emphasis on bodies in relation, helps us to see queerness in the Arab context as not a sexual identity only or exclusively (a description), but rather as a strategy of filiation (a direction). Writing on frottage, Macharia invites us to consider how relations of proximity, both desirable and painful, can disrupt heteronormative tropes of the Black diaspora.[7] He uses frottage to explore the conceptual and affective proximity between bodies, how the rub and press of bodies against one another "might offer a richer, queerer account of how diaspora functions as intimacy."[8] Rather than produce the diaspora via genealogy, these relations of proximity offer new ways to think and feel racial identity. As I explored in the introduction and throughout, it is difficult to articulate how we might come to define any one of the key subject terms of this study: queer Arab women. The construction of queer Arab lives and identities (such as they are), as well as the sexual freedom of queer subjects in any location, is predicated on the collaborative and collective organizing of those subjects across national and cultural lines. The transnational, fricative emergence of queerness and queerness as a liberatory project was particularly evident in chapter 4, in the discussion of activist-published accounts of queer Arab life in Lebanon and Palestine. In those accounts the writers' and editors' struggle with language, naming, and location indicated a double, sometimes triple consciousness from which they lived and imagined their queerness. In response, the activist organizations resisted homonational determinations of identity and focused instead on creating community projects and solidarity building with multiple kinds of minority subjects, across geographic and linguistic boundaries. While the transnational does not erase the national project itself (as we will see with the case of Nöl Collective and its efforts in Palestine), constructing a transnational collective recognizes the limited efficacy of isolated national projects, particularly in the case of the "Arab world," which continues to be impacted by colonial reverberations and ongoing Western imperialism wherein many postcolonial and independent Arab nations fail their queer and nonnormative subjects via a commitment to heteronationalist patriarchy. Transnational allows space from which to join subjects based not on national identity but instead, queerly as Cohen tells us, via their relationship to various oppressive gender and sexual normative structures, structures which include, but are not limited to, the state.[9] Queerness in an Arab context is produced in transit, transnationally.

Thus far I have suggested that sahq operates as a description for queer Arab life as well as a directive against authenticity politics and toward transnational collective organizing. Now I foreground the "vulgarity" of sahq and of grinding as a sexual act to urge us to reject respectability politics. I somewhat jokingly refer to sahq as aromatic scissoring, but in truth this interpretation brings us firmly back to Black or Brown bodies that have been othered both in the exotification of their bodies, hair, and skin and in the outright hostility at "ethnic" foods/bodies that "stink." These bodies are also rendered sexually deviant, either overtly sexual or impossibly repressed. Sahq reminds us that at stake in our queer organizing and actions against heteronormativity and patriarchy is not an idyllic, "respectable" future where "Arab queers are just like white ones" or "Arab queers are just like straight people." At stake is the radical freedom of such Black and Brown subjects.

Sahq describes and directs us toward a rejection of respectability. I draw the concept of respectability politics from Black feminist and queer radical critique. In Black feminist theory, Evelyn Brooks Higginbotham coined the "politics of respectability" to discuss the Black Baptist church in the progressive era. Higginbotham notes how some African American social and political actors promoted certain ideals, like politeness and purity, as reform strategies. As examples of "uplift politics," she suggests these strategies were aimed both at African Americans to encourage them to be respectable and at white communities to convince them of Black respectability.[10] Despite challenges and criticisms of the practice, in many ways respectability offered Black women especially one means by which they navigated hostile public spheres and the violence they experienced therein.[11]

In queer critiques, respectability is at best a stratagem or tactic and at worst a way of life, which refers to attempts by LGBT communities to assimilate or fit into straight sexual cultures. In *The Trouble with Normal*, Michael Warner articulates respectability as a response to gay shame, an affect that both haunts and bedrocks queer life.[12] In "Thinking Sex," Gayle Rubin narrates how heteropatriachal culture's sex negativity positions LGBT communities in an immoral sexual hierarchy, wherein movements toward "normal" sexual practices like marriage and monogamy might reform their moral failure.[13] Thus, respectability was an attempt to mitigate the violence and exclusion LGBT people faced, particularly in the 1980s–1990s, as the community reeled from the dominant culture's malignant neglect of and outright hostility toward the AIDS crisis.

For Arab communities, the topic of respectability comes to the fore within Western nations in the discursive construction of Good versus Bad Muslims in the post-9/11 context. "Bad" Muslims or Arabs are those who have failed to assimilate enough to erase their permanent foreignness and/or are impossibly yoked to terrorism by virtue of their Muslimness.[14] "Good" Arabs and Muslims are those whose ethnic or religious identity is superseded by their fidelity to the Western nation-state who explicitly and actively disavow "extremist" Muslim groups, and who practice Islam in a digestible fashion for non-Muslim onlookers. They might also be Christian and use that religious difference to distance themselves from other Arab or Muslim communities. As in the previous examples, respectability attempts to mitigate violence experienced by Arabs and Muslims at the hands of colonial and imperial nations while creating dangerous divisions among them.

Yet, respectability does not produce safety for communities of color or queer communities, and particularly does not for Black and Brown queer subjects at their intersection. Responses to Higginbotham's work note how respectability might function as class policing. Respectability "tended to reinforce status distinctions within the African American community. These distinctions were about class, but they were defined primarily in behavioral, not economic, terms. By linking worthiness for respect to sexual propriety, behavioral decorum, and neatness, respectability served a gatekeeping function, establishing a behavioral 'entrance fee,' to the right to respect and the right to full citizenship."[15] Similarly, in LGBT communities, the turn toward respectability often results in what Duggan calls homonormativity.[16] Homonormativity describes an LGBT subject who imagines their subjectivity aligns with the hegemonic in all ways except sexual orientation (e.g., white, cis, abled, middle-class who just happens to be gay). Within queer communities, the further subjects stray from this ideal, the less palatable they are to mainstream (or even some gay and lesbian) contingents, the less protected they become by the already insufficient safety nets in place for queer people.

Though some modes of respectability might act in resistance or produce safety for some subjects, it is often the case that respectability leaves behind some of the most vulnerable members of any given community. Respectability leaves behind members of the community who cannot, will not, or do not perform respectability: the housing insecure, sex workers, those with HIV/AIDS, "nonpassing" trans people, nonbinary people, visible Muslims, effeminate men. Respectability creates within minority communities "good" and "bad" examples of the culture. Unfortunately, respectability neither addresses the underlying economic, legal, or other structural disparities that impact minority communities nor does it "save" those respectable practitioners. In *Beyond Respectability*, Brittney C. Cooper theorizes respectability as an inherently bodied process that produces gender for Black women who were stripped of it during slavery. She suggests that respectability can route humanity back into Black and Brown bodies, sometimes via gendered and sexual performance. In our case, respectability might attempt to bring humanity back to Arabs and Muslims through an ethnonational alignment with the US settler colony or Arab nationalist paradigm. As with the cultural politics of authenticity, respectability relies on distancing oneself from gendered and sexual stereotypes that have been damning for the community, but in turn, that distance can abject vulnerable, nonnormative community members.

The work of sexual liberation and queer futures relies then on the refusal of respectability as the benchmark for which subjects deserve to live freely and which subjects do not. I suggest we reject here the Scheherazadian version of Arab femininity outlined in chapter 1. Instead of attempting to assuage the dominant culture with assimilatory gestures—be good minorities who lose their accent and internalize white supremacy or be good gays who keep it in the bedroom with their husbands—sahq calls for the rejection of respectability for women and queers on the whole. It embraces sex and sex work, flamboyance, bodily autonomy. It is aromatic scissoring, a loud, pungent act that takes up space. Sahq neither requires nor recommends subjects take up traditional normative iterations of their identities in order to fit in with or appease the dominant community. Rejecting respectability allows for more expressions of gender and sexuality that fail to clearly align with iterative sexual identities, a process that has already seen purchase in queer Arab communities (see chapters 3 and 4).

Because sahq is so literally grounded in the body, because it emphasizes the relation between bodies, it can challenge the damages of respectability on a few fronts. Here sahq's description and direction are entwined: the attention to the "vulgar" body breaks the cultural taboo on frank discussions of sex and gender. Second, through its emphasis on sexuality and as a description of friction, it reminds us to think about bodies in relation. Through the frame of sahq, we can prioritize sexual and gendered education as a cultural necessity for all genders and sexual practices—not simply for nonnormative communities. Finally, because sahq relishes in the smell of sex, in the grind of bodies that work and live and fuck outside normative lines, it challenges the moral stigma of عيب (aib) and كلام الناس (kalam il nas) as justifications against sexual diversity, divorce, gender fluidity, and so on. "Aib" is an Arabic word that roughly translates to shame. Because of its ubiquitous usage, aib is best understood as a way to police behavior, particularly gendered and sexual behavior. It is also sometimes a means by which people delineate the public from the private; for example, it is aib to have romantic or sexual intimacy in public, even for heteronormative couples, because sex and romance are private constructions. When something is called aib, it is understood as shameful and reflects not only on the individual practitioner (usually women) but on the "reputation" of the family. Aib operates through a heteropatriarchal respectability economy where one must avoid anything aib to maintain respectability and be spared from kalam il nas (the people's talk).[17] Aib and kalam il nas are thus mechanisms of respectability that would police and limit nonnormative gendered and sexual expression. In short, by rejecting respectability, sahq resists queer Arab erasure.

Sahq reminds us, as I have throughout the book, that queerness is not restricted to that which resists heterosexuality; rather it is an opposition to heteronormativity and patriarchy, which are part cultural construction and part national infrastructure. Positioning identity formation and coalitional politics across national lines poses a challenge to national organizations in this study where the emphasis resides in the circuitry between nations rather than the individual "ends" of the transnational, the nations themselves. As such, emphasizing transnational collectivity is a queer project. Rejection of respectability is perhaps more evidently queer because it resists the hetero-normative construction of a respectable subject as the center around which politics are organized. Instead, it prioritizes proliferations of sexual discourse that prefer education, openness, and autonomy as the goals of sexual subject formation. Finally, I would suggest that since authenticity often relies on sexual and gendered expectations, particularly for the women in the culture, a refusal to engage in the cultural politics of authenticity disrupts those heteronormative directives. Sahq emphasizes new connections to and narrations of the culture by artists and writers that include but are not limited to homoerotic and same-sex iterations.

Sahq describes a queer Arab presence, and through transnational collective organizing and the rejection of respectability and authenticity politics, seeks a future where queers reject the old Orientalisms, Arab heteronational projects, and normative Western gay and lesbian culture. It is a future where Arab queers carve out new paths and traditions. As both a descriptive term for queer Arab cultures and a directive regarding how we might exist and resist, sahq links intimacy between bodies to collective and collaborative attempts at reeducating, disrupting, and shifting Orientalist and Arab cultural discourses about queer sexualities. In transnational collectives organized by subjects' relationship to power, the rejection of respectability and authenticity politics brings forward and addresses the needs of the most vulnerable members of the community, which includes queers but is not limited to them. We seek neither a whitewashed nor an assimilated queer Arab culture. We seek a sweaty, loud future where vulgarity is prized over respectability.

In the remainder of this chapter, I suggest that sahq is already at work in banat's creative and political labor. Sahq offers transnational Arab subjects a guide map to work against the limiting discourses of Orientalism, hetero-normativity, heteronationalism, and so on. Sahq produces a nonnationalist, anti-assimilationist, and sexually radical future for queer Arab subjects. As we continue, I urge readers to remember Scheherazade, our earlier feminine divining rod from which we determined normative expectations of Arab femininity and around which many Arab creatives organized their depictions of Arab women. The kinds of feminine subjects in this chapter stand in sharp contrast with the book's earliest study through their rejection of the respectability and authenticity Scheherazade symbolized. I turn now to artists and collectives whose work embodies the principles of sahq. In the following three sections I will discuss how *Bar Bahar*, Nöl Collective, and Maamoul Press practice sahq and advocate for transnational collectivity, the rejection of respectability politics, and the refusal of cultural authenticity.

"Ya Habibti Itlahlahi": Visualizing Pleasure
and Resistance in *Bar Bahar*

Maysaloun Hamoud's 2016 narrative film *Bar Bahar* presents women's intimacy as the most radical political act available, particularly for subjects
under national and heteropatriarchal state occupation. In this sense, the film
reasserts the primacy of women's intimacy discussed in chapter 2. It rejects
respectability and authenticity, and imagines transnational queer possibility.
Additionally, it asserts the importance of pleasure to our survival and futures.
Bar Bahar asks us how Arab women can live, and live well, amid the ongoing
assault on their mobility and freedom. The film follows three Palestinian
roommates, Laila, Selma, and Nour, who are living in Tel Aviv. Laila is a
lawyer representing Palestinians in Israeli courts. Selma is a queer DJ from a
conservative Christian family. Nour is a computer science undergraduate and
practicing Muslim. While the film uses each character's romantic entanglements as its guiding action, the intimate friendship between the women is
the film's central love story. At the same time, the film acknowledges and
constructs the social realities of Arab women's homoerotic life within Arab
communities. Though the queer character Selma ultimately chooses to leave
Palestine after a painful estrangement from her family because of her sexuality, the film's overall radical move is to reject heteronormativity and patriarchy writ large and focus instead on queer kinship, intimacy, and love for
and between banat.

Sahq is evident in the film first through its antinormative emphasis on
women and their friendships, and second through categorical rejection of
hetreropatriarchal respectability. Numerous mundane instances in the film
support the women's primacy toward one another: the first night Selma
meets Donia, her soon-to-be lover, she chooses to take a drunk Laila home
rather than go home with Donia; in an early scene, Selma fixes Laila her morning coffee; Laila picks up Nour from her home to help her move her things
back into the apartment after a brief hiatus elsewhere; all three regularly
share cigarettes, joints, and food. These everyday intimacies and small acts of
service are kinds of care work or access intimacy that mark a different mode
of ethical and interdependent relationship between intimates, particularly
those who lack heteronormative or biological ties to one another. In *Care
Work*, Leah Lakshmi Piepzna-Samarasinha suggests that these forms of intimacy are often performed by femmes and, rather than be undervalued or taken

for granted, are the fiber of our most radical relationships.[18] Like Piepzna-Samarasinha, I understand this intimacy as queer particularly because it challenges normative social structures that are more usually organized via sex and procreation, but at the same time, their relationship with one another is not homoerotic or sexual in nature (in this instance). As I did in chapter 2, I suggest this primacy between women resists heteropatriarchal imaginings of women's lives where they are in service to men and instead positions their relationship to one another as the primary focus. This repositioning has powerful effects.

Bar Bahar suggests that women's intimacy and care for one another is transformational work. Underscoring the transformative impact of the women's care for one another is a fun, fleshy scene in the film: during her stressful exams, Nour "shakes it off" with an impromptu dance party. At the start of the scene, Nour is home alone and tentatively puts music on during a break from her studies. She begins to dance and smile to herself. The scene is well lit and uses close-ups to emphasize Nour's smile and relaxed movements. Laila arrives home, sees Nour dancing, and joins her. The two dance and laugh with the music for the remainder of the song before flopping on to the couch, during which Laila asks Nour about herself, her plans for her future, and so on.

Bar Bahar uses intimacies and friendship between women to displace Orientalist framing of women's spaces. The dance scene cements Laila and Nour's friendship in the film. When Nour first joins Laila and Selma in their apartment, Nour is painted with a conservative brush. She is the only hijabi among them. When she first arrives at the house, Laila and Selma look down the stairwell at her—physically and metaphorically—taken aback by her appearance and her appearance at the house. The song playing during their dance, "Azza" by Yasmine Hamdan, is played once earlier in the film in a scene between Laila and Selma, the film's two original roommates and friends. Replaying the song during Laila and Nour's time together echoes the Laila and Selma scene and establishes their friendship. As in the Egyptian films of chapter 2, Laila's watching of Nour is rendered with wonder and love, and her position as spectator and then participant replaces both an Orientalist scopophilia organized around unveiling as well as a male gaze oriented toward men's pleasure. Because what follows Nour's dance is an actual insight into Nour's character, desires, and selfhood, the tokenization of her in an Orientalist or male gaze perspective is impossible. She is not an object in the film whose only purpose is for the spectator's pleasure. She is a vocal and dimensional character.

The portrayal of pleasure in this scene is an example of sahq, where Nour's rejection of respectability leads her toward her own pleasure. This scene also reminds us of the embodied nature of sahq: that it is enacted through the body and has tangible repercussions on how women experience and own their bodies. Nour and Laila rub against each other as roommates, but rather than antagonize, their friction leads Nour to "open up" over the course of the film—something she does in the safety of her apartment and friendships with Laila and Selma, and on her own timeline. Her "opening" serves her own fulfillment and not that of men or unveiling enthusiasts. Finally, within the arc of the film, the scene cements the women's friendship and sets the stage for Laila's unwavering support of Nour.

Bar Bahar predicates its enactment of transformational justice on the intimacy between women, rather than via recourse to legal or disciplinary structures. The strongest examples of the women's love for one another are tied to the central crisis of the film: Nour is raped by her fiancé, Wissam. Throughout the film Wissam has been given a religious, conservative edit, and on this particular evening he is railing against Nour's unwillingness to leave her current living situation. Wissam lectures her that her roommates are loose women, whores. Nour's resistance to Wissam's tyranny regarding her roommates is one rejection of respectability in the film. When she defends them, his anger erupts and he calls her a whore, like her roommates, before forcing himself on her. Meanwhile, Laila and Selma are out drinking, and Laila is exceptionally drunk. Rather than abandon her to head home alone, Selma leaves the company of a new paramour and takes Laila home, where they are met with the sobering image of Nour crying in the bathroom. They help her shower, hold her, cry with her. They care for her physically and emotionally. In the crucial moments, punished with violence from her "respectable" fiancé, Nour defends Laila and Selma against Wissam, and the women choose each other over other lovers, friends, or family. Nour's choice to defend her friends and refusal to capitulate to Wissam are direct rejections of respectability. In this sense, one of the lessons the film teaches us about sahq is that a rejection of respectability is a way to choose women and vulnerable people over heteropatriarchal "safety" or inclusion.

Because the film foregrounds Nour's desires over public opinion and respectability, it offers us an example of sahq. After the assault, the roommates plan to extricate Nour from her relationship with Wissam. Laila and Selma ask Nour what she wants and proceed from there. Laila seeks out Wissam's support as a pillar of his religious community. In their meetings, Wissam comes on to Laila, and Selma gets photographic evidence. Evidence in hand,

Nour demands an end to their relationship and forces Wissam to explain their breakup to her father. What Nour wants, it turns out, is extraction from Wissam, and this is what she gets. Nour's choice to end her engagement is an example of sahq's rejection of respectability, since broken engagements often leave a rough mark on women's reputations.

In rejecting respectability and rendering control back to the sexual assault survivor, *Bar Bahar* imagines other paths toward healing, freedom, and justice for women. Nour's choice of justice (freedom from Wissam) and her friends' support can tell us a great deal about how intimacy and care between banat produce agential subjects and new futures. In the film, Laila undergoes conservative drag in order to convincingly trap Wissam. Looking in a mirror as she prepares to head to Nour's hometown, she mutters to herself, "ما كنتش أعرف حالي ... مش سامع حالي" ("I don't recognize myself . . . I can't hear myself"). Laila tolerates this temporary erasure of self in service of Nour's needs, and this is contrasted by her refusal to do so for her boyfriend. When her erstwhile boyfriend requests a similar conservative drag in order to introduce Laila to his sister, Laila drops him. She refuses to change her appearance, often profane language choices, and habit of chain-smoking to make herself more respectable or conservative. The justice the women seek—not revenge, as some critics have suggested—is predicated on Nour's wants and needs, not a carceral or punitive system.[19] Though we cannot imagine what Nour might have done outside the realm of a heteropatriarchal society, that her roommates afford her this simple gift—the decision of how to manage her trauma—invites viewers to render agency back to survivors of violence rather than into other hands. The women's care for one another operates as a rejection of respectability; the film reveals how Wissam's respectability is an empty patriarchal endeavor that inevitably binds him.

The film also practices sahq via transnational collectivity and rejection of authenticity. Notably, *Bar Bahar* relocates oft-overlooked Palestinian women to the center of the Palestinian narrative. The film's opening scene features Selma DJing a very vibrant party with Laila and others in the crowd. The scene is remarkable because it establishes an oft-unheard story—Palestinian Arabs in Tel Aviv who are having a really good night. Against the dominant Orientalist or Arab nationalist representations of Arabs, the dancing, alcohol, music, and drug use set this group apart. Against Israeli erasure, *Bar Bahar* asserts the presence and authenticity of Arabs in occupied Palestine. *Bar Bahar* is a deeply Palestinian film. Though labeled "Israeli" in international circuits (Hamoud lives in occupied Palestine and holds Arab-Israeli citizenship), the film narrates its Palestinian identity through its language choice, its music, its use of Palestinian protagonists, its exploration of Palestinian landscapes, and its rejection of the Israeli version of Palestinian identity. By focusing on vibrant, diverse women who are not only alive but living, *Bar Bahar* rejects an "authentic" image of Palestinian life that corroborates either Israeli or Orientalist imaginations of Palestine—where Palestinians are dangerous suicide-bombing men, sobbing victims of violence, or trapped in their own extremist cultures.

The styling and narrative of Selma's character performs sahq by refusing to allow "authenticity" to dictate her queer Arab identity. Selma is visually set apart as a pierced and tattooed DJ. Her day jobs—first a line cook and then a bartender—seem to be a way to pay the bills for her truer passion in music. Selma is also very busy thwarting multiple marriage plots, convincing her parents she is simply picky rather than queer. During a family dinner with a new potential fiancé, Selma brazenly brings her current girlfriend home and her mother witnesses them kissing in the kitchen. Her mother informs her father, and her Christian parents turn, kick out the girlfriend, and attempt to trap Selma in the hopes of sending her off somewhere to be cured. Selma escapes from her parents' home during the night and makes the decision to leave Palestine entirely to pursue her career in Berlin.

This portrayal of Selma allows us to consider how authenticity is an intersected cage: first, it isn't only her sexuality that drives her out of Palestine. It's the economic and social realities. Selma quits her job as a line cook after being scolded by the management for speaking Arabic. She gets her job as a bartender from a Western-looking man who thinks it's "cool" that she's Palestinian. Selma's choice to leave Palestine is not only then about her experiences as a queer woman, but inextricably about her experience as a Palestinian queer. It's not that she cannot find love with a woman—she can and does. It's that she cannot seem to live at all—in her profession, as a Palestinian, with her family. As a Palestinian queer, Selma's life is foreclosed in Tel Aviv, the pinkwashed alleged liberal democracy of Israel. Her parents' rejection of her, while painful, stands in stark contrast to Nour's "conservative" Muslim parents' acceptance of the dissolution of her engagement with Wissam, who take her side unequivocally and throw Wissam out of their shop and lives. Selma's experiences underscore the messaging from *Haqi* and *Waqfet* in chapter 4: queer women's oppression in Palestine is intersectional and never simply a question of homophobia alone. Selma's choice to leave Palestine comes with a great deal of pain—loss of her family, her roommates, and the life she knows. She makes the choice to leave with the hope that another world is possible. In leaving, she becomes an explicitly transnational subject.

5.1 The closing scene of *Bar Bahar*: Selma, Nour, and Laila share a quiet moment.

Bar Bahar exemplifies sahq as it emphasizes the power of intimacy between banat in the face of a damning heteropatriarchal and settler oppression. In interviews about the film, Hamoud remarks that people who think every story has been told have forgotten that women's stories have not. She defends the film's "provocations" regarding drugs, morality, and sexuality and asserts the film is about women and the solidarities between them. She refutes the edict to exclusively narrate Palestinian lives by centering Israel.[20] The occupation of Palestine is part of the film, but the Palestinian women remain its protagonists. In a critique of patriarchy, the women choose one another. The film's closing scene underscores the centrality of their friendship. On the night of Selma's going away party, the women leave their bustling apartment independently and make their way up to the roof to spend time with one another. The film closes with a wide shot of them together against the night sky, sharing a cigarette. Their physical cohesion is both undeniable and ambivalent. We do not know what will come next, given Selma's upcoming departure, but we do know that for now, their solace derives from each other. The protagonists experience many kinds of violence and meet it not by capitulating but by forming genuine bonds with one another. *Bar Bahar* amplifies sahq's messages of collectivity and anti-respectability as it underscores women and women's intimacy as a path toward love and freedom. Like *Bar Bahar*, Nöl Collective challenges authenticity and respectability and imagines a transnational collective community.

"Every Rose Has Its Thowra":
Nöl Collective in Palestine and Beyond

In this section, I discuss how Nöl Collective exemplifies sahq through its transnational formation, its challenge to gender and sexual normativity, and its construction of dynamic Palestinian subjects. Nöl Collective is a Palestinian clothing production company with a social justice focused mission.[21] The brand celebrates femininity as a source of strength. Significant to Nöl Collective's mission is how it produces its clothing and to what end its profits are used. Specifically, Nöl Collective describes itself as an intersectional feminist and political fashion collective based in Ramallah, Palestine.[22] Nöl Collective works to challenge gender oppression in Palestine and resist fast fashion through local and ethical production. It also hosts events and runs education campaigns in the community. Nöl Collective achieves this mission in a few ways. First, design and fabrication of products occur by Palestinian artists and manufacturers. The company's apparel is produced in Gaza by a family-run factory and shipped from Gaza to Palestine and beyond. Nöl Collective also works with a women's cooperative in Beit Duquu to produce jewelry, as well as other factories and makers in the occupied West Bank. By centering production in Gaza and other occupied Palestinian cities, Nöl Collective pushes material gains back into its communities and finds bigger audiences for Palestinian artisans and factories. Through production policies it also challenges fast fashion and disposable labor. Profits from sales get redistributed to the local industry. Nöl Collective's labor and profit distribution mobilizes a transnational collective community to reallocate resources to local economies.

How Nöl uses its profits in the community demonstrates another facet of sahq: challenging gender and sexual normativity via the refusal of respectability. A portion of company profits go toward Nöl Collective's multiple social education and awareness campaigns; the most prominent of these is its Menstruation Education Campaign (MEC). MEC is an example of sahq through its challenge to respectability. Using 10 percent of sales proceeds as well as individual donations, Nöl Collective produces menstruation education materials for adolescents at puberty. It created a guidebook to menstruation and distributed it along with pads and other materials.[23] The guidebook is itself of note: rather than a sterile illustration with unrelatable figures and images, the guidebook uses colloquial Arabic, warm colors, and floral diagrams that animate reproductive organs and processes more joyfully.

This works directly against the silence and misinformation about menstruation and reproductive processes that Palestinian women and girls usually experience.[24]

The MEC initiative and education process is a rejection of aib and its attendant respectability. By openly educating girls about menstruation and recasting the process in more approachable language and illustration, Nöl Collective asserts openness and positivity against the dominant messaging around women's bodies in public. Teaching adolescents (mostly girls but not exclusively) about these processes is an initial step in changing the notion that menstruation is a secret or shameful process, and it categorizes it as worthy of frank discussion. Making menstruation an open, transparent bodily function is an example of sahq's direction against respectability, which erases and silences women's bodies.

At the same time, MEC practices sahq by rejecting an Arab cultural authenticity rooted in girls' behaviors and policed through aib. In other words, if authenticity rests on gendered performances, then rejection of aib, which polices gender, also rejects normative iterations of Arab identity. Instead, Nöl Collective offers a different Palestinian woman narrative: emphasizing transparency and banats' bodily autonomy through knowledge and access to materials. To arrive at an embodied, self-aware subject, girls are encouraged to reject the idea that ignorance about their bodies is the respectable Arab status quo. Instead, the girls become themselves through their embrace of their not-so-dirty secrets. MEC makes a seemingly private topic, policed through aib, a public and less shameful one.

Like sahq, MEC also undermines respectability by emphasizing physicality and women's bodily autonomy. Part of the MEC includes a T-shirt with the words بلا عيب (bela aib) on it around a line drawing of a body with breasts and a vagina. "Bela aib" translates literally to "without shame" and figuratively to "forget shame" or "pffft shame." The shirt underlines the message of the workshop, where aib is replaced with open knowledge and representation of women's bodies. Similarly, another piece is embroidered with the text سمعتي ذهب الزبالة مش شغلك (Sumaatee ~~thahab zibala~~ mish shuglak/My reputation is ~~gold garbage~~ none of your business). The strikethroughs go over the white embroidered text with a pink slash. While girls' and women's reputations are subject to a great deal of scrutiny and oversignified with familial and cultural "honor," Nöl Collective reclaims their bodies and lives from public space and returns them to the wearer. This is a useful moment to remember the physical and embodied dimensions of sahq, where a rejection of respectability impacts one's experience and ownership of one's body. Further, because the shirt uses first person, it can be worn by users of any gender expression and is modeled as such, underscoring how aib and kalam il nas relate to many kinds of bodies.

The reputation tees also construct a dynamic Palestinian subject that resists essentialism and authenticating projects. The use of embroidery on the tees can be seen as a tribute to تطريز (tatreez/Palestinian embroidery), and it underscores the ways Nöl Collective reclaims Palestinian cultural legacy and narrates it to include multiple kinds of contemporary Palestinian identities. This is aligned with its interest and investment in historical Palestinian textile practices, evident in their name Nöl (loom).[25] At Nöl Collective, the use of tatreez, which historically only appears on women's clothing, doesn't reify a dated gendered binary but becomes open to multiply gendered subjects. In this way, Nöl Collective performs sahq in its joint rejection of gendered authenticities and respectability.

Another way Nöl Collective pushes against respectability politics is through its cultural education campaign, supported by products and community workshops. Many of Nöl Collective's shirts, bags, and other items take common turns of phrase and highlight women's significance within them, or alternately subvert normative tropes about femininity to reclaim and rewrite feminine scripts from suppression to empowerment. The hallmark example is "not your habibti." Habibti is an endearment that translates to "my love" or "my dearest." Because Arabic uses feminine articles, habibti refers to women and femininity, versus habibi for men and masculinity. The T-shirt addresses a broad "you," proclaiming the wearer is no person's love or dear, rejecting the notion of women and their bodies as subject to public policing. Another example, "Every Rose Has Its ثورة" (thowra), plays off the English "Every rose has its thorn." "Thowra" is the Arabic word for revolution. The switch thus transforms the negative association of "thorn"—wherein beauty has a painful cost—to "thowra," wherein the feminine rose experiences a revolution. What that revolution entails, whether it be around beauty standards, Palestinian liberation, or women's oppression, is available for the wearer's decree. Copy on the sale page of the tee offers this interpretation: "This is our response to men on the street who call women 'warda,' which is the Arabic word for 'flower,' and usually implies delicacy or vulnerability. The phrase 'every rose has its thorn' has been transformed into 'every rose has its thowra' which in Arabic means revolution to illustrate that women are not to be underestimated."[26] Nöl Collective thus uses fashion to interrupt catcalling on one level, and on a broader level, implications about women's roles and significance in public spaces. Here sahq lives in the queering of normativity and in the delightful movement from feminine beauty to beautiful feminine revolutions.

Another example of how Nöl Collective rejects heteropatriarchal respectability and authenticity is in its turn against cis-normative renditions of women's identities. Nöl Collective curates a distinctly Palestinian subject whose authenticity is not measured by its modeling of normative gender roles, but rather an engagement with feminist pasts and an accountability to a feminist/feminine future. This turn is evident and can be read in its هي المستقبل (hiyal mustaqbal) line. Hiyal mustaqbal translates to "She is the future." This nonessentialist take on "the future is female" includes subjects who identify with femininity rather than asserting a biological identification. Nöl Collective's attempt to offer less binary-gendered representations of Palestinians is also apparent in its production of unisex clothing options and in its choice to use men to model shirts with distinctly feminine suffixes and phrases adorning them. For example, one T-shirt is printed with poppy flowers (indigenous to Palestine) and the words موءددة محررة (mouadida mouharira, which means "buried free"). The copy on the tee suggests Nöl Collective is attempting to draw attention to the plight of female infanticide. By having men model the shirt, it offers opportunities for many groups, not only childbearing ones, to identify with and support femininity and feminist causes. Additional pieces feature quotes from famous Palestinian writers like Fadwa Touqan and Mahmoud Darwish. Like the use of tatreez, the use of indigenous Palestinian flowers and reference to Palestinian writers takes an "authentic" cultural touchstone and signifies it for a more capacious representation of Arab gender identities.

This dynamic construction of a Palestinian subject not conscribed by authentic limits also contributes to the deconstruction of gender and sexual norms for Palestinian femininity. Nöl Collective's models portray gender diversely, and it does not designate gendered versions of the clothes (or name if the models are men, women, cis, trans, nonbinary). It also features models of multiple sizes and models with different skin colors (black, olive, white). Because authenticity is often measured through both gendered normativity and specifically racialized subjects, the impact of this diversity is to imagine multiple kinds of Palestinian bodies and presentations and undermine the monolithic representation of Palestinians that does not include Black people. Moreover, I would suggest that the dominance of feminine and femme of center representations on the page does a certain kind of representational work around images of Palestinian femininity that have usually been represented as tragic, stuck in time, violent, or subdued. The models in the campaigns stare directly into the camera. They may or may not wear hair covers. They may have piercings, tattoos, straight or curly hair. They look, frankly, like contemporary young adults and thus offer a rupture of the saturation of static images of Palestinians or representations of them as dead or near-death subjects.[27]

Another aspect of Nöl Collective that aligns with sahq is its attendance to transnational organizing. For example, Nöl Collective attempts to fundraise for Palestinian youth across national boundaries. It calls other communities into service of Palestine while it supports initiatives beyond Palestine through sharing their calls for donations and raising awareness around their stories. Before its platform became primarily clothing-based, Nöl Collective (again, as Babyfist) also conducted workshops in the United States and Palestine around sexual violence, assault, and healing through its "Typewriter Project." During these workshops, Nöl Collective founder Yasmeen Mjalli typed up stories shared with her by various women about gendered oppression and sexual misconduct.[28] She collected and shared these stories on social media (Nöl has 52,800 followers on Instagram at the time of this writing), in exhibitions, and potentially in a forthcoming book. This project, like the MEC, puts vulnerable community members at the center of the practice and asks interlocutors to be accountable to them in a different capacity: by witnessing, by contributing to mutual aid, by raising awareness.

Nöl Collective fosters transnational collective engagement with Palestinians by speaking to its broad diaspora. The community Nöl Collective created around its brand is mobilized in a number of useful ways. For example, early in the COVID-19 crisis, Nöl Collective used its factory contacts and large consumer base to raise money for mask production in Gaza, which was/is severely underresourced for such a crisis. In a matter of days, Nöl Collective raised over $33,000 for mask production in Gaza, which eventually led to the distribution of approximately 62,000 masks to refugee camps and to sanitation and hospital workers in April 2020. The capacity to make an abrupt pivot in production is enabled by Nöl's personal connections with production industries and its established consumer base. On the one hand, the necessity for Nöl Collective's intervention in personal protective equipment for Palestinians witnesses the oppressive apparatus of the Israeli state, which denies fundamental care to Palestinians, particularly Gazans—an apparatus that is omnipresent and thrown into sharp relief during crisis. At the same time, Nöl Collective's capacity to meet some of the extraordinary needs of Palestinians during the crisis emphasizes the significance and utility of transnational collective organizing in the face of extraordinary obstacles.

Nöl Collective's processes of production, its community education and accountability, and its investment in challenging Palestinian heteropatriarchy and Israeli apartheid model the tenets of sahq: transnational collective organizing and the rejection of authenticity politics and respectability politics. Nöl Collective's work models ways to resist dominant scripts about Arab identity and offers strategies for imagining and producing a more equitable and queer community. Nöl Collective's sahq is not queer futurity as we are conditioned to see it in gay pride or visibility. It works at the root of Palestinian oppression, with people, with production, and with the occupied land to reorient Palestinians and Palestinian supporters to a new kind of Palestine: one where women are neither shamed nor repressed for their bodies, where people with multiple gendered identities work together toward social freedoms, where Palestine and its people are diverse and varied. Moreover, it works toward an anti-Zionist Palestine, in which Palestinians are able to create of and from their land and traditions, and cement their survival in an unoccupied future. Like Nöl Collective, our next collective, Maamoul Press, uses sahq-centered art practices to produce radical queer futures.

"A Woman's Voice Is a Revolution":
Maamoul Press and Transnational Queer Commons

Through its organization and the work it features, Maamoul Press takes an anti-essentialist and antinormative stance on gender and sexuality while constructing a sense of transnational community. Maamoul Press is a small multidisciplinary art collective that supports the production and circulation of creative works in the genres of comics, printmaking, and book arts. In response to an arts community that deprioritizes these genres and the marginalized communities that make them, Maamoul Press emphasizes "storytelling by us, for us"; "forging the arts spaces we need"; and "generating knowledge through community."[29] As such it is not only a space that responds to and challenges dominant representation to foreground inclusion, it is additionally attuned to how dominant representation is often inaccessible or impossible for minority communities. Maamoul Press uplifts lateral learning, community-based knowledge and skill share, and works that do not require elite or otherwise inaccessible art practices. Through its platform it not only offers a venue for emerging and established artists but imagines a creative community in fellowship—an alternative commons, one that works against and supersedes structural, national, and oppressive barriers of artistic creation. At present, Maamoul Press names three cofounders: Leila Abdelrazaq, Aya Krisht, and Zeinab Saab, in addition to twenty-one artist members. The twenty-four members of Maamoul Press hail from multiple locations, are of varying ethnic and racial descent, include diverse gendered and sexual expression, and represent multiple religious backgrounds. In this sense, Maamoul Press embodies the ethos of transnational collective organizing and, within its mission, highlights the significance of holding diasporic and home artists alongside one another as a salve to fractured community. Within its diverse roster it aims to allow artists to tell their own stories rather than allow discourses like Orientalism and racism to narrate them. Maamoul, an Arab pastry, also emerges from the root word عمل ('amal), meaning work or action. The choice of an Arabic signifier and a name that necessitates process underscores how Maamoul Press creates the community that it seeks to represent. At the same time, the emphasis on 'amal recognizes that the work of community is indeed work. Maamoul Press reminds us of sahq as practice, as grind.

Maamoul Press practices sahq through its refusal of authenticity as the central metric of Arab identity. Even in its overarching framework, Maamoul Press works to disrupt the notion of recounting an authentic Arab subject and instead favors a collaborative organization of community that shares political, social, and cultural investments. Maamoul Press is explicit in resisting the notion of a predefined community "monolith" and instead emphasizes one forged in opposition to "racism, sexism, homophobia, zionism, Islamophobia, classism, and other forces of oppression that seek to keep us silenced and marginalized."[30] The membership roster underlines this commitment to a vibrant and nonessentialist community identity. The commitment to thinking about Arab community inclusive of diaspora and Arab nations is also evident in the use of Arabic and English on the website. As I noted in the introduction, one site of contention with regard to the "authenticity" of diaspora Arabs is whether those living outside Arab nations can speak, read, or write Arabic. The absence of fluency in the language is often taken to reveal diaspora Arabs' inauthenticity. Maamoul Press uses Arabic and English to explain the press name and lists many of its prints and book titles in both Arabic and English. As in Nöl Collective, the use of multiple languages on the site and in some of its art allows participation by multiple kinds of creators and consumers, whose recognition of the work and organization as relevant to them comes not through language mastery or even identification with Arab identity but via other kinds of identification: with the topic, with the mission, with the artists.

I want to look at some of the texts published by the press as case studies for the collective, anti-essentialist, and anti-respectability approach Maamoul Press takes. First, I want to discuss the print "صوت المرأة ثورة" ("A Woman's Voice Is a Revolution") by Lina Habazi. It emerged from a contest Maamoul Press held in 2017 under the theme "Resisting Orientalism" in which a call was circulated to artists on various digital platforms to submit a print that Maamoul Press would produce and sell. Habazi's print emphasizes sahq through its rejection of respectability and authenticity. As the press's first (and currently only) contest, the selection of "A Woman's Voice Is a Revolution" encapsulates some of its political and creative commitments. The winning print features a feminine-presenting figure dressed in a ثوب (thowb), an embroidered garment that Palestinian women wear. She is wearing large hoop earrings, her hair is down, her nose is broad. She has full eyebrows and freckles or acne. She is taking a knee, with one arm at her side and another resting on the knee. Her gaze meets the viewer directly, though her head is slightly turned. The phrase "A Woman's Voice Is a Revolution" is written in Arabic along the right of the print, which is done in black, white, and red (all traditional tatreez colors). Prominent in the frame is the woman's right foot, which juts forward in her crouched stance. On it she wears a recognizable white Adidas sneaker with three black stripes along its sides. The pairing of the thowb, quote, color scheme, and sneaker is a direct volley against Orientalist representations that mire Arab women into silent, dying, or oppressed figures. This figure is wholly of the present, with her hoops and sneakers. Her sneakers and earrings make her a cross-cultural, transnational figure, one unmoored from heteronational imaginings of an authentic, respectable Arab women. Here there is no Arab subject sealed into a past or wholly detached from it. She is neither in the "there" of the homeland or "here" of the diaspora. She is both. At the same time, she is also clearly and directly connected to her matriarchal past, via the reference to the thowb. As in the earlier discussion of Nöl Collective, the use of the thowb and tatreez colors resignify historical touchstones of Arab femininity for a new subject. Finally, her voice is the subject of the quote—and her voice is a revolution. Even in the image's silence, her gaze and stance speak volumes. To resist Orientalism here is not to become a pliant respectable subject but to become a defiant, present one who meets Orientalism and sexism with challenge.

The second Maamoul Press item that embodies sahq through its rejection of heteropatriarchal respectability is the "Love and Death" series by Aya Krisht. "Love and Death" consists of four black-and-white linocut prints featuring common Arabic phrases around love that have a macabre undertone. They include the English translations and a focal point illustration. The four phrases featured are "تقبرني؟" ("Touqburnee/Will you bury me?"); "بتدوبلي قلبي" ("Bitdowibli Kulbee/You melt my heart"); "بموت فيك" ("Bamoot Feek/I die in you"); and "انت عمري" ("Anta Omri/You are my life span"). The illustrations use flowers and hearts as the primary motifs. There are also human hands on two illustrations and human figures on one. The series comments on heteronormative expectations for love in an indirect manner. By invoking the literal meanings of the phrases with illustration, Krisht draws attention to the somewhat threatening and toxic undercurrent of romantic love as it is represented in Arabic idioms. Krisht also takes the most macabre translations for the work. For example, "Anta Omri" could easily translate to a still difficult but less evocative "You are my life," a sentiment that is expressed in heteronormative Western romance as well. Instead, Krisht leans into the morbidity of the sentiment, illustrating the piece with one hand dropping ashes into another. The remains of one life, one's life span, reduced to dust. "Bitdowibli Kulbee" features a loosely anatomically rendered heart with a flame, as though the heart is literally melting, its matter dripping down. In "Bamoot Feek," two bodies cross at their pelvises to form an X, and a small bouquet sits atop them. The illustration shows the bodies as though they are fused into one another, and the figures are falling backward in pain or surrender. Lastly, "Touqburnee" features two hands holding the handle of a shovel, which appears to be speared into the ground, cleaving a cluster of flowers. These abstract and simultaneously embodied renditions of love demonstrate how normative romance and sexuality are mapped and experienced on the body itself.

The "Love and Death" series challenges us to reconsider how we articulate intimacy and how it operates within our lives and to move away from the kind of sacrificial love the idioms evoke. Krisht's selection of the idioms and their literal translations paired with the beautiful but wrecked bodies offers a compelling take on romantic love that renders it as consuming, devastating, and in some ways fatal. Though Krisht may not have intended a critical rendition, the eerie quality of the prints causes viewers to consider more closely the kinds of love and sentiment we take for granted as "common" or "normal." Though most often applied to romantic love, these phrases might also be uttered between other intense intimates (a parent to their child, between friends). Even in these instances, the suggestion remains that love comes at the cost of the lover, and that rather than inspired or romantic, these iterations of feeling cause pause. I consider this gesture in the work nonnormative regarding intimacy, especially for seemingly respectable and normative iterations of love.

For Maamoul Press's books and comics, we begin with a comic that directly challenges respectability and authenticity as it is imagined for Arab women. Christina Atik's "مش حلو لبنت" ("Mish Hilu La Bint/It's Not Nice for a Girl") collects phrases frequently targeted at girls and women that attempt to discipline their behavior and model them into typical feminine subjects. The idea that it's "not nice" ties into our earlier discussion of aib and kalam il nas, where many women's behaviors and bodies are subject to policing via respectability and heteropatriarchal iterations of ideal Arab femininity. The title of the collection uses speech bubbles under each of the words to denote the presence of a third party saying the phrases. The speech bubbles are not closed, which allows Atik to imply the omnipresence and commonality of the phrases in common discourse. The collection's afterword suggests the series is inspired by "conversations that almost every woman hears from family and society, dictating how she needs to live, look, and act in order to be a proper woman."[31] Atik thus makes explicit the pressure and impact dominant norms have on the illustrations. Each illustration also uses an animal to deliver the phrases to the figures in the illustration. The nonhuman speaker reminds us how heteronormative discourses become woven into the social fabric so deeply they become part of our imagination of the "natural" landscape. The choice of the animal in each illustration and the illustrations of the figure juxtaposed offer a contradicting message and cause us to question the verity of the phrases offered.

On the front cover, there is also an illustration of a feminine figure with each word of the title as it appears in Arabic (three total). The image changes from right to left with the title. "مش" ("Mish/It's Not") features a figure on her knees with one hand on the ground and the other holding her face. "حلو" ("Hilu/Nice") features the same figure who has removed her hand from her face, placed it on the ground, and has begun to raise her head. "لبنت" ("La Bint/For a Girl") straightens the figure's back and raises her head, changing her gaze from the ground to look back at the other two figures. The subtle shift in the figure's posture from desolate to erect visualizes an embodied act of resistance or rejection of the prescriptions to her behavior. The sense of defiance carries through each illustration in the work and offers a strong example of the embodied nature of sahq as an activist practice, particularly when it involves the rejection of respectability.

As with Nöl Collective's critiques of aib, what is considered "not nice" here is inherently linked to women's autonomy over their lives and bodies. Atik's

5.2 The cover image of "Mish Hilu La Bint/It's Not Nice for a Girl." Image courtesy of the artist, Christina Atik.

illustrations find figures rejecting respectability and through that rejection delivering themselves back to pleasure and ownership of their bodily experiences. Atik's first illustration claims "مش حلو هالمنخار لبنت" ("Mish hilu hal munkhar la bint/This nose isn't nice for a girl") and pairs an image of a girl with a prominent nose and nose ring alongside two toucans. One of the toucans seems to glare at the girl while another looks on more gently from its perch on her shoulder. The glaring bird is delivering the news to the girl about her nose. The illustration pokes fun at the common beauty standard by implying the hypocrisy of the toucan's declaration given its own prominent beak. The second illustration uses a similar technique by having an owl, a nocturnal animal, deliver the edict "مش حلو لبنت تتأخر بالليل" ("Mish hilu il bint titakhar bil leil/It's not nice for a girl to stay out late") to a young woman on a scooter. The woman in the illustration looks at the owl from the corners of her eyes and smirks. These small facial details do a great deal to underline the absurdity of the edicts. A similar hypocrisy is used in another image where a torso grows trees and plants from which a goat is grazing. The goat tells her "مش حلو لبنت يكون عندها شعر" ("Mish hilu il bint ikoon 'andha sha'ar/It's not nice for a girl to have body hair"). Despite finding sustenance through the woman's body, the goat attempts to discipline it and tell her body hair is not nice. The placement of the foliage on the woman's breasts allows us to think through the various ways breasts are imagined as both sexual and maternal and thus reminds us of the double bind women must navigate regarding their embodiment, which is ultimately an impossible goal. In the illustration the woman's torso is the only thing visible, and her breasts arch up while her stomach concaves. The arched back and erect nipples in the illustration imply the woman is experiencing pleasure in her body despite the sanctions around it. As such, the illustration rejects respectability in favor of autonomy and pleasure.

One illustration rejects respectability and cultural authenticity when it is used to condemn same-sex desire between banat. In it, a crow pronounces, "مش حلو لبنت تحب بنت" ("Mish hilu il bint itheb bint/It's not nice for a girl to like another girl") to two banat. The women are gazing at one another out of the corner of their eyes despite their heads being turned away from one another. Their linked gazes and raised eyebrows offer an illicit tension between the two figures, wherein the bird is delivering the condemnation even as the bad behavior occurs underneath its beak.

On pleasure as the right of women rather than a source of shame, Atik is also clear. Another illustration features a disheveled figure wearing a slouching shirt laying on her back while a snake weaves through her limbs. The snake suggests, "مش حلو لبنت تقول شو بتحب" ("Mish hilu il bint tokoul sho bidha/It's not nice for a girl to say what she likes"). The use of the snake (a common phallic image), its placement, and the nudity of the figure take the comment to the sexual, chastising the woman for not only having sexual desires, but voicing them. The snake also invariably evokes Eve, who is punished for her desire for knowledge. The knowing of the girl in the image is thus as troubling as her articulation of her desires. When women voice or act on what they like in these illustrations, they are met with censure. But the illustrations show the women desiring in any case and push against the policing respectability (here "niceness") necessitates.

In many of Atik's illustrations, the use of the figure's gaze creates an intimacy between the reader and the illustrated girls. The gaze draws the reader into the subject's rejection of the animal and the edict it delivers. Importantly, in each illustration the girl is not an example of why it is "not nice" for the girl to do the thing, but rather the illustrations highlight the girl's success and pleasure in doing just that, despite the animal's concerns. As we saw in

5.3 "It's Not Nice for a Girl to Love Another Girl" in "Mish Hilu La Bint/It's Not Nice for a Girl." Image courtesy of the artist, Christina Atik.

Bar Bahar, the women's pleasure is itself a redress of respectability and draws the figures back into their bodies as autonomous subjects.

   In the complete illustrations of "Mish Hilu" only one image does not deliver the success of the girl doing the opposite of the edict, but it does see the figure reject shame and niceness as a necessary condition of women's freedom and healing. This image depicts a turkey vulture perched in a tree, informing her "مش حلو البنت تخبر حدا" ("Mish hilu il bint tokhbir hada/It's not nice for a girl to tell anybody"). The illustration is of a woman crouched on the ground with her face in her hands (a duplicate of the first of the three cover images). Here the girl's suffering highlights how the prescription "not to tell" actually results in her harm. In one of the more detailed drawings, the girl is cast in the shadow of the tree and the bird. But the girl is not completely shadowed. The top of her head is touched by the light, which is indicated through a color change in her hair (red in the light, dark auburn in the shadow). Because this image is a double of the cover, we can imagine her in the cover sequence. We know her posture will change and become more assertive, which will bring light to her face. The sequence, plus the use of light in the image, allow us to imagine how the girl will "bring to light" whatever occurred to her and in that telling reject or recover from some of the pain of the silence, the event, and the edict against speaking. Like Nöl Collective's emphasis on transparent menstrual education, here Atik rejects niceness, respectability, and shame as the private means by which women's bodies and suffering are managed and perpetuated. The turn to speech is not about performance for an audience, but about allowing women's bodies and voices to occupy space, and in so doing, challenge heteropatriarchal violence.

In sum, the images and text in Atik's "Mish Hilu La Bint" offer resistance to dominant narratives around heteronormative femininity for Arab women and guide the girls within the illustrations toward pleasure and power in their refusal to comply. As one of Maamoul Press's earliest published texts, "Mish Hilu" establishes some of the collective's ethos and its commitment to challenging sexism and homophobia with its work, work that falls squarely within the queer labor of sahq, especially as it challenges respectability.

My last example of Maamoul Press's sahq is visible in Leila Abdelrazaq's short comic "The Fig Tree." "The Fig Tree" does the work of creating a transnational Palestinian community, rejecting respectability, choosing pleasure regarding gender and sexual expectations, and rewriting identity and community inclusion against cultural politics of authenticity. In it, the comic's protagonist uses the imagery of the fig, including its lush pink center, to narrate her exile from Palestine and the ways her matrilineal connections keep her tethered to her home and to her own pleasure. The story begins with a postcard from a friend visiting her family's ancestral home, to which the narrator is barred from returning. The narrator mourns her inability to access her home and wonders, "How do you keep alive the spirit of a place you never knew and can't go to?" The remainder of the comic answers this question. The narrator comments that traditions hold communities together and enable them to survive in hostile conditions. The illustration tells the story of one such tradition: the process of making tea. The narrator comments that the act of "reproducing" the culture often falls to women and child bearers. The comic illustrates an older woman teaching the narrator how to make tea and emphasizes the stirring of the tea. The gesture to stir the tea is then mimicked as the narrator masturbates. The two-page panel of her masturbating includes an illustration of a ripe fig being held and opened by a set of hands. The illustration also uses the same color of the fig, a rich pink (the only color in the black-and-white comic) for the color of the tea and the increased pleasure the narrator experiences as she continues to masturbate. The next two-page illustration is simply the image of a fig split in two, followed by an image of the narrator topless, smiling, with her eyes closed in ecstasy, awash in the pink of the fig. These images are coupled with the narrator's exposition, which suggests we should not assume feminine rituals like preparing tea are merely for outsiders, a kind of social obligation, but that the rituals might have been and continue to be in service of the women's own bodies and pleasures. Both the text and the illustrations in "The Fig Tree" claim an explicit feminine Arab heritage, one that is unashamedly linked to pleasure as both an inheritance and a survival mechanism. To illustrate and narrate masturbation so openly and name it as part of her Arab heritage challenges gender-normative notions of both cultural authenticity and respectability.

To elaborate on the embodied aspect of sahq and how it moves us toward queer futures, it is useful to consider how the fig tree functions symbolically within the text, given its history as an oversignified image. Figs have multiple meanings assigned to them. They can be read as hyperfeminine symbols, where the fig's elongated top, exterior skin, and sweet pink center represent a vagina, especially when the fruit is dissected. Abdelrazaq seems aware and engaged with this symbolism in the comic, particularly on pages 9–10, which depict the masturbation story panel and the fig splitting. The fig's pink interior with white seeds is also represented on the post-masturbation page, where the narrator lies against the pink and white, looking satisfied. But Abdelrazaq is quick to undermine the association of the fig, matrilineal descent, and pleasure with biological essentialism or equivocate the vagina with women's identities. The dedication of the comic uses a small illustration of an open fig and leaf along with the words "for all palestinian womxn, with or without pussies."[32] Despite then the use of the fig as evocation of the pussy, Abdelrazaq celebrates Palestinian trans and cis women together and does not excise trans women from feminine and matrilineal histories and inheritances. Maamoul Press rejects authenticity both in the experiential definition of Palestinian identity and in the explicit call to include all women against cis-normative exclusion.

As a metonym for Palestine, the fig offers a connection to Palestinian heritage without reifying exclusionary and essential definitions of Palestinian identity. The fig is one of the oldest fruit trees known to contemporary civilization, and indigenous to Palestine. Abdelrazaq's comic employs all these discourses associated with the fig. The knowledge the maternal figure shares

BUT WHAT IF, INSTEAD OF PERFORMING THESE RITUALS STRICTLY FOR OTHERS, WE DID THEM FOR OURSELVES?

FOR OUR OWN PERSONAL PLEASURE?

5.4 From "The Fig Tree." Image courtesy of the artist, Leila Abdelrazaq.

with her is both social and carnal, and in neither case a cause for shame, but rather a source of connection to her homeland and to pleasure. The fig and tea rituals depicted are also faith acts for the narrator, one of the ways she "keep[s] alive the spirit of a place [she] never knew and can't go to." Abdelrazak uses the fig as metonym for Palestine and its diaspora, creating a mode of identification with Palestine that is not reliant on traditional metrics of cultural authenticity. It attributes Arabness instead to inheritance and ancestry, a shared experience of the homeland that is possible in one's exile from or presence therein.

"The Fig Tree" is in many ways the perfect example of sahq: it features a heavily signified image with multiple competing discourses; it reclaims and rewrites the fig as a feminine and femme of center symbol of Palestinian history and resistance; it emphasizes the body and its movement, joy, and pain; it centers that pleasure as one way to connect to our past and fight for our future; it is "vulgar" in its explicit depiction of sexuality; it creates and imagines a transnational collective of trans and cis Arab women; it rejects respectability; and it offers new ways of imagining an Arab identity that do not rely on divisive and exclusionary authenticating metrics. These acts of imagining I locate within sahq precisely because they reject and repudiate normative gender and sexuality in pursuit of a capacious and joyful future.

All four of Maamoul Press's texts engage in a critical deconstruction of gendered and sexual norms in Arab cultures, some more directly and explicitly, like "The Fig Tree" and "Mish Hilu," and some by forcing the viewer to interrogate commonplace assumptions and reconsider normative thinking, like "A Woman's Voice" and the "Love and Death" series. The most remarkable aspects of Maamoul Press, in addition to its grassroots collective structure, is precisely how this structure enables a new version of Arab femininity, often a queer one, to emerge on its pages. I want to be clear that I do not know how many or if any of the Maamoul Press artists identify as queer. But their work as a collective upholds and enables a queer future by virtue of its capacity to interrogate the structures that would forbid it (such as heteronormativity), and in that interrogation opens space for queer subjects (both person and topic) to emerge. As we saw in chapter 4, rigid sexual definitions that are predicated on homosexual and heterosexual binary identities (gay, lesbian, etc.) are only useful insofar as individuals might find them such. Rather, what emerged in that chapter and is evident here is the utility of renegotiating gendered and sexual norms in Arab culture to allow a plethora of sexual and gendered expressions to emerge, with or without identity labels. I again assert that the radical work of women in this chapter is precisely their love for and accountability to women as the primary and most significant subjects of their community. The primacy of women's intimacy is evident in the individual texts of Maamoul Press, its mission, and its diverse roster of artists.

In short, Bar Bahar, Nöl Collective, and Maamoul Press are all examples of sahq in action, in movement toward queer futures. They imagine transnational Arab communities and collectives. They reject respectability. They narrate a nonessentialized view of Arab identity that does not recreate authenticity policing. These strategies, this sahq, challenge the erasure and rejection of queer Arab life by resisting heteronormative iterations of Arab identity and making space for queer Arabs to emerge. Ultimately, Bar Bahar, Nöl Collective, and Maamoul Press are geared toward a queer Arab future whose ethnic, sexual, and gender politics point toward collective liberation rather than community gatekeeping and social erasure. They do so by centering diverse voices, substantiating a future in which queer Arabs not only exist and experience pleasure, but whose existence, pleasures, and activisms are essential to a sexually free future.

☾

I chose sahq as the concluding chapter of this monograph because it offers concrete strategies for imagining queer Arab futures. While the first chapter emphasized limiting discourses, the second recuperated queer pasts, and the third and fourth investigated our queer present, sahq envisions queers and their kin at the forefront of our new world. In this trajectory, the work of this book has been threefold: First, to outline the multiple discourses and obstacles that obfuscate queer Arab subjects, particularly banat, femmes, and women. For banat, the horizon of possibility is egregiously eclipsed by essentialisms and nationalisms that abject queerness from Arab culture, by ongoing Orientalist erasure of a mobile and shifting Arab culture, and by blatant anti-Arab, misogynist, and homophobic sentiment in the Arab world and its diaspora. Despite the discursive and material threats that impact queer Arab life, it persists. As such, the second aim of this book has been to catalogue how queer Arab life can be located in heteronormative spaces and how queer Arabs animate and narrate themselves. *Between Banat* creates a queer Arab archive from which to begin to ground our histories and present. The archive itself is ambivalent, fluid, and gestural, much as queer sexuality appears in Arab cultures. Lastly, drawing on artists and creators who are both aware of the limiting discourses that frame queer Arab life and committed to representing it with joy and pleasure, the book offers sahq as the collection of the strategies and activisms necessary to hold and create a queer Arab future.

With its emphasis on transnational collectivity, sahq asks us to radically decenter the self and imagine a collective accountable to one another. In the midst of the ongoing violence and erasure visited on queer Arabs, we can use sahq to grind against heteronormative and national violence, to survive, and to imagine otherwise. For queer Arab subjects who already face disproportionate patriarchal and state violence, the mere act of existence is a radical and stubborn activism that enables futurity. With its rejection of respectability and authenticity, sahq urges us to not volley for tolerance, homonormativity, or heteronational inclusion. Homonormativity should not be the goal toward which queer Arabs organize. Arab national projects will sacrifice queer lives over and over. Western perceptions of queer Arab life will not hold us in our complete subjectivity, but rather will be overdetermined by new and old Orientalist tropes designed to other Arabs and Arab queers. Rather, our capacity to live and experience pleasure and joy are bound to one another, even and especially across a transnational spectrum. Our capacities to love and live rest on strident and unwavering interruptions of heteronormativity and its attendant respectability politics. Our capacity to imagine an Arab identity that does not rely on heteronormative exclusions is precisely the capacity to imagine a queer Arab future at all.

When we are stifled by limiting discourses, grow weary of the excavation process of our pasts, or continue to feel hemmed or unrepresented in the realities of right now, I suggest sahq can push us forward into a queer future. Following Muñoz, the future is itself a queer project.[33] Queerness is the insistence of the potentiality of another world: a world in which queer Arabs not only survive but thrive. A world where Palestine is free. A world where we are at home in the world and the world is a home for us. In the face of receding horizons of possibility for minority subjects—in almost every nation-state is a nation that seeks to disappear us—the task of rewriting the future is an essential one. But as Muñoz reminds us, it is not an optimistic or simple endeavor. It is sahq, a grind, work. It is not easy to form and maintain transnational solidarity in an increasingly fractured and isolationist world order. It is not easy to free our bodies from the self-correction of respectability, and to reject visiting it upon others, when for so long it has seemed hopeful to strive for respect. It is disorienting (pun intended) to pursue our identities without recourse to authenticating measures, to imagine our lives and stories are enough without the erasure of others. Yet we can. The archive of work in this book, and the work of this book, are attempts to teach us how.

notes

Introduction

1 Ngai, *Ugly Feelings*, 8.
2 Ahmed, *The Promise*, 121–59.
3 Alsultany, *Arabs and Muslims*, 71–99.
4 Georgis, "Thinking Past Pride," 233–51.
5 Nash, *Black Feminism*, 1–32.
6 Cvetkovich, *An Archive*, 1–14.
7 Arondekar, *For the Record*, 3–4.
8 Rodríguez, *Sexual Futures*, 6.
9 Muñoz, "Ephemera as Evidence," 6.
10 Arondekar et al., "Queering Archives," 213.
11 Arondekar, *For the Record*, 20.
12 Hartman, "Venus," 11.
13 This phrase comes from Scott, "The Evidence."
14 This phrase comes from Spivak, *In Other Worlds*.
15 Naber, "Introduction," 5.
16 Shohat and Alsultany, "Cultural Politics," 20.
17 For a discussion of the shifting name and political valence of such terms, see Cainkar, "Fluid Terror Threat, " 27–28.
18 As evidenced by countless studies that situate their research within the nation-state as subject.
19 The flattening of the national and ethnic diversity of the SWANA region to Arab and Muslim only is strident in the United States, particularly after 9/11. For commentary on this, see Abdulhadi, Alsultany, and Naber, *Arab and Arab*

American Feminisms; Chan-Malik et al., "A Space for the Spiritual"; and Asultany, Arabs and Muslims. For more on the racialization of Arabs in the United States specifically, see Gualtieri, Between Arab and White; and Jamal and Naber, Race and Arab Americans.

20 For an example outside the United States, we need look no further than France and its Islamophobic ban on veils.

21 Abdulhadi, Alsultany, and Naber, Arab and Arab American Feminisms, xxiv.

22 Fadda-Conrey, Contemporary, 24–25.

23 Fernandes, Transnational, 6.

24 Gualtieri, Between, 2.

25 Naber, "Introduction," 30.

26 Amin, "Anti-Blackness."

27 Elhillo in Alsous et al., "Beyond the Land," 187.

28 El-Zein, "Introduction"; for more from this forum, see: https://csalateral.org /archive/forum/cultural-constructions-race-racism-middle-east-north-africa -southwest-asia-mena-swana/.

29 El-Rouayheb, Before Homosexuality; Merbet, Queer Beirut; Hayes, Queer Nations; Habib, Female Homosexuality and Arabo-Islamic Texts; Amer, Crossing Borders.

30 Duggan, "The New Homonormativity," 187–90.

31 Al-Samman and El-Ariss, "Queer Affects: Introduction," 205.

32 Puar, Terrorist Assemblages, xxv.

33 Massad, Desiring Arabs, 16–62, 48–50.

34 Kozma, Policing Egyptian Women, xv–xvi.

35 Kandiyoti, "Some Awkward Questions," 271.

36 Naber, Arab America, 44–48, 63–65.

37 Ferguson, Aberrations in Black, 139.

38 Amireh, "Afterword," 635.

39 Baron and Pursley, "Editorial Foreword," 203.

40 Kuntsman and Al-Qasimi, "Introduction," 2.

41 Cohen, "Punks."

42 Rodríguez, Sexual Futures, 13.

43 Gopinath, Impossible Desires, 16.

44 Tinsley, Thieving Sugar, 7–10.

45 Kahf, "The Pity Committee," III–12.

46 Said, Orientalism.

47 Spivak, "Can the Subaltern Speak?," 21.

48 Abu-Lughod, Do Muslim Women.

49 Alsultany, Arabs and Muslims, 71–99.

50 Jarmakani, Imagining Arab Womanhood, 3–4, 45–49.

51 Amireh, "Palestinian Women's Disappearing Act," 33.

52 Saliba, "Arab Feminism," 1089–92.

53 Alarcón, Kaplan, and Moallem, "Introduction."

54 Connell, Gender and Power, 184–85.

55 Pyke and Johnson, "Asian American Women."

56 Schippers, "Recovering the Feminine Other," 94.
57 Gopinath, *Impossible Desires*, 15.
58 Hoskin and Taylor, "Femme Resistance," 282.
59 See Simpson, "On Ethnographic Refusal"; Teves, *Defiant Indigeneity*.
60 Muñoz, "Thinking Beyond," 826.
61 Abdulhadi, Alsultany, and Naber, *Arab and Arab American Feminisms*, xxxi.

Chapter One. A Thousand and One Scheherazades

1 Since "Scheherazade" is transliterated, it is open to multiple spellings. I use "Scheherazade" unless I am directly quoting a source with another spelling.
2 *The Thousand and One Nights* is sometimes referred to or translated as *The Arabian Nights*. I use *The Nights* here for ease and consistency.
3 Burton, *A Plain and Literal*; Haddawy, *The Arabian Nights*.
4 Naber, *Arab America*, 81–82.
5 Said, *Orientalism*.
6 For more on how Orientalism invokes gender and sexuality as sites of regulation for "Eastern," specifically Arab, bodies, see Said, *Orientalism*; Yegenoglu, *Colonial Fantasies*; Massad, *Desiring Arabs*; Shohat and Stam, *Unthinking Eurocentrism*; and Boone, "Vacation Cruises."
7 I chose these two translations because of their prominence in the translation history of the Nights. *The Nights* as we know them now, a collection of magical realist folk tales over which Scheherazade presides, only appears in collected, written form in the second half of the thirteenth century. The thirteenth-century manuscript was copied and regenerated for subsequent renditions and is considered the "authentic," albeit now lost, form. It contained the frame story of Scheherazade and approximately eleven other stories that occur over the course of two hundred and eighty-two nights. Two versions of *The Nights* grew from this historical seed, one Syrian and one Egyptian. The Syrian copy is kept in the Bibliothèque nationale in Paris, while the Egyptian version proliferated endlessly, often deviating in dramatic ways from the Syrian and, consequently, from the thirteenth-century version. The content in *The Nights* shifted considerably in the Egyptian edition during the period of Ottoman reign, which is often considered a waning of Arab culture and traditions. The travel of the manuscript to the European context would alter the stories even more, particularly in the hands of the first French translation, performed by Antoine Galland in 1704. Galland collaborated with Hanna Diab in 1709 to add approximately twelve new stories to the collection, most famously, the stories of Aladdin, Ali Baba, and Sinbad (Haddawy, *The Arabian Nights*, xvi). It is due to this dilution of *The Nights* in the Egyptian context that many scholars of the text refer to the Syrian copy at the Bibliothèque nationale as the most authentic version of the text and thus the most referential of Arab culture. Eventually, the collection would make its way into English based on the success of Galland's French translation, most famously

in the ten-volume work of Richard Burton, circa 1850. Haddawy bases his translation on the definitive Arabic edition of the text by Muhsin Mahdi in 1984, who based his work on the Syrian edition in the Bibliothèque nationale. By claiming its proximity to the original collection, Haddawy views his collection as the more authentic representation of the Arab world, though we must also understand it as correcting what he understands as the failed and damaging *Nights* presented by Burton and the like.

8 Joseph, "Gender and Citizenship," 9. See also Parker et al., *Nationalisms and Sexualities*; Kaplan, Alarcón, and Moallem, *Between Woman and Nation*; Sharoni, *Gender and the Israeli-Palestinian Conflict*; Hatem, "The Enduring Alliance."

9 Sinha, "Gender and Nation," 258–59.

10 Burton, *A Plain and Literal*, 15.

11 Haddawy, *The Arabian Nights*, 15.

12 Sinha, "Gender and Nation," 159–60; Kandiyoti, "Bargaining with Patriarchy," 279.

13 Najmabadi, "Crafting," 95–97.

14 Tétreault and al-Mughni, "Gender," 71.

15 El-Geressi, "Racism in the Arab World." A recent issue of *Lateral* explores facets of anti-Blackness in the Arab world via articles on blackface, hip hop, constructions of whiteness, and more and is useful further context for this phenomenon. See El Zein "Introduction."

16 Ozcelik, "Introduction"; Kakande, *Slave States*; Fernandez, "Racialised."

17 Tayeb, "What Is Whiteness?"

18 While the generic diversity of the three texts is interesting, this chapter focuses on Scheherazade's uses in the narrative of each text rather than focusing on the texts' formal diversity. Scheherazade's original rhetorical use as a frame story makes her a compelling figure to compile writers, as in *Scheherazade's Legacy* and *E-mails from Scheherazad*, and as a collector and through line for multiple stories, as in *The Night Counter*.

19 Since this section focuses on Arab American texts, I will not comment on Mernissi's *Scheherazade Goes West* or Haddad's *I Killed Scheherazade*. However, it is useful to note that Mernissi valorizes Scheherazade for her intellect and cunning as a literary ancestor in many of the same ways that *Legacy* and *E-mails* do, while Haddad chooses to "murder" Scheherazade as a means of liberating herself from the sexual and gendered expectations Scheherazade's idealized femininity creates for Arab women.

20 For more on Arab American racialization, there is a rich body of literature, including, but not limited to, Jamal and Naber's edited collection *Race and Arab Americans Before and After 9/11*; Gualtieri's *Between Arab and White*; Cainkar's *Homeland Insecurity*; and Berman's *American Arabesque*.

21 For more on how these events queered Arabs, see Puar, *Terrorist Assemblages*; and Puar and Rai, "Monster, Terrorist, Fag."

22 Said, *Orientalism*, 103.

23 Praeger, "About," accessed February 14, 2013, www.greenwood.com/praeger .aspx.

24 Palumbo-Liu, *Ethnic Canon*.

25 Ferguson, *Aberrations in Black*.

26 Aziz, "Preface," xii.

27 Ferguson, *Aberrations in Black*, 25.

28 Aziz, "Preface," xiii.

29 Jarmakani, "Arab American," 235.

30 Lloyd, "Race," 265–66.

31 Aziz, "Preface," xii.

32 Aziz, "Preface," xv.

33 This poem does not appear in the anthology.

34 Darraj, *Scheherazade's Legacy*, 1.

35 Darraj, *Scheherazade's Legacy*, 2.

36 Darraj, *Scheherazade's Legacy*, 2–3.

37 Darraj, *Scheherazade's Legacy*, 3.

38 For more on Arabs and Muslims as expendable, see Razack, *Casting Out*.

39 There is another anthology, *Dinarzad's Children*, edited by Khaled Mattawa and Pauline Kaldas, that invokes Scheherazade. I have not included it in my analysis because its focus is Scheherazade's sister, Dinarzad.

40 Two useful examples that analyze the national anxiety around raced bodies that do not perform heterosexuality are Puar, *Terrorist Assemblages*, and Eng, *The Feeling of Kinship*. In *Terrorist Assemblages*, Jasbir K. Puar details the construction of the terrorist as a sexual deviant (homosexual, fag). In *The Feeling of Kinship*, David L. Eng questions the significance of miscegenation in the historic sodomy case *Garner v. Texas* (which involved an interracial couple). Meanwhile, numerous queer scholars critique the marriage movement in LGBT politics as assimilationist to white, hegemonic paradigms of US citizenship. In "Punks," Cohen indicates the similarities in the construction of racially and sexually marginal subjects as one reason for their coalition in politics.

41 Somerville, *Queering*, 3.

42 Naber, *Arab America*, 6–7, 82.

43 Suheir Hammad, who appears in this collection, is the author of *Born Palestinian, Born Black*. She writes about the positionality of Palestinians in the United States as comparable and in solidarity with Blackness.

44 Kahf, "E-mail," lines 19–20.

45 Kahf, "E-mail," line 17. Dinarzad is also referred to as Dunyazad in some translations of *The Nights*.

46 Kahf, "Thawrah," line 83.

47 For more on colonial feminism in the Arab and Muslim context, see Abu-Lughod, *Do Muslim Women Need Saving?*; and Ahmed, *Women and Gender in Islam*.

48 Naber, *Arab America*, 82.

49 Abdelrazek, *Contemporary Arab*, 113.

50 Kahf, "I Can Scent," lines 17–18.

51 Kahf, "Hijab Scene #1," line 1.

52 Kahf, "Hijab Scene #2," line 1.

53 Kahf, "Hijab Scene #2," line 3.

54 Cohen, "Punks," 439.

55 Naber, *Arab America*, 95.

56 Alarcón, Kaplan, and Moallem, "Introduction," 4. For sati debates, see Mani, "Contentious Traditions."

57 Yunis, *The Night Counter*, 68.

58 Yunis, *The Night Counter*, 85.

59 Yunis, *The Night Counter*, 195.

60 For more on this double bind, see Naber, "Arab American Femininities."

61 Yunis, *The Night Counter*, 353.

62 For a queer critique of "love the sinner, hate the sin," see Jakobsen and Pelligrini, *Love the Sin*; for a queer critique of tolerance more generally, see Warner, *The Trouble with Normal*.

63 Yunis, *The Night Counter*, 210.

64 Yunis, *The Night Counter*, 216.

65 Pickens, "Modern Family," 138.

66 Yunis, *The Night Counter*, 217.

67 Yunis, *The Night Counter*, 26.

68 Yunis, *The Night Counter*, 24.

Chapter Two. Between Women

1 For work on men's homosexuality in Egyptian film, see Hassan, "Real Queer Arabs"; Kiernan, "Cultural Hegemony and National Film Language"; and Van Eynde, "Men in the Picture."

2 Menicucci, "Unlocking the Arab," 32–36.

3 Shafik, *Popular Egyptian Cinema*.

4 Mansour, "Egyptian Film," 11.

5 Shafik, *Arab Cinema*, 12.

6 Shafik, *Arab Cinema*, 20–21.

7 Shafik, *Arab Cinema*, 26.

8 Said, "Farewell," 34.

9 Gopinath, *Impossible Desires*, 15.

10 Doty, *Making Things*, 3; and White, *Uninvited*, 2.

11 White, *Uninvited*, xv.

12 Gopinath, *Impossible Desires*, 15–17, 21–22.

13 Muñoz, *Disidentifications*, 4.

14 Najmabadi, "Reading," 219–20.

15 Halberstam, *In a Queer Time*, 6.

16 Eng, *The Feeling*, 15–16.

17 Gopinath, *Impossible Desires*, 25.

18 Sedgewick, *Between Men*, 26–27.

19 Najmabadi, "Reading," 210–13.

20 Najmabadi, "Reading," 220.

21 See Shah, *Stranger Intimacy*; and Somerville, *Queering the Color Line*.

22 Freeman, *The Wedding Complex*, xi; and Frye, *Anatomy*, 182.

23 Gopinath, *Impossible Desires*, 93–130.

24 McRuer, *Crip Theory*, 26–28.

25 Knight, *Disintegrating*, 14–17.

26 Shafik, *Popular Egyptian Cinema*, 166–67.

27 Van Nieuwkerk, *A Trade*, 129.

28 Anecdotally, Samia Gamal and Tahia Carioca, who play Samra and Zakia, were trained at the same nightclub by Badia Masabni. The women were subject to much gossip during their lives, which reports them as sometimes friends and sometimes foes. This is the only film in which they appear together.

29 Azza's Tunisian status becomes important later because as a Tunisian she can reside in Egypt on a visa for six months at a time.

30 Menicucci, "Unlocking the Arab," 34.

31 McRuer, *Crip Theory*, 24–26.

32 In Western films, this tendency is documented in *The Celluloid Closet*. Gopinath notes similar tendencies in Bollywood.

33 Rostom also dies, but his death is a given since he's a criminal.

34 Boym, *The Future*, xv–xvi.

35 Berlant, *The Queen*, 3–5.

36 Muñoz, *Cruising Utopia*, 37–38.

37 Windle, "'It Never Really Was,'" 24.

Chapter Three. Longing in Arabic

1 Some examples of queer Arab English-language literature focused on women and girls include Randa Jarrar's *Map of Home* and Etel Adnan's many poetry collections. Representation in film is slightly more common, including Shamim Sarif's *I Can't Think Straight* and Rolla Selbek's *Three Veils*. There are also many short pieces with queer centers (e.g., Etel Adnan's punching nonfiction essay "First Passion"), or longer works with queer secondary characters, including but not limited to Zeinab Hifni's novel *Malamih*; Cherien Dabais's film *May in the Summer*; and Nadine Labaki's film *Caramel*.

2 Massad, *Desiring Arabs*.

3 Puar, *Terrorist Assemblages*.

4 Amer, "Naming," 386.

5 I will discuss sahq at length in chapter 5.

6 Habib offers a round up of these assumptions in her review of *Ana Hiya Inti*, "Historical," 207.

7 Al-Ghafari, "The Lesbian Subjectivity," 7.

8 Hassan, "Toward a Theory," 22.

9 Siddiq, *Arab Culture*, 1.

10 Hassan, "Toward a Theory," 30.

11 Shaaban, *Voices Revealed*, 14.

12 Al-Id, "Introduction"; Elsadda, *Gender, Nation, and the Arabic Novel*, xx.

13 Majaj, Sunderman, and Saliba, "Introduction"; Malti-Douglas, *Men*.

14 Qualey, "Homosexuality."

15 Shomali, "Pulse," 319–22.

16 Multiple writers discuss the silencing of Arab and Muslim women through Orientalist tropes and the production of the hypermasculine, violent Arab man. Of particular note are the essays in Abdulhadi, Alsultany, and Naber, *Arab and Arab American Feminisms*.

17 Boone, *The Homoerotics*.

18 See Puar, *Terrorist Assemblages*; Puar and Rai, "Monster, Terrorist, Fag."

19 El-Rouayheb, *Before Homosexuality*, 19.

20 See Clarke, "Lesbianism"; Rich, "Compulsory Heterosexuality"; Hoskin, "Femme Theory."

21 Halabi, *Unmaking*, 150.

22 Halabi, *Unmaking*, 151. Halabi uses the term "chick lit." I find that "chick lit" rings in a distinctly US/UK register that is not necessarily transferable or useful for an Arab context. I use women's literature to avoid unnecessary valence while recognizing that "women's literature" is an unevenly applied term that designates works produced by and about women, that center women's voices, emotions, experiences, and lives.

23 Hanna, *Feminism*, 9.

24 Mansour, *I Am You*, 135–37. A note about citations for the novels: I read the books in the original Arabic and their English translations. The Arabic version of the texts I had access to, living outside the Arab nations in which they were published, were digital copies with no page numbers. Arabic versions of *Ana Hiya Inti* and *Ra'ihat il Kirfa* are both out of print. One can purchase an e-reader version of *Al Akharuun*, but it does not include page numbers. English translations with pagination were purchased or procured through library systems. To allow for reference, I cite here and below the page numbers in the English translations.

25 Al-Herz, *The Others*, 138.

26 Yazbek, *Cinnamon*, 84–85.

27 For a discussion of queer childhood sexualities, consider Stockton, *The Queer Child*.

28 Yazbek, *Cinnamon*, 68.

29 Yazbek, *Cinnamon*, 72.

30 Yazbek, *Cinnamon*, 71.

31 Mansour, *I Am You*, 113.

32 Mansour, *I Am You*, 35.

33 Habib, "Historical," 213–15.

34 Halabi, *The Unmaking*, 135, 148.
35 Halabi, *The Unmaking*, 152.
36 Al-Herz, *The Others*, 23.
37 Al-Herz, *The Others*, 153–55.
38 I draw "misogynoir" from Bailey and Trudy, "On Misogynoir"; and Bailey, *Misogynoir Transformed*.
39 Guardi, "Female Homosexuality," 20.
40 Yazbek, *Cinnamon*, 50–52.
41 Yazbek, *Cinnamon*, 70.
42 Yazbek, *Cinnamon*, 70–71.
43 Yazbek, *Cinnamon*, 50–53.
44 Yazbek, *Cinnamon*, 60.

Chapter Four. Love Letters

1 *Haqi* was released in Arabic, while *Waqfet* was released simultaneously in Arabic and English. *Bareed* was originally released in English and later released in Arabic. Translations of *Haqi* are mine. For quotes, I defer to the writers and editors of the collections and use the English language version of *Waqfet Banat*, unless I am making an explicit note about the differences between the two editions and the significance of the translation choices. I use the English-language version of *Bareed* because it is the original. I will further discuss the politics of translation in the second section of this chapter.
2 Felman, "Education," 6.
3 Smith, *Decolonizing*, 34.
4 Ahmed and Stacey, "Testimonial," 5.
5 Meem, *Bareed*, 7–8.
6 Aswat, *Haqi*, 11–12.
7 Aswat, *Haqi*, 99.
8 Aswat, *Waqfet*, 9–11. English version.
9 Caruth, "Introduction," 11.
10 Meem, *Bareed*, 1.
11 Palestinian Central Bureau of Statistics, "Illiteracy."
12 Aswat, *Haqi*, 12.
13 Aswat, *Haqi*, 61. My translation.
14 Aswat, *Waqfet*, 6–7. Arabic version. My translation.
15 Aswat, *Waqfet*, 6–9. Arabic version. My translation.
16 Aswat, *Waqfet*, 104. Arabic version. My translation.
17 Amer, "Naming," 393.
18 Meem, *Bareed*, 6.
19 I would consider all the following versions of Arabish: the translation of English words into Arabic via transliteration (e.g., a phonetic spelling of "queer"); rapid code switching; and combining English and Arabic words (e.g., adding "ing" to an Arabic verb).

20 Meem, *Bareed*, 124.

21 Meem, *Bareed*, 110.

22 Moussawi, "(Un)critically Queer," 595.

23 Many queer Arab groups are closed for privacy and safety.

24 Georgis, "Thinking Past Pride," 234–35.

25 Aswat, *Haqi*, 67, 69.

26 Aswat, *Haqi,* 67–72.

27 Aswat, *Waqfet*, 47. English version.

28 Meem, *Bareed*, 98–99.

29 Aswat, *Waqfet*, 152–54. English version.

30 Aswat, *Waqfet*, 155–57. English version.

31 For more on pinkwashing, see Mikdashi, "Gay Rights as Human Rights"; Schulman, "A Documentary Guide to 'Brand Israel' and the Art of Pinkwashing"; and Shafie, "Pinkwashing."

32 Aswat, *Waqfet*, 74. English version.

33 Aswat, *Waqfet*, 125–26. English version.

34 Georgis, "Thinking Past Pride," 237.

35 Aswat, *Haqi*, 28.

36 Aswat, *Haqi*, 51.

37 Aswat, *Haqi*, 95–99.

38 Meem, *Bareed*, 95.

Chapter Five. Sahq

1 Cvetkovich, *An Archive*, 7–9.

2 Amer, "Medieval," 216.

3 Habib, *Female Homosexuality*, 17–18.

4 Naber first introduces this concept in "Arab American Femininities," 90–91.

5 Musser, *Sensual Excess*, 14.

6 Musser, *Sensual Excess*, 5.

7 Macharia, *Frottage*, 3.

8 Macharia, *Frottage*, 5.

9 Cohen, "Punks."

10 Higginbotham, *Righteous Discontent*, 187.

11 For a recent genealogy of Black feminist thought on respectability, see Cooper, *Beyond Respectability*.

12 Warner, *The Trouble*, 30–37.

13 Rubin, "Thinking Sex," 178.

14 On good/bad Muslims, see Mamdani, "Good Muslim, Bad Muslim"; and Gotanda, "The Racialization of Islam in American Law."

15 Harris, "Gatekeeping," 213.

16 Introduced in Duggan, "The New Homonormativity."

17 As I said earlier, aib is a ubiquitous concept in Arab culture—I would be shocked if anyone subject to Arab sexism and heteronormativity did not

have familiarity with the concept. For scholarship on the concept, however: Georgis, "Thinking Past Pride"; Naber, *Arab America*; al-Khayyat, *Honour and Shame*; and Eltahawy, *Headscarves and Hymens*.

18 Piepzna-Samarasinha, *Care Work*. For further discussions of care work's radical potential for resisting heteropatriarchy and capitalism, see Schalk, *Bodyminds Reimagined*; and the following blog posts on Leaving Evidence by Mia Mingus: "Access Intimacy: The Missing Link" (May 5, 2011), https://leavingevidence.wordpress.com/2011/05/05/access-intimacy-the-missing-link; "Feeling the Weight: Some Notes on Disability, Access, and Love" (May 8, 2012), https://leavingevidence.wordpress.com/2012/05/08/feeling-the-weight-some-beginning-notes-on-disability-access-and-love; and "Access Intimacy, Interdependence, and Disability Justice" (April 12, 2017), https://leavingevidence.wordpress.com/2017/04/12/access-intimacy-interdependence-and-disability-justice.

19 Reviews that frame *Bar Bahar* as a "revenge fantasy" include Felsenthal, "Maysaloun Hamoud's *In Between*"; Scott, "Review"; and Kermode, "*In Between* Review."

20 Hamoud in Felsenthal, "Maysaloun Hamoud's *In Between*."

21 It is important to note that Nöl Collective used to operate under the name Babyfist. Many of the initiatives discussed in this chapter were started by Babyfist. Some have continued under the new name while others have not. I use Nöl Collective for the most up-to-date rendition of its work but reference some of the retired Babyfist initiatives. The transition announcement can be found on Instagram, accessed September 28, 2020, https://www.instagram.com/p/CFr4yD9BGJW.

22 From Nöl Collective's "About Us" page, accessed May 2019, https://nolcollective.com/slow-political-fashion-in-palestine.

23 From Nöl Collective's "Menstruation Education Campaign" page, accessed May 2019, https://nolcollective.com/menstruation-campaign-2019.

24 Shalabi-Abbas et al., "Knowledge."

25 From Nöl Collective's "Weaving Threads of Palestinian History" page, accessed May 2019, https://nolcollective.com/get-inspired/nol-weaving-threads-of-palestinian-history.

26 At the time of the first draft of this chapter, Nöl Collective was selling this print on numerous garments under the label Babyfist. At this time, the print is no longer for sale. You can see an example of this print, as well as the buried and free print discussed next, in various articles about the brand. Megan Giovanetti, "How This Ramallah Shop Teaches Women to Fight against Harassment," July 15, 2019, https://www.al-monitor.com/originals/2019/07/palestinian-clothing-brand-goes-to-schools.html; Liana Satenstein, "Supporting Local Business and Gender Equality," January 29, 2020, https://www.vogue.com/vogueworld/article/palestinian-label-babyfist-women-yasmeen-mjalli; FDM, "Babyfist, the Palestinian Brand of Clothing Challenging Street Harassment," accessed May 6, 2022, http://moroccanladies.com/fashion-news/babyfist-palestinian-brand-clothing-challenging-street-harassment-25659.

27 For how Palestinian women are portrayed as dead or dying, see Amireh, "Palestinian Women's Disappearing Act."

28 Manka, "In Conversation."

29 From Maamoul Press's "About" page, accessed May 2019, https://maamoulpress.com/About.

30 From Maamoul Press's "About" page, accessed May 2019, https://maamoulpress.com/About.

31 Atik, "Mish Hilu," 9.

32 Abdelrazaq, "The Fig Tree," 1.

33 Muñoz, *Cruising Utopia*, 1.

bibliography

Abdelrazaq, Leila. "The Fig Tree." N.p.: Maamoul Press, n.d.

Abdelrazek, Amal. *Contemporary Arab American Women Writers: Hyphenated Identities and Border Crossings.* Amherst, NY: Cambria Press, 2007.

Abdulhadi, Rabab, Evelyn Alsutany, and Nadine Naber. *Arab and Arab American Feminisms: Gender, Violence, and Belonging.* Syracuse, NY: Syracuse University Press, 2011.

Abu-Lughod, Lila. *Do Muslim Women Need Saving?* Cambridge, MA: Harvard University Press, 2013.

Adnan, Etel. "First Passion." In *Queer 13: Lesbian and Gay Writers Recall Seventh Grade,* edited by Clifford Chase. New York: Rob Weisbach Books, 1998.

Ahmed, Leila. *Women and Gender in Islam.* New Haven, CT: Yale University Press, 2021.

Ahmed, Sara. *The Promise of Happiness.* Durham, NC: Duke University Press, 2010.

Ahmed, Sara, and Jackie Stacey. "Testimonial Cultures." *Cultural Values* 5, no. 1 (2001): 1–6.

Akash, Munir, and Khaled Mattawa, eds. *Post-Gibran: Anthology of New Arab American Writing.* Syracuse, NY: Syracuse University Press, 1999.

Alarcón, Norma, Caren Kaplan, and Minoo Moallem. "Introduction: Between Woman and Nation." In *Between Woman and Nation: Nationalisms, Transnational Feminisms, and the State,* edited by Caren Kaplan, Norma Alarcón, and Minoo Moallem, 1–18. Durham, NC: Duke University Press, 1999.

Al-Ghafari, Iman. "The Lesbian Subjectivity in Contemporary Arabic Literature: 'An Absent Presence' Disciplined by the Gaze." *Al-Raida Journal,* nos. 138–40 (Summer/Fall/Winter 2012–2013): 6–18.

Al-Herz, Seba. *Al Akharuun.* Beirut: Dar Al Saqi, 2006.

Al-Herz, Seba. *The Others.* Anonymous translator. New York: Seven Stories Press, 2008.

Al-Id, Youmna. "Introduction to Special Edition of Hasanat al-Hub." Al-Diya, 2002.

Al-Khayyat, Sana'a. *Honour and Shame: Women in Modern Iraq.* London: Saqi Books, 1990.

Al-Samman, Hanadi, and Tarek El-Ariss. "Queer Affects: Introduction." *International Journal of Middle East Studies* 45, no. 2 (2013): 205–9.

Alsous, Zaina, et al. "Beyond the Land of Erasure: A Roundtable of Poets from the Arabic-Speaking and Muslim Worlds." *Iowa Review* 49, no. 1 (2019): 168–87.

Alsultany, Evelyn. *Arabs and Muslims in the Media: Race and Representation after 9/11.* New York: New York University Press, 2012.

Amer, Sahar. *Crossing Borders: Love Between Women in Medieval French and Arabic Literature.* Philadelphia: University of Pennsylvania Press, 2008.

Amer, Sahar. "Medieval Arab Lesbians and Lesbian-Like Women." *Journal of the History of Sexuality* 18, no. 2 (2009): 215–36.

Amer, Sahar. "Naming to Empower: Lesbianism in the Arab Islamicate World Today." *Journal of Lesbian Studies* 16, no. 4 (2012): 381–97.

Amin, Bahira. "Anti-Blackness in the Arab World." *Scene Arabia*, June 10, 2020. https://scenearabia.com/Life/Arab-Anti-Blackness-Racism-and-the-Violence -that-Doesn-t-Get-A-Hashtag.

Amireh, Amal. "Afterword." GLQ: *A Journal of Lesbian and Gay Studies* 16, no. 4 (2010): 635–47.

Amireh, Amal. "Palestinian Women's Disappearing Act: The Suicide Bomber through Western Feminist Eyes." In *Arab and Arab American Feminisms: Gender, Violence, and Belonging,* edited by Rabab Abdulhadi, Evelyn Alsultany, and Nadine Naber, 29–45. Syracuse, NY: Syracuse University Press, 2011.

Arondekar, Anjali. *For the Record: On Sexuality and the Colonial Archive in India.* Durham, NC: Duke University Press, 2009.

Arondekar, Anjali, Ann Cvetkovich, Christina B. Hanhardt, Regina Kunzel, Tavia Nyong'o, Juana María Rodríguez, Susan Stryker, Daniel Marshall, Kevin P. Murphy, and Zeb Tortorici. "Queering Archives: A Roundtable Discussion." *Radical History Review* 2015, no. 122 (2015): 211–31.

Aswat, ed. *Haqi: An A'ish, An Akhtar, An Akoon* [*My Right: To Live, To Choose, To Be*]. N.p.: Aswat, 2007.

Aswat, ed. *Waqfet Banat* [*Women's Stand*]. Arabic. N.p.: Aswat, 2010.

Aswat, ed. *Waqfet Banat.* English. N.p.: Aswat, 2011.

Atik, Christina. "Mish Hilu La Bint/It's Not Nice for a Girl." N.p.: Maamoul Press, n.d.

Aziz, Barbara. "Preface." In *Scheherazade's Legacy: Arab and Arab American Women on Writing,* edited by Susan Muaddi Darraj, xi–xvi. Westport, CT: Praeger, 2004.

Bailey, Moya. *Misogynoir Transformed: Black Women's Digital Resistance.* New York: New York University Press, 2021.

Bailey, Moya, and Trudy. "On Misogynoir: Citation, Erasure, and Plagiarism." *Feminist Media Studies* 18, no. 4 (2018): 762–68.

Baron, Beth, and Sara Pursley. "Editorial Foreword." *International Journal of Middle East Studies* 45, no. 2 (2013): 203–4.

Berlant, Lauren. *The Queen of America Goes to Washington City*. Durham, NC: Duke University Press, 1997.

Berman, Jacob. *American Arabesque: Arabs and Islam in the Nineteenth-Century Imaginary*. New York: New York University Press, 2012.

Boone, Joseph. *The Homoerotics of Orientalism*. New York: Columbia University Press, 2014.

Boone, Joseph. "Vacation Cruises; or, the Homoerotics of Orientalism." *PMLA/Publications of the Modern Language Association of America* 110, no. 1 (1995): 89–107.

Boym, Svetlana. *The Future of Nostalgia*. New York: Basic Books, 2008.

Burton, Richard. *A Plain and Literal Translation of the Arabian Nights' Entertainments, Now Entitled the Book of the Thousand Nights and a Night: With Introduction, Explanatory Notes on the Manners and Customs of Moslem Men, and a Terminal Essay upon the History of The Nights*. Vol. 10. London: Burton Society for Private Circulation, 1900.

Cainkar, Louise. "Fluid Terror Threat." *Amerasia Journal* 44, no. 1 (2018): 27–59.

Cainkar, Louise. *Homeland Insecurity: The Arab American and Muslim American Experience after 9/11*. New York: Russell Sage Foundation, 2009.

Caruth, Cathy. "Introduction." In *Trauma: Explorations in Memory*, edited by Cathy Caruth, 3–12. Baltimore, MD: Johns Hopkins University Press, 1995.

Chan-Malik, Sylvia (moderator), Evelyn Alsultany, Su'ad Abdul Khabeer, and Maryam Kashani. "'A Space for the Spiritual': A Roundtable on Race, Gender, and Islam in the United States." *Amerasia Journal* 40, no. 1 (2014): 17–33.

Clarke, Cheryl. "Lesbianism: An Act of Resistance." In *This Bridge Called My Back: Writings by Radical Women of Color*, edited by Cherríe Moraga and Gloria Anzaldúa, 128–37. Albany: State University of New York Press, 1981.

Cohen, Cathy. "Punks, Bulldaggers, and Welfare Queens: The Real Radical Potential of Queer Politics?" *GLQ: A Journal of Lesbian and Gay Studies* 3, no. 4 (2005): 437–65.

Connell, Raewyn. *Gender and Power: Society, the Person and Sexual Politics*. Hoboken, NJ: John Wiley and Sons, 1987.

Cooper, Brittney C. *Beyond Respectability: The Intellectual Thought of Race Women*. Champaign: University of Illinois Press, 2017.

Cvetkovich, Ann. *An Archive of Feelings*. Durham, NC: Duke University Press, 2003.

Darraj, Susan Muaddi, ed. *Scheherazade's Legacy: Arab and Arab American Women on Writing*. Westport, CT: Praeger, 2004.

Doty, Alexander. *Making Things Perfectly Queer*. Minneapolis: University of Minnesota Press, 1993.

Duggan, Lisa. "The New Homonormativity: The Sexual Politics of Neoliberalism." In *Materializing Democracy*, edited by Russ Castronovo and Dana D. Nelson, 175–94. Durham, NC: Duke University Press, 2002.

El-Geressi, Yasmine. "Racism in the Arab World: An Open Secret." *Majalla*, June 12, 2020. https://eng.majalla.com/node/91756/racism-in-the-arab-world -an-open-secret.

El-Rouayheb, Khaled. *Before Homosexuality in the Arab-Islamic World, 1500–1800*. Chicago: University of Chicago Press, 2009.

Elsadda, Hoda. *Gender, Nation, and the Arabic Novel: Egypt, 1892–2008*. Edinburgh: Edinburgh University Press, 2012.

Eltahawy, Mona. *Headscarves and Hymens: Why the Middle East Needs a Sexual Revolution*. New York: Farrar, Straus and Giroux, 2015.

El Zein, Rayya. "Introduction: Cultural Constructions of Race and Racism in the Middle East and North Africa/Southwest Asia and North Africa." *Lateral* 10, no. 1 (2021): n.p.

Eng, David Lee. *The Feeling of Kinship: Queer Liberalism and the Racialization of Intimacy*. Durham, NC: Duke University Press, 2010.

Fadda-Conrey, Carol. *Contemporary Arab-American Literature: Transnational Reconfigurations of Citizenship and Belonging*. New York: New York University Press, 2014.

Felman, Shoshana. "Education and Crisis, or the Vicissitudes of Teaching." In *Trauma: Explorations in Memory*, edited by Cathy Caruth, 13–60. Baltimore: Johns Hopkins University Press, 1995.

Felsenthal, Julia. "Maysaloun Hamoud's *In Between* Is a Palestinian Feminist Revenge Fantasy." *Vogue*, January 5, 2018.

Ferguson, Roderick. *Aberrations in Black: Toward a Queer of Color Critique*. Minneapolis: University of Minnesota Press, 2003.

Fernandes, Leela. *Transnational Feminism in the United States*. New York: New York University Press, 2013.

Fernandez, Bina. "Racialised Institutional Humiliation through the Kafala." *Journal of Ethnic and Migration Studies* (2021): 1–18.

Freeman, Elizabeth. *The Wedding Complex*. Durham, NC: Duke University Press, 2002.

Frye, Northrop. *Anatomy of Criticism*. Princeton, NJ: Princeton University Press, 1957.

Georgis, Dina. *The Better Story: Queer Affects from the Middle East*. Albany: State University of New York Press, 2013.

Georgis, Dina. "Thinking Past Pride: Queer Arab Shame in *Bareed Mista3jil*." *International Journal of Middle East Studies* 45, no. 2 (2013): 233–51.

Gopinath, Gayatri. *Impossible Desires: Queer Diasporas and South Asian Public Cultures*. Durham, NC: Duke University Press, 2005.

Gotanda, Neil. "The Racialization of Islam in American Law." *The ANNALS of the American Academy of Political and Social Science* 637, no. 1 (2011): 184–95.

Gualtieri, Sarah. *Between Arab and White: Race and Ethnicity in the Early Syrian American Diaspora*. Berkeley: University of California Press, 2009.

Guardi, Jolanda. "Female Homosexuality in the Contemporary Arabic Novel." *Deportate, esuli, profughe* 25 (2014): 17–30.

Habib, Samar. *Arabo-Islamic Texts on Female Homosexuality: 850–1780 A.D.* Amherst, NY: Teneo Press, 2009.

Habib, Samar. *Female Homosexuality in the Middle East*. New York: Routledge, 2007.

Habib, Samar. "The Historical Context and Reception of the First Arabic-Lesbian Novel, *I Am You*, by Elham Mansour." *EnterText* 5, no. 3 (2005): 201–35.

Haddad, Joumana. *I Killed Scheherazade: Confessions of an Angry Arab Woman*. Chicago: Lawrence Hill Books, 2010.

Haddawy, Husain, trans. *The Arabian Nights*. Edited by Muhsin Mahdi. New York: Norton, 1995.

Halabi, Zeina. *The Unmaking of the Arab Intellectual: Prophecy, Exile, and the Nation*. Edinburgh: Edinburgh University Press, 2017.

Halberstam, Jack. *In a Queer Time and Place: Transgender Bodies, Subcultural Lives*. New York: New York University Press, 2005.

Hammad, Suheir. *Born Palestinian, Born Black*. Brooklyn: UpSet Press, 2010.

Hanna, Kifah. *Feminism and Avant-Garde Aesthetics in the Levantine Novel*. New York: Springer, 2016.

Harris, Paisley Jane. "Gatekeeping and Remaking: The Politics of Respectability in African American Women's History and Black Feminism." *Journal of Women's History* 15, no. 1 (2003): 212–20.

Hartman, Saidiya. "Venus in Two Acts." *Small Axe* 12, no. 2 (2008): 1–14.

Hartmann, Michelle. "Grandmothers, Grape Leaves and Kahlil Gibran: Writing Race in Anthologies of Arab American Literature." In *Race and Arab Americans Before 9/11: From Invisible Citizens to Visible Subjects*, edited by Amaney Jamal and Nadine Naber, 170–203. Syracuse, NY: Syracuse University Press, 2008.

Hassan, Omar. "Real Queer Arabs: The Tension between Colonialism and Homosexuality in Egyptian Cinema." *Film International* 8, no. 1 (2010): 18–24.

Hassan, Waïl S. "Toward a Theory of the Arabic Novel." In *The Oxford Handbook of Arab Novelistic Traditions*, edited by Waïl S. Hassan, 19–48. Oxford: Oxford University Press, 2017.

Hatem, Mervat. "The Enduring Alliance of Nationalism and Patriarchy in Muslim Personal Status Laws: The Case of Modern Egypt." *Feminist Issues* 6, no. 1 (1986): 19–43.

Hayes, Jarrod. *Queer Nations: Marginal Sexualities in the Maghreb*. Chicago: University of Chicago Press, 2000.

Hifni, Zeinab. *Malamih*. Beirut: Dar Al Saqi Press, 2006.

Higginbotham, Evelyn Brooks. *Righteous Discontent: The Women's Movement in the Black Baptist Church, 1880–1920*. Cambridge, MA: Harvard University Press, 1994.

Hoskin, Rhea Ashley. "Femme Theory: Femininity's Challenge to Western Feminist Pedagogies." MA thesis, Queen's University (Canada), 2013.

Hoskin, Rhea Ashley, and Allison Taylor. "Femme Resistance: The Fem(me)inine Art of Failure." *Psychology & Sexuality* 10, no. 4 (2019): 281–300.

Jakobsen, Janet, and Anne Pelligrini. *Love the Sin: Sexual Regulation and the Limits of Religious Tolerance*. New York: New York University Press, 2003.

Jamal, Amaney, and Nadine Naber, eds. *Race and Arab Americans Before and After 9/11: From Invisible Citizens to Visible Subjects*. Syracuse, NY: Syracuse University Press, 2008.

Jarmakani, Amira. "Arab American Feminisms: Mobilizing the Politics of Invisibility." In *Arab and Arab American Feminisms: Gender, Violence, and Belonging*, edited by Rabab Abdulhadi, Evelyn Alsultany, and Nadine Naber, 227–41. Syracuse, NY: Syracuse University Press, 2011.

Jarmakani, Amira. *Imagining Arab Womanhood: The Cultural Mythology of Veils, Harems, and Belly Dancers in the US*. New York: Springer, 2008.

Jarrar, Randa. *Map of Home*. New York: Other Press, 2008.

Joseph, Suad. "Gender and Citizenship in the Arab World." *Al-Raida Journal* 129–130 (Spring/Summer 2010): 8–18.

Kadi, Joe, ed. *Food for Our Grandmothers: Writings by Arab-American and Arab-Canadian Feminists*. Cambridge, MA: South End Press, 1994.

Kahf, Mohja. "E-mail from Scheherazad." In *E-mails from Scheherazad*, 43. Gainesville: University Press of Florida, 2003.

Kahf, Mohja. "Hijab Scene #1." In *E-mails from Scheherazad*, 41. Gainesville: University Press of Florida, 2003.

Kahf, Mohja. "Hijab Scene #2." In *E-mails from Scheherazad*, 42. Gainesville: University Press of Florida, 2003.

Kahf, Mohja. "I Can Scent an Arab Man a Mile Away." In *E-mails from Scheherazad*, 29–30. Gainesville: University Press of Florida, 2003.

Kahf, Mohja. "The Pity Committee and the Careful Reader." In *Arab and Arab American Feminisms: Gender, Violence, and Belonging*, edited by Rabab Abdulhadi, Evelyn Alsultany, and Nadine Naber, 111–23. Syracuse, NY: Syracuse University Press, 2011.

Kahf, Mohja. "Thawrah." In *E-mails from Scheherazad*, 64–68. Gainesville: University Press of Florida, 2003.

Kakande, Yasin. *Slave States: The Practice of Kafala in the Gulf Arab Region*. Washington, DC: John Hunt, 2015.

Kandiyoti, Deniz. "Bargaining with Patriarchy." *Gender & Society* 2, no. 3 (1988): 274–90.

Kandiyoti, Deniz. "Some Awkward Questions on Women and Modernity in Turkey." In *Remaking Women: Feminism and Modernity in the Middle East*, edited by Lila Abu-Lughod, 270–88. Princeton, NJ: Princeton University Press, 1998.

Kaplan, Caren, Norma Alarcón, and Minoo Moallem, eds. *Between Woman and Nation: Nationalisms, Transnational Feminisms, and the State*. Durham, NC: Duke University Press, 1999.

Kermode, Mark. "*In Between* Review—the Struggle of Free Spirits Trying to Fly." *Guardian*, September 24, 2017.

Kiernan, Maureen. "Cultural Hegemony and National Film Language: Youssef Chahine." *Alif: Journal of Comparative Poetics* 15 (1995): 130–52.

Knight, Arthur. *Disintegrating the Musical*. Durham, NC: Duke University Press, 2002.

Kozma, Liat. *Policing Egyptian Women: Sex, Law, and Medicine in Khedival Egypt*. Syracuse, NY: Syracuse University Press, 2011.

Kuntsman, Adi, and Noor Al-Qasimi. "Introduction to Special Issue: Queering Middle Eastern Cyberspace." *Journal of Middle East Women's Studies* 8, no. 3 (2012): 1–13.

Lloyd, David. "Race Under Representation." In *Culture/Contexture: Explorations in Anthropology and Literary Studies*, edited by E. Valentine Daniel and Jeffrey M. Peck, 249–72. Berkeley: University of California Press, 1996.

Macharia, Keguro. *Frottage: Frictions of Intimacy across the Black Diaspora*. New York: New York University Press, 2019.

Majaj, Lisa Suhair, Paula Sunderman, and Therese Saliba. "Introduction." In *Intersections: Gender, Nation, and Community in Arab Women's Novels*, edited by Lisa Suhair Majaj, Paula Sunderman, and Therese Saliba, xvii–xxx. Syracuse, NY: Syracuse University Press, 2002.

Malti-Douglas, Fedwa. *Men, Women, and Gods*. Oakland: University of California Press, 2018.

Mamdani, Mahmood. "Good Muslim, Bad Muslim: A Political Perspective on Culture and Terrorism." *American Anthropologist* 104, no. 3 (2002): 766–75.

Mani, Lata. "Contentious Traditions: The Debate on Sati in Colonial India." *Cultural Critique* 7 (Autumn 1987): 119–56.

Manka, Claudia. "In Conversation with Yasmeen Mjalli at Babyfist." *PETRIe Inventory*. http://www.petrieinventory.com/in-conversation-with-yasmeen-mjalli-at-babyfist. Accessed May 6, 2022.

Mansour, Dina. "Egyptian Film Censorship: Safeguarding Society, Upholding Taboos." *Alphaville: Journal of Film and Screen Media* 4 (Winter 2012): 1–16.

Mansour, Elham. *Ana Hiya Inti: Riwaya*. Beirut: Riad El Rayyes Books, 1991.

Mansour, Elham. *I Am You: A Novel on Lesbian Desire in the Middle East*. Translated and edited by Samar Habib. Amherst, NY: Cambria Press, 2008.

Massad, Joseph. *Desiring Arabs*. Chicago: University of Chicago Press, 2008.

Mattawa, Khaled, and Pauline Kaldas, eds. *Dinarzad's Children: An Anthology of Contemporary Arab American Fiction*. Fayetteville: University of Arkansas Press, 2009.

McRuer, Robert. *Crip Theory*. New York: New York University Press, 2006.

Meem. *Bareed Mista3jil: True Stories*. Self-published, 2008.

Menicucci, Garay. "Unlocking the Arab Celluloid Closet: Homosexuality in Egyptian Film." *Middle East Report* 206 (Spring 1996): 32–36.

Merbet, Sofian. *Queer Beirut*. Austin: University of Texas Press, 2014.

Mernissi, Fatema. *Scheherazade Goes West: Different Cultures, Different Harems*. New York: Washington Square Press, 2001.

Mikdashi, Maya. "Gay Rights as Human Rights: Pinkwashing Homonationalism." *Jadaliyya*, December 16, 2011. https://www.jadaliyya.com/Details/24855.

Moussawi, Ghassan. "(Un)critically Queer Organizing: Towards a More Complex Analysis of LGBTQ Organizing in Lebanon." *Sexualities* 18, nos. 5–6 (2015): 593–617.

Muñoz, José Esteban. *Cruising Utopia: The Then and There of Queer Futurity*. New York: New York University Press, 2009.

Muñoz, José Esteban. *Disidentifications: Queers of Color and the Performance of Politics*. Minneapolis: University of Minnesota Press, 1999.

Muñoz, José Esteban. "Ephemera as Evidence: Introductory Notes to Queer Acts." *Women & Performance* 8, no. 2 (1996): 5–16.

Muñoz, José Esteban. "Thinking Beyond Antirelationality and Antiutopianism in Queer Critique." *Publications of the Modern Language Association of America* 121, no. 3 (2006): 825–56.

Musser, Amber Jamilla. *Sensual Excess*. New York: New York University Press, 2018.

Naber, Nadine. "Arab American Femininities: Beyond Arab Virgin/American (ized) Whore." *Feminist Studies* 32, no. 1 (2006): 87–111.

Naber, Nadine. *Arab America: Gender, Cultural Politics, and Activism*. New York: New York University Press, 2012.

Naber, Nadine. "Introduction." In *Race and Arab Americans Before and After 9/11: From Invisible Citizens to Visible Subjects*, edited by Amaney Jamal and Nadine Naber, 1–45. Syracuse, NY: Syracuse University Press, 2008.

Najmabadi, Afsaneh. "Crafting an Educated Housewife in Iran." In *Remaking Women: Feminism and Modernity in the Middle East*, edited by Lila Abu-Lughod, 91–125. Princeton, NJ: Princeton University Press, 1998.

Najmabadi, Afsaneh. "Reading 'Wiles of Women' Stories as Fictions of Masculinity." *Iranian Studies* 32, no. 2 (1999): 203–22.

Nash, Jennifer. *Black Feminism Reimagined: After Intersectionality*. Durham, NC: Duke University Press, 2018.

Ngai, Sianne. *Ugly Feelings*. Cambridge, MA: Harvard University Press, 2005.

Ozcelik, Burcu. "Introduction: Confronting the Legacy and Contemporary Iterations of Racial Politics in the Middle East." *Ethnic and Racial Studies* 44, no. 12 (2021): 2155–66.

Palestinian Central Bureau of Statistics. "Illiteracy Rates in Palestine Reduced from 13.9% in 1997 to 3.7% in 2013." Press release, September 8, 2014. http://www.pcbs.gov.ps/portals/_pcbs/PressRelease/Press_En_IntLitDy2014E.pdf.

Palumbo-Liu, David. *The Ethnic Canon: Histories, Institutions, and Interventions*. Minneapolis: University of Minnesota Press, 1995.

Parker, Andrew, Mary Russo, Doris Sommer, and Patricia Yaeger, eds. *Nationalisms and Sexualities*. New York: Routledge, 2018.

Pickens, Therí A. "Modern Family: Circuits of Transmission between Arabs and Blacks." *Comparative Literature* 68, no. 2 (2016): 130–40.

Piepzna-Samarasinha, Leah Lakshmi. *Care Work: Dreaming Disability Justice*. Vancouver: Arsenal Pulp Press, 2018.

Puar, Jasbir K. *Terrorist Assemblages: Homonationalism in Queer Times*. Durham, NC: Duke University Press, 2018.

Puar, Jasbir K., and Amit Rai. "Monster, Terrorist, Fag: The War on Terrorism and the Production of Docile Patriots." *Social Text* 20, no. 3 (2002): 117–48.

Pyke, Karen D., and Denise L. Johnson. "Asian American Women and Racialized Femininities: 'Doing' Gender across Cultural Worlds." *Gender and Society* 17, no. 1 (2003): 33–53.

Qualey, M. Lynx. "Homosexuality and the Arab Novel: The Triumph of Mockery." *ArabLit*, September 4, 2015. https://arablit.org/2015/09/04 /homosexuality-and-the-arabic-novel.

Razack, Sherene. *Casting Out: The Eviction of Muslims from Western Law and Politics.* Toronto: University of Toronto Press, 2008.

Rich, Adrienne. "Compulsory Heterosexuality and Lesbian Existence." *Signs: Journal of Women in Culture and Society* 5, no. 4 (1980): 631–60.

Rodríguez, Juana María. *Sexual Futures, Queer Gestures, and Other Latina Longings.* New York: New York University Press, 2014.

Rubin, Gayle S. "Thinking Sex." In *Sexualities II: Some Elements for an Account of the Social Organisation of Sexualities,* edited by Ken Plummer, 188–202. London: Routledge, 2002.

Said, Edward. "Farewell to Tahia." *Al-Raida* 16, nos. 86–87 (1999): 34–36.

Said, Edward. *Orientalism.* New York: Vintage Books, 1978.

Saliba, Therese. "Arab Feminism at the Millennium." *Signs* 25, no. 4 (2000): 1087–92.

Schalk, Sami. *Bodyminds Reimagined: Disability, Race, and Gender in Black Women's Speculative Fiction.* Durham, NC: Duke University Press, 2018.

Schippers, Mimi. "Recovering the Feminine Other: Masculinity, Femininity, and Gender Hegemony." *Theory and Society* 36, no. 1 (2007): 85–102.

Schulman, Sarah. "A Documentary Guide to 'Brand Israel' and the Art of Pink-washing." *Mondoweiss*, November 30, 2011. https://mondoweiss.net/2011/11/a -documentary-guide-to-brand-israel-and-the-art-of-pinkwashing/.

Scott, A. O. "Review: 'In Between' Tells of Three Women Fighting Partiarchy in Tel Aviv." *New York Times*, January 4, 2018.

Scott, Joan W. "The Evidence of Experience." *Critical Inquiry* 17, no. 4 (1991): 773–97.

Sedgwick, Eve Kosofsky. *Between Men: English Literature and Male Homosocial Desire.* New York: Columbia University Press, 1985.

Shaaban, Bouthaina. *Voices Revealed: Arab Women Novelists 1898–2000.* Translated by Jeff Shalan. Boulder, CO: Lynne Rienner Publishers, 2009.

Shafie, Ghadir. "Pinkwashing: Israel's International Strategy and Internal Agenda." *Kohl: A Journal for Body and Gender Research* 1, no. 1 (2015): 82–86.

Shafik, Viola. *Arab Cinema: History and Cultural Identity.* Cairo: American University in Cairo Press, 2007.

Shafik, Viola. *Popular Egyptian Cinema: Gender, Class, and Nation.* Cairo: American University in Cairo Press, 2006.

Shah, Nayan. *Stranger Intimacy: Contesting Race, Sexuality, and the Law in the North American West.* Berkeley: University of California Press, 2011.

Shakir, Evelyn. *Bint Arab: Arab and Arab American Women in the United States.* Westport, CO: Praeger, 1997.

Shalabi-Abbas, Eatimad, Saba Dweikat, Israa Al Gazawy, and Sajeda Draghmah. "Knowledge and Self Care Practices in Adolescent Girls Living in Nablus District During Menstruation: A Cross-Sectional Study." *The Lancet*, 2018. doi:10.1016/S0140-6736(18)30376-3.

Sharoni, Simona. *Gender and the Israeli-Palestinian Conflict: The Politics of Women's Resistance*. Syracuse, NY: Syracuse University Press, 1995.

Shohat, Ella, and Evelyn Alsultany. "The Cultural Politics of the Middle East in America: An Introduction." In *Between the Middle East and the Americas: The Cultural Politics of Diaspora*, edited by Ella Shohat and Evelyn Alsultany, 3–41. Ann Arbor: University of Michigan Press, 2013.

Shohat, Ella, and Robert Stam. *Unthinking Eurocentrism: Multiculturalism and the Media*. New York: Routledge, 2014.

Shomali, Mejdulene. "The Pulse of Queer Life: Arab Bodies in Gay Bars." In *Sajjilu Arab American: A Reader in SWANA Studies*, edited by Amira Jarmakani, Pauline Homsi Vinson, and Louise Cainkar, 317–25. Syracuse, NY: Syracuse University Press, 2022.

Siddiq, Muhammad. *Arab Culture and the Novel: Genre, Identity and Agency in Egyptian Fiction*. New York: Routledge, 2007.

Simpson, Audra. "On Ethnographic Refusal: Indigeneity, 'Voice' and Colonial Citizenship." *Junctures: The Journal for Thematic Dialogue* 9 (December 2007): 67–80.

Sinha, Mrinalini. "Gender and Nation." In *Feminist Theory Reader*, edited by Carole R. McCann, Seung-kyung Kim, and Emek Ergun, 155–68. New York: Routledge, 2021.

Smith, Linda Tuhiwai. *Decolonizing Methodologies*. London: Zed Books, 2013.

Somerville, Siobhan. *Queering the Color Line: Race and the Invention of Homosexuality in American Culture*. Durham, NC: Duke University Press, 2000.

Spivak, Gayatri Chakravorty. "Can the Subaltern Speak?" In *Can the Subaltern Speak? Reflections on the History of an Idea*, edited by Rosalind Morris, 21–80. New York: Columbia University Press, 2010.

Spivak, Gayatri Chakravorty. *In Other Worlds: Essays in Cultural Politics*. New York: Routledge, 2012.

Stockton, Kathryn Bond. *The Queer Child*. Durham, NC: Duke University Press, 2009.

Tayeb, Leila. "What Is Whiteness in North Africa?" *Lateral* 10, no. 1 (2021): n.p.

Tétreault, Mary Ann, and Haya al-Mughni. "Gender, Citizenship and Nationalism in Kuwait." *British Journal of Middle Eastern Studies* 22, no. 1–2 (1995): 64–80.

Teves, Stephanie Nohelani. *Defiant Indigeneity: The Politics of Hawaiian Performance*. Chapel Hill: University of North Carolina Press, 2018.

Tinsley, Omise'eke Natasha. *Thieving Sugar: Eroticism between Women in Caribbean Literature*. Durham, NC: Duke University Press, 2010.

Van Eynde, Koen. "Men in the Picture: Representations of Men and Masculinities in Egyptian Cinema since 1952." PhD diss., Katholieke Universiteit Leuven, 2015.

van Nieuwkerk, Karin. *A Trade Like Any Other: Female Singers and Dancers in Egypt.* Austin: University of Texas Press, 1995.

Warner, Michael. *The Trouble with Normal: Sex, Politics, and the Ethics of Queer Life.* Cambridge, MA: Harvard University Press, 2000.

White, Patricia. *Uninvited: Classical Hollywood Cinema and Lesbian Representability.* Bloomington: Indiana University Press, 1999.

Windle, Elisabeth. "'It Never Really Was the Same': Brother to Brother's Black and White and Queer Nostalgia." *Melus* 41, no. 4 (2016): 6–31.

Yazbek, Samar. *Cinnamon.* Translated by Emily Danby. London: Haus, 2013.

Yazbek, Samar. *Ra'ihat il Kirfa.* Beirut: Dar Al Adab, 2008.

Yazbek, Samar. *A Woman in the Crossfire: Diaries of the Syrian Revolution.* Translated by Max Weiss. London: Haus, 2012.

Yegenoglu, Meyda. *Colonial Fantasies: Towards a Feminist Reading of Orientalism.* Cambride: Cambridge University Press, 1998.

Yunis, Alia. *The Night Counter.* New York: Three Rivers Press, 2009.

index

Arabian Nights, The. See Thousand and One Nights, The

Arabic (language), 7, 21, 89–91, 100, 118, 139, 148, 154, 162–65, 183n1; classical, 102, 131; colloquial, 122, 126, 130–31, 156; formal, 126; and gender terminology, 15, 20, 158; and neologisms, 20, 125–26, 128–29, 131, 137; and queer terminology, 1, 24–25, 94–95, 120–37, 140–42; and transcription, 30; and translation, 122, 125, 182n24, 183n19; and transliteration, 14, 122–32, 136–37, 141–42, 183n19

Arabish, 21, 122, 131, 183n19

Arab League, 7

Arab men, 13, 43, 45–48, 101, 182n16. See also masculinity

Arab nationalism, 3–4, 8, 10–11, 16, 23, 26, 29, 112, 147, 173. See also heteronationalism; homonationalism

Arabness, 29, 49, 60–61, 171; and Blackness, 9, 34–35, 42; and queerness, 3, 6, 18–22, 26, 37, 59, 122, 125, 135–36, 142; and transnationalism, 7–8, 21–22, 26, 125, 136, 139

archives: queer, 4, 14, 18–19, 62–63, 89; queer Arab, 2–6, 19, 22–24, 36–37, 58–59, 63–68, 91, 117–18, 173. See also ephemera

Arondekar, Anjali, 5

assimilation, 47–48, 57, 62, 107, 109, 125, 130, 143, 146–47; resisting, 12, 20, 35–36, 56, 119, 142, 149; Western, 2, 14, 38–39, 53, 95, 99, 110, 128, 137, 179n40

Aswat, 15, 119–20, 122, 126, 128–31, 134–35. See also Haqi: An A'ish, An Akhtar, An Akoon; Waqfet Banat

Atik, Christina: "Mish Hilu La Bint/ It's Not Nice for a Girl," 15, 165–69, 172

Atrash, Farid al, 61

authenticity: cultural politics of, 12, 29, 42, 57, 142–43, 147, 149, 169; rejecting, 3, 25, 140, 142–43, 145, 149–50, 153–63, 165, 167, 170, 172–73

autobiography: essay collections of, 24–25, 35, 92, 119–21; ontological insistence of, 122–25; translations of, 125–32. See also individual titles

Aziz, Barbara Nimri, 38–40

Babyfist. See Nöl Collective

Badr, Abd al Muhsin Taha, 99, 101–2

Bahrain, 7

banat: and Arabic texts, 24, 89–91, 94, 96, 105–6, 116, 120, 134, 139, 167; in film, 79, 150, 153, 155; and queer Arab critique, 26, 59, 64; and sahq, 25, 140–41, 149, 173; use of term, 14–16, 18–19, 22

Bar Bahar (In Between), 139, 140, 149, 150–55, 168, 172

Bareed Mista3jil, 120, 122–26, 128–34, 136–37

bathhouses, 108

Beirut, Lebanon, 50, 53, 62

Beit Duqqu, Palestine, 156

belly dance, 16, 27, 59–61, 63, 65, 68–78, 85. See also Habibi al Asmar (My Dark Darling); Sigara wa Kass (A Cigarette and a Glass)

Bend It Like Beckham, 67

Berlant, Lauren, 3, 88

Berlin, Germany, 62, 154

Bibliothèque nationale, 177–78n7

bint, 15. See also banat

Black Arabs, 9, 34, 42, 143

Blackness, 9, 33–34, 41–42. See also anti-Blackness

Bollywood, 62, 64, 181n32

Boone, Joseph, 101

Boym, Svetlana, 88

Brooklyn, NY, 62

Burton, Richard, 28–29, 31–33, 178n7

Carioca, Tahia, 61, 63, 68–69, 181n28

Celluloid Closet, The, 181n32

chick lit, 182n22

Christianity, 134, 146, 150, 154

classism, 109, 114, 116, 162

clothing, 156–61

Cohen, Cathy, 13, 64, 145, 179n40

flipped homoerotic triangulation, 23, 59, 64–67, 78–83, 87, 89
Food for Our Grandmothers, 36
Freeman, Elizabeth, 66
frottage, 144

Galland, Antoine, 177n7
Gamal, Samia, 63, 67–69, 79–80, 181n28
Gay International (Massad concept), 11–12
gay women (term), 1, 10–11
Gaza Strip, 135, 156, 160
genre, 41, 97–99, 102, 105, 161; and methodology of book, 19–21, 24, 92
Georgis, Dina, 4, 133
gesture, 4–5, 13–14, 18, 20, 64, 147
Golden Era film. *See* Egyptian film (Golden Era)
Google, 61
Gopinath, Gayatri, 13–14, 18, 62, 64–68, 181n32
graphic novels, 21, 25, 97, 137. *See also individual titles*
Gualtieri, Sarah, 9
Guapa, 62

Habazi, Lina, 163, 172
Habib, Samar, 10, 140–41
Habibi al Asmar (My Dark Darling), 63, 66–70, 76–79, 82–83, 85–86
Haddad, Joumana, 178n19
Haddawy, Husain, 28–29, 31–33, 178n7
Halabi, Zeina G., 102, 112
Halberstam, Jack, 65
Hamdan, Yasmine, 151
Hammad, Suheir, 39, 179n43
Hamoud, Maysaloun, 139, 150, 155. See also *Bar Bahar* (In Between)
Hanna, Kifah, 102
Haqi: An A'ish, An Akhtar, An Akoon, 120, 122, 124–30, 132–36, 154, 183n1
harems, 16, 27, 30–31, 39–40, 66
Hartman, Saidiya, 5
Hayes, Jarrod, 10
heteronationalism, 16–17, 48, 57, 59–60, 63–64, 67–70, 101, 110, 139, 145; and Arab femininity, 23; and cultural au-

thenticity, 142; definition of, 12, 17, 29, 142; queerness beyond, 90, 117, 120–21, 163; resistance to, 20, 22, 87–90, 121–22, 140, 149, 173; and Scheherazade, 23, 28–29, 34–35, 37, 56
heteronormative time, 65, 69, 72
heteropatriarchy, 1, 24–25, 114, 134, 161; and violence, 57, 90, 96–97, 114, 120, 169
Hifni, Zenab, 181n1
Higginbotham, Evelyn Brooks, 145–46
hijabs, 44–47, 151
HIV/AIDS, 146–47
homoeroticism: in autobiography, 120, 126, 133; and dance, 72, 73, 74, 75, 76, 78, 87; in film, 59, 63–69, 72–76, 78, 80–83, 87, 89, 91; intergenerational, 105–9; between men, 65–66, 101; in novels, 91–95, 98, 100, 105–14, 115–18; and queerness, 10, 12–14, 18, 37, 139, 149–51. *See also* flipped homoerotic triangulation
homonationalism, 11–12, 94, 145
homonormativity, 4, 9, 11–13, 88, 93, 106, 147, 173
homosociality, 14, 18, 37, 63, 65–66, 68–69, 87, 93, 105–9, 116
Hoskin, Rhea, 18
Human Rights Campaign, 129
hypersexuality, 16, 27, 30–32, 34, 43, 51, 101, 113

imperialism. *See* colonialism; Orientalism
India, 48
Indigenous peoples, 13, 20, 123, 159, 170
intersectionality, 9, 100, 116, 132, 154, 156
Iran, 33, 48
Iraq, 7, 61
Islam, 10, 37, 45–46, 134, 146. *See also* Muslim women
Islamophobia, 136, 143, 162, 176n20. *See also* anti-Arab racism
Israel, violence of, 44, 153, 160–61; occupation of Palestine, 25, 125, 128, 134–36, 150, 155

novels: Arabic, 24, 90, 97–105; critics of queer Arab, 93–95, 98, 101–2, 105, 115; lesbian Arab, 92–93, 97–98; narration in, 96–97, 102–5, 107–8, 116; translations of, 98, 182n24; as Western form, 98–99. *See also individual titles*
Nye, Naomi Shibab, 39

occupation. *See* Palestine
Odalisques, 44–45
Oman, 7
Orientalism: and anti-Arab racism, 16, 23, 25, 37–38, 42–43, 46, 56–57, 87, 101, 173; and Arabic novels, 90–91, 93–94, 101, 105–7, 109, 117; and Arab subjects, 9, 20, 173; and Arab women, 15–17, 182n16; and autobiography, 120–23; in film, 59–60, 62–64, 66–67, 87–89, 151, 153–54; and queerness, 1–4, 12, 25; rejection of, 7, 149, 162–63; and Scheherazade, 28–31, 34–35, 37–38, 40, 42–46, 48–51, 55–57
Ozcelik, Burcu, 34

Palestine: activist organizations in, 15, 21, 24, 119–20, 131–32, 134; and Arab League, 7; in *Bar Bahar*, 150, 153–55; fig as symbol of, 170–71; Israeli occupation of, 25, 125, 128, 134–36, 150, 155; literacy in, 126; and the Nöl Collective, 163; queer people in, 117, 124, 128–29, 145, 174; refugees from, 135, 136, 169, 179n43
Palumbo-Liu, David, 38
Pickens, Therí, 53
Piepzna-Samarasinha, Leah Lakshmi, 150–51
Pinterest, 62
Planned Parenthood, 129
poetry, 21, 33, 35, 38, 98. See also *E-mails from Scheherazad*; *individual titles*
postcolonialism, 12–13, 29, 98, 128, 142, 145
Post-Gibran: Anthology of New Arab American Writing, 36
Praeger, 38
precolonialism, 10, 12, 29, 59, 62–63, 88–89, 93, 99, 128, 142

prints, 21, 25, 137, 139, 162–64
Puar, Jasbir K., 11, 94, 179n40
Pyke, Karen, 17

Qatar, 7
queer Arab critique, 2–6, 9–14, 22–23, 64–67, 110, 132. *See also* flipped homoerotic triangulation; queer containment; queer space and time; queer spectatorship
queer Arab futures, 2–3, 19, 25–26, 138, 140, 145, 172–74. *See also* queer futures
queer Arab studies, 2, 10
queer Arab women (term), 2, 6, 18, 114. *See also* banat; mithliya; sahaqiya; sahq
queer containment, 23, 59, 64, 66–67, 70, 83–87, 89, 139
queer futures, 2–3, 19, 22–23, 25, 137, 140–41, 147, 161, 170, 172, 174. *See also* queer Arab futures
queer kinship, 65, 68–69, 150–51
queer of color critique, 12–13, 21–24, 26, 41, 59, 63
queer space and time, 23, 59, 64–68, 70, 78, 85, 87, 89, 139
queer spectatorship, 23, 59, 64–65, 67, 81, 83, 87, 89, 154, 172
queer studies, 10–12. *See also* queer of color critique
queer time. *See* queer space and time
Quran, 7

Race and Arab Americans Before and After 9/11, 9
racialization, 4, 8–9, 34–36, 42, 113
racism. *See* anti-Arab racism; anti-Blackness; racialization
Ra'ihat il Kirfa (The Scent of Cinnamon), 91–92, 96–99, 104–5, 108–9, 113, 115–17, 182n24
Ramallah, Palestine, 156
rape. *See* violence
Rauda, 135
refugees, 7, 113–14, 126, 135, 160
respectability: in Arabic literature, 93, 107, 114; definition of, 145–47; in

Egyptian film, 70; in essay collections, 125, 133–34, 136; rejection of, 3, 25, 140, 145–50, 152–53, 155–59, 161, 163, 165–69, 172–74; and Scheherazade, 31, 36, 47, 57

Rima, 135

Rodríguez, Juana María, 5, 13–14, 64

Rubin, Gayle, 146

Saab, Zeinab, 162

sahaqiya, 1, 10–11, 125, 127–30, 140–41, 143

sahq, 94–95, 127, 129, 181n5; in *Bar Bahar*, 150–55; definition of, 23, 25, 140; as description versus direction, 140–49; and Nöl Collective, 156–61; and Maamoul Press, 161–73; rejecting authenticity, 25, 140–50, 153–74; rejecting respectability, 25, 140, 145–58, 161–74; and transnational collectivity, 25, 140–41, 144–45, 148–49, 153, 155–62, 172–73. *See also* queer Arab futures; queer futures; sahaqiya

Said, Edward, 16, 30–31, 36, 61. *See also* Orientalism

Saliba, Therese, 16–17, 100

Samirah, 134

Sarif, Shamim, 181n1

Saudi Arabia, 7, 24, 91, 96, 98, 102, 107, 112, 116

Scheherazade: and anti-Blackness, 28–29, 31, 35, 37, 52–53, 57; in Arab American literature, 35–57, 139, 178nn18–19; and femininity, 23, 29–35, 51, 56, 147, 149, 178n19; literary history of, 23, 27–28, 57; spelling of, 177n1; in the United States, 36, 43, 46, 50, 53. See also *Thousand and One Nights, The*

Scheherazade's Legacy, 29, 35, 37–44, 48–49, 56, 92, 178n18

Second Gulf War, 37

Sedgwick, Eve Kosofsky, 65–66

Selbak, Rolla, 181n1

sentimentality, 3, 102

sexual assault. *See* violence

sexuality: nonnormative, 42, 51, 56, 59, 110–11; normative, 33, 41, 46, 48

sex work, 147

Shaaban, Bouthaina, 99

shaatha, 1, 10–11

Shafik, Viola, 59, 68

Shahryar, 27, 32, 43–44, 50, 53–54, 58

Shakir, Evelyn, 15

shame: and disability, 112; and menstruation, 157; and queer Arab life, 4, 53, 94, 123, 132–34; rejection of, 167–71. *See also* aib

Shi'i Islam, 107, 112

shuthooth, 94–95, 127

Sigara wa Kass (A Cigarette and a Glass), 63, 65–76, 79–86

Sinha, Mrinalini, 32–33

Smith, Linda Tuhiwai, 123

Somalia, 7

Somerville, Siobhan B., 41–42, 47, 53

Soueif, Ahdaf, 40

South Sudan, 9

Southwest Asia and North Africa (SWANA), 7, 9, 11, 24, 175n19

Spivak, Gayatri Chakravorty, 16

Stacey, Jackie, 123

state violence. *See also* violence: state

subjects, queer Arab (term), 2–6, 9–10, 22. *See also* queer Arab critique

Sudan, 7, 9

Suleiman, Haya, 135

Sunni Islam, 112, 116

Syria, 7, 24, 61, 91, 96–98, 104, 114, 116, 177n7

tatreez, 158–59, 163

Tayeb, Leila, 34

Taylor, Allison, 18

Tel Aviv, 150, 154

terrorism, 16, 27, 101, 146

testimony, 122–24. *See also* autobiography

Tétreault, Mary Ann, 33

Thousand and One Nights, The: frame story of, 23, 27–35, 57, 177–78n7; legacy of, 30; translations of, 28–34, 40, 56, 177–78n7. *See also* Dinarzad; Scheherazade; Shahryar

Tinsley, Omise'eke Natasha, 13–14, 64